PERGAMON INTERNATIONAL LIBRARY
of Science, Technology, Engineering and Social Studies
*The 100-volume original paperback library in aid of education,
industrial training and the enjoyment of leisure*
Publisher: Robert Maxwell, M.C.

Methods of Learning
Communication Skills

SOCIAL WORK SERIES

Editor: JEAN P. NURSTEN

Methods of Learning Communication Skills

BY

P. R. DAY

Lecturer in Applied Social Studies,
University of Hull

245614

PERGAMON PRESS

OXFORD . NEW YORK . TORONTO
SYDNEY . PARIS . FRANKFURT

U. K.	Pergamon Press Ltd., Headington Hill Hall, Oxford OX3 0BW, England
U. S. A.	Pergamon Press Inc., Maxwell House, Fairview Park, Elmsford, New York 10523, U.S.A.
CANADA	Pergamon of Canada Ltd., 75 The East Mall, Toronto, Ontario, Canada
AUSTRALIA	Pergamon Press (Aust.) Pty. Ltd., 19a Boundary Street, Rushcutters Bay, N.S.W. 2011, Australia
FRANCE	Pergamon Press SARL, 24 rue des Ecoles, 75240 Paris, Cedex 05, France
WEST GERMANY	Pergamon Press GmbH, 6242 Kronberg-Taunus, Pferdstrasse 1, Frankfurt-am-Main, West Germany

First Edition 1977

Library of Congress Cataloging in Publication Data
Day, Peter Russell, 1933-
Methods of learning communication skills.

(Social work series)
Bibliography: p.
1. Personnel service in education. 2. School social work. 3. Oral communication. I. Title.
LB1027.5.D35   371.4'6   76-57946
ISBN 0-08-018954-7 (Hard cover)
ISBN 0-08-018953-9 (Flexi cover)

Printed in Great Britain by A. Wheaton & Co., Exeter

Contents

Preface

This book describes and analyses different kinds of learning experiences and raises questions about their use by people engaged in social work training and education. It is based on the assumption that there are elements of skill in different forms of communication between people and that learning experiences can be organised in ways that enable people to develop some of these skills. We are beginning to face the difficult problem of identifying and analysing basic skills in non-verbal and verbal communication and how they may be developed and I believe it will be useful to assess the present position.

This work has developed from an earlier exploration of communication processes in social work and I have used the plan of that book in this review of learning experiences. I am grateful to Dr. Martin Bloom of Washington University for the suggestion which led to the venture and for sharing ideas with me and to Mrs. Jean Nursten for her help in many ways. I thank other colleagues for helpful discussions and criticisms, including Mrs. Ruth Fanner and Mrs. Pat Gooderham, formerly tutors to the Lincoln social work course, former students and Mr. Colin Akhurst. Like its predecessor this book contains material which has been disguised to safeguard people's privacy and I should like to thank those people who are not identified by their real names. My thanks are again due to my father for help with illustrations and my wife for support in trying times, including those when I have tried her patience.

I thank the Open University Press Ltd. and Mr. T. G. B. Howe, Head of John Smeaton High School, Barwick Road, Leeds, for permission to use the material from the Open University book *Language in the Classroom*. The reader will find other material included as illustrations and acknowledgement is made to the original sources and these are quoted in the text. Clearly in fast-growing fields one is indebted to many people and I am grateful for the generous help I have received.

January 1977   PETER R. DAY

CHAPTER 1

Learning Experiences and Communication in Social Work

In the first part of this chapter I give an introduction to the subject by means of illustrations. These are taken from everyday situations including a description of a series of events in a waiting room which contains the elements of the process which is the subject of this book. This leads to a short section on communication and social systems, also illustrated by a short passage. Next, problems found in social life and families are discussed in terms of communication processes. My purpose in this first section is to take a first look at the question how communication and systems theories enlarge our understanding of social work practice. In other words I want to examine the practical implications of these theories on the assumption that communication skills are central in social work and in education. In this way I hope to give a practical introduction to the theoretical complexities which inevitably arise for the student of human interaction.

The next part of the chapter deals with some of these under the headings of communication, language and learning, models and imitative learning, social skills, and human relationships and communication skills. This chapter thus contains the main themes, and concludes with an outline of how they are dealt with in subsequent chapters.

1. INTRODUCTION

In order to justify another book about social work it is advisable to start with practice and our experience as human beings. Often people talk of "problems of communication" at work, in school or at home.

Messages and people often "get lost in the hierarchy" or in the complexities of social systems. Inadequacies in communication skills, it is said, plague social workers who feel unable to "get through" to someone else because of social or psychological barriers or both. Because they feel unable to "get through" or to "get alongside" people they find it difficult to provide help. It is evident that social workers face and react to criticism. Committees of inquiry refer to failures of communication, failure to consult, and lack of co-ordination. Colleagues, other professionals, and other people such as journalists and authors, comment on poor quality, lack of clarity, discipline and credibility in social workers' verbal and written communications. The problems do not even stop here. A common feature of large health and social service organisations is their inefficiency. A common sign of this is over-communication. It is as if there is pressure on staff to engage almost endlessly in debilitating dialogues and discussions more often because of fear of offending colleagues rather than because of genuine need for consultation in order to carry out a task. The excessive expenditure of time and energy in meetings is an indication of the problematic nature of obtaining co-operation. I have quoted a number of examples to introduce one reason why the use of communication theory is of practical importance. It is simply that we are beset by a range of communication problems. We are not particularly good at understanding them even when we recognise them. I will go on to quote some more examples and discuss them to support my argument. But it may be worth bearing in mind other practical questions, namely the consequences of our failure to see communication as problematic sometimes.

Most of what I have written so far can be confirmed by much of our recent everyday experience. Some people in the early 1970s might go further and say that it is sickeningly familiar and prosaic, and I would accept that point. But it is important to add two things. It is worth bearing in mind the practical problems which arise from our failure to see communication as sometimes problematic and equally, the dangers of facile labelling of problems as ones of communication and suggesting that they are obviously insoluble as a consequence. This far, I have suggested that one justification for learning about communication (or anything else for that matter) is that it is perceived as problematic. The next step is to examine the problems in more detail and an illustration is presented as a focus for further discussion.

Illustration

He was sprawled in his chair in the waiting room and turning over the pages of the magazine when she opened the door quietly and walked in. He noticed the colour and movement of her skirt although at first he did not look at her directly: and he also perceived the faint scent of perfume or powder. He straightened up and pulled in his legs and looked up. He observed more about the girl and studied her face and looked quickly at the rest of her body. She looked at him and he turned as if he was looking at the clock on the wall. The receptionist and the girl spoke to each other. The girl then sat down fairly near him and picked up a paper. They were silent but both wanted to break the tension. He said he hoped they would not have to wait too long. She responded by agreeing with him and added that you could get worried if you had to wait a long time: often you got fed up hanging around. Her comments encouraged him and he smiled at her, as he replied. The conversation continued and they both felt more confident about talking to each other.

This process of information exchange is dynamic and if a complete circuit is considered the receiver becomes a sender-back to the original sender (and receiver). This applies to groups of two people and also to groups of more than two. The encounter I have described is a very common kind of occurrence. People find themselves in such situations frequently. Broadly speaking communication refers to the transmission of information from one unit in a system to another unit. The story above contains the main elements of a communication theory. They can be recognised immediately. First, you can see how information about each of the people was received and interpreted by both of them. At first the man obtained information about the girl through noticing her skirt and its colouring "out of the corner of his eye" and he used this and other cues (e.g. scent) to decide on the sex of the person who came in. She saw him first relaxed in his chair and then saw him straighten up. Perhaps she thought he did this to create a favourable impression on her: later events might confirm that this interpretation was correct. The two people had to pay attention to other things which were going on in the situation, for example, the brief conversation with the receptionist (another exchange of information) was a distraction. The girl chose to sit quite near the man: they both seemed to sense the wish to speak to each other to break a silence in which tension could have increased. The man's remark allowed her to continue the conversation by involving herself to a greater or lesser extent. Her reply indicated that she chose a greater degree of involvement. The story does not exhaust the variety of the means of interpersonal communication but it does illustrate such aspects as postures, dress, gestures, tone of voice, silence, noise (or distractions in this story) and verbal conversation. The anecdote illustrates what happens in communication in every-day life. By trying to "make sense" of what happened here, we may be able to extend our understanding of more complex communications and perhaps be helped in recognising subtler information processing.

The story suggests that it may be important to regard the sending and receiving of messages as a complete circuit, each actor in the system taking both roles. This suggestion is assigned importance in later discussion. The man sends a message: the woman sends another message, a reply to the man's message. The interchange of messages at that early stage in the relationship has a meaning to the two people but it is not necessarily a shared meaning. But as the interchanges continue meanings come to be shared, and as interdependence grows further relationships also develop. In the anecdote the context of the meeting is referred to briefly. This enabled us to concentrate on the interchange of messages between the two principal actors: this single complete circuit is the foundation of communication theory. To relate it to real life the complexity of a variety of networks has to be comprehended, and theory thus becomes more complicated to correspond to the reality it seeks to "explain". Communication theory encourages the helping professional to see client problems in the context of a system of interacting forces. The output of one person or group is part of the input of another and this results in some form of mutual accommodation (possibly ranging from agreement and co-operation to conflict). After a normal conversation commences between the man and the woman perhaps the man's pulse rate returns to normal while his role changes in adjusting to the new context. His personality system remains largely untouched by the brief encounter (but it could be changed over a period of time). From the perspective of communication every act has some repercussions at all levels. As information leaves from one point (for example, the signalling mechanisms of the man) there is sometimes confusion as to which level is communicating. Are the man's sexual feelings being communicated or is the message one of interest in developing the broader social aspects of friendship? Or is he trying to help the woman (and perhaps himself as well) to feel more comfortable in a strange situation with no intentions beyond that? These messages are not, as it happens, incongruent with one another. They are all friendly messages and are not therefore exclusive: is the man sending a combination of them? Content and affect flow together and the man may be trying to be sociable and helping the girl to feel at ease and at the same time sending a message at a different level. As well as being difficult theoretically systems are complicated matters in practice. The interaction between the two people constitutes one system, and their membership of society constitutes membership of another system. The illustration shows how communication starts at one point in the system and circulates through all of the intersecting systems. Information about the presence of the girl we may guess activates the boy's physical system. It is not necessary to consider all of the consequences for his physiological state — his increased pulse rate and so on — nor is it possible to consider all of the consequences for his "personality system"; his role as stranger in the waiting room alters for example.

Communication and social systems

Wider relationships develop and are involved in the mutual interdependence of the sender-receiver and receiver-sender which is illustrated here. From the simple communication circuit shared frames of reference for communication are clarified. People, individually and in groups, are information-processing systems: they communicate physically and symbolically to live. In social life people can be thought of as systems communicating within systems. "Society" is the biggest system. Different groups permit variations in patterns of communication so long as the needs of the larger unit are served.

Individuals and groups have different goals according to their experiences in development and cultural setting. Systems theory provides a convenient way of looking at a person in his various interactions. It is a way of looking at the "parts of things" while bearing in mind the danger of fragmentation and also the danger of ignoring problems which do not fit easily into simple mechanical schemes. The short illustration which follows is of another commonplace situation: everyone may experience conflict of this nature and is often aware of its possible repercussive effects.

Illustration

Susan Smith had telephoned earlier in the week for an appointment. She was a dark haired, socially poised and attractive girl and she talked fluently in the interview. She expressed a considerable amount of feeling which seemed to me to be appropriate for a 19-year-old whose circumstances are like hers. When she had sat down she said emphatically that she wanted to get married and her mother opposed the idea. Miss Smith does not want to disappoint her mother. This is why she came to talk to us. She heard of the department through a friend who had a similar kind of problem.

This short anecdote has several points of interest. We notice, among them, that the interviewer (about whom we are told nothing) found Susan an attractive person able to express ideas and feelings and apparently behaving in ways one might expect, given her circumstances. (We are not given the reasons for this opinion; because this is a short illustration we are being asked to accept that quite an amount of information has been omitted but that there is some supporting evidence.) We also notice that Susan has certain expectations of herself in her relationships with other people who are important to her. She has views about what they expect of her. She expresses concern about the conflicting expectations of her future husband, her mother and herself. Finally, we notice that her expectations of the department have been affected by what her friend had told her. Points like these help to put the communications between Susan Smith and the other people, particularly the interviewer, in their social context. Essentially the idea of role comes from the performance expectations in the social system. Most social relationships involve certain standards of conduct or norms of social behaviour. Some behaviour is appropriate and acceptable in a situation where other behaviour is inappropriate and unacceptable. The essential thing about a role is that it cannot be performed alone. One person affects the behaviour of others who are interacting with him. The child of an anxious and confused mother will be affected by the mother's behaviour so that the child's role performance is threatened. Social prescriptions for role behaviour are often vague. There are wide areas of diversity for individual and group interpretations of how roles should be carried. Parents are supposed to care for their children. A child is supposed to respect adult authority. In the individual's own small and tight social network role expectations come to be more specifically defined between him and his role partners. In these closer-knit circuits people work out what each is supposed to do and what each is supposed to get out of this. It is satisfying to the people involved if things work out happily; it is, of course, a fact of life that conflict and frustration are involved if they do not. This is illustrated in various aspects of social life, the family being one location.

Problems in social life and problems of communication
 Frequently in cases of family conflict we find, not always surprisingly, that individuals are not communicating with each other. People find themselves in the roles of husband, wife, or child without ever really being clear what is expected of them in the family. People know in a general sort of way and get along quite well until there is a disagreement or a small incident. Then there is friction and each may feel the other is unreasonable. They discover that they have been taken for granted that they understand what is expected of each other only to find that there are really many things on which they disagree. These areas of disagreement may need to be looked at objectively in order to disentangle the complicated processes of family life, and also to understand the attitudes partners bring into their new families which they learned in their families of origin. With well-adjusted couples communication is almost automatic and requires little conscious

attention. Each partner is familiar with the words and gestures of the other and able to sense changes in mood. But even for the most compatible couples there are some areas of experience that are resistant to communication. This may create crisis in the lives of relatively well-adjusted people. Clearly where differences between people include differences in social and cultural background and in every aspect of experience (and even in language itself) communication becomes a major problem.

Faulty communication is a major source of family dysfunctioning and improvement in communication is often a specific goal of treatment. Change in communication requires changes in the perceptions and responses of the individuals who compose the interpersonal system, that is, changes in individuals' personality systems. The nature of a particular perception depends upon the actual event perceived and how the person interprets it. The interpretation depends on the social and cultural context in which the individual places the event, his role expectations, and any distortions due to emotional factors such as ego defence mechanisms for example. It is surprising that people generally communicate as well as they do because the potential complexity of ordinary communication is so enormous. Somehow much of the guesswork is taken out of ordinary discourse perhaps because of the various networks of shared norms and habits that provide standard expectations and shared interpretations. Attention needs to be given to both the inter-personal system (for example, relationships between members of a family) and to the personality systems of the people who are in the inter-personal system. When there is dysfunctioning in the inter-personal system for this to change there need to be changes in the perceptions of participants and in their responses to each other. These perceptions and responses depend on and create the quality of communication between the individuals in the system. An individual's personality has changed, if only to a small degree, if he learns to perceive certain situations differently. If his perception of himself, or his self-control, his ability to cope with difficulties differently, or his defences, for example, change these are all aspects of personality change and altered perceptions.

For many social workers there seems to be too great a distance between theory and practice and empirical research is now indicating a gap between the supposed aims of intervention and its outcome. In what ways, then, do communication and systems theories enlarge our understanding of social work practice? Every act by a social worker is a communication act and potentially social workers' communications can shape clients' perceptions. The fact that communication is such a familiar activity is well seen in the way we take language very much for granted. This familiarity tends to conceal the need for systematic attempts to further understanding, but the basic assertion stands. This ordinary activity is a central process (or *the* process) in social work. In modern society no one can manage his life without relying on other people whether in formal organisations or not. The opportunities for role conflict are increased because of the fragmentation of relationships through multiple institutions and the resulting increase in the different roles carried by each person. Difficulties in social functioning arise in various ways and it does not seem possible today to approach a "case" as if it were independent of the circumstances of life surrounding it. It is necessary to see how individuals act on each other and to try to understand their interdependence. It is necessary to see a case as a system of interacting forces all having reciprocity and feedback with each other.

One advantage of the communication perspective is that it can be related to a wide range of other theoretical perspectives (and of course it draws on them too). Perhaps one of the most helpful ways of illustrating its practical utility is through the analogy of the jigsaw puzzle. Here, the puzzle represents the social problem and the pieces represent items of information which are needed to "see" the picture. I hope that the considerable limitations of this analogy are self-evident but in any case this analogy provides a useful stimulus in thinking about practice. Its possibilities seem considerable as an intellectual exercise. If you are setting out to solve a crossword puzzle you fill in your answers to the clues that are there to guide you. What you write is limited by the squares and blanks on the puzzle and they determine the logic of your answers. If, on the other hand, you are trying to set or construct a puzzle you create both the structure and the meaning at the same time. They influence each other. The social worker is involved in the flow of information about a problem and information changes as the client and the social worker jointly explore the problem. The social worker is assessing and reassessing situations continually, that is, formulating and revising hypotheses. "If I assume that I am correct about this person (client) then if I do X he will do Y and the effect of that action could be Z or W." This "open" type of formulation differs from one based on other models. "This client has a neurosis. He will therefore be likely to engage in certain kinds of pathological behaviour." Such an expectation may turn out to be a self-fulfilling prophecy because the social worker is set to perceive the pathological behaviour. This expectation may help to produce it because, sometimes unknowingly, the social worker may reward the pathological behaviour. This argument does not lead, of course, to the fashionable complete denunciation of the medical model. It cannot, since different perspectives are appropriate for different situations and this enables social workers to try to be discriminating about different forms of help. However, it alerts us again to the importance of feedback, and to the way in which various factors, existing information and language among them, lead people to structure their perceptions of "reality" in certain ways. A point which is often found in the literature of the profession and which is repeated several times in this book is that communication skills are central in the helping process. The extent to which people are able to convey their thoughts and feelings to each other, either verbally or non-verbally, is an important aspect of interaction. Defences interfere with the process and since it occurs on different levels, attitudes expressed verbally may be contradicted by non-verbal behaviour. But another person may misinterpret bodily movements and posture, tone of voice and the words of the other because of his psychological needs. The basic elements of a social work communication model are the continuing make up of one person (the personality of one individual or the structure of a group), an output system (that is the internal processes necessary for the transmission of information such as the individual's vocal chords or the group's spokesman), the channel (such as air for sound waves, paper to write on, or a tape recorder) an input system (such as the sense organs, ears and nose, of the other person(s)), and again, the output systems and channels back to the original sender. Thus you have feedback. Finally, a communication occurs in a context of time and space (including social organisation).

2. COMMUNICATION, LANGUAGE AND LEARNING

Communication can be regarded as a form of the learning process, and it can be described as the discriminatory response of an organism to a stimulus (Stevens, 1950). This description is not entirely adequate but it will be helpful to pursue this line of thought in part of this introduction. Communicators often wish to produce learning in receivers, or to make use of the receiver's existing habitual responses and to send messages which take them into account. Learning can thus be thought of as equivalent to communication. A message can be thought of as a stimulus: when a message is decoded the receiver is perceiving it as a stimulus. When a stimulus is interpreted the receiver is responding to it although the process may not be observed in his behaviour: it is taking place in his brain. This internal response stimulates the formulation of a new message. When a person interprets a stimulus he operates as a receiver and as a communication source.

These relationships may be expressed diagrammatically:

Ingredients in learning	*Ingredients in communication*
Organism	Channel
Stimulus	Message
Perception of stimulus	Decoder
Interpretation of stimulus	Receiver-source
Overt response to stimulus	Encoder
Consequence of response	Feedback

The accompanying figure (Fig. 1) is a model of the relationships between communication and meaning.

Communication with oneself can also be used to illustrate this. In writing this chapter I have some ideas which I want to convey to people, many of whom I do not know personally. I am operating as a communication source, and in producing the writing on this sheet of paper, an encoder. Now I read the message as encoded. I decode it; I retranslate it and interpret it and receive the message. Thus I am the source, the encoder, decoder and receiver; only the message and the marks on the paper are external to me. This kind of intrapersonal communication goes on continuously and it demonstrates the relationship between communication and learning models. All the ingredients of the two processes are contained in it. The process of intrapersonal communication is equivalent to the learning process. When a person communicates with himself the messages he encodes are fed back into this system by his decoding mechanism. Feedback is important in assessing the effectiveness of communication and the achievement of learning objectives.

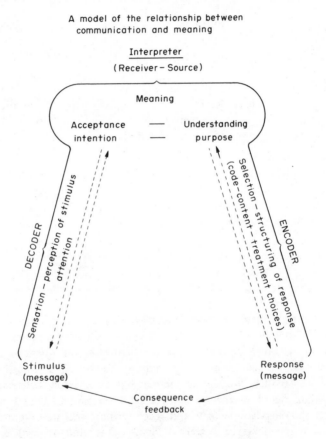

Fig. 1. A model of the relationship between communication and meaning.
(From Berlo, D. K. (1960) *The Process of Communication.* Holt, Rinehart and Winston.)

It will be seen that feedback is a particular aspect of receiver reaction. The source can use the reaction of the receiver as a check on his own effectiveness and thus as a guide to his future actions. The reaction of the receiver is a consequence of this and it serves as a feedback to the source. Feedback provides the source with information concerning his success in accomplishing his objective: in this way it affects future messages which the source encodes. The audience exerts control over future messages by the responses it makes. Action-reaction relationships are thus important in analysing communication. In communication between people symbols are used to anticipate how others will respond to their messages and to develop expectations about their own behaviour and the behaviour of others. The concept of expectations is important in human communication (Day, 1974). People tend to match the style of what they say and do to what they think are the expectations of their hearers. It is difficult to say precisely when children learn to match what they say to the person they say it to. In some families, for example, learning that you do not talk to Grandma as you do to your mother may come very early indeed. Partly this is a matter of choosing what to say so as to tell people what they need to know. What aspects of the social context are likely most to affect teachers', school children's, or students' use of language? Perhaps the most important aspect of an audience is whether it is seen as alien and critical or as comfortable and accepting. A great deal of time is spent in talking to people who one knows quite well about familiar topics. Part of remaining a human being is confirming that "my world" is still "your world" and that we share enough of a common reality to make life possible. Talking to friends is a valuable context in which to approach new, difficult or threatening ideas. They are likely to be tolerant and to be willing to accept lack of coherence in "thinking out loud". Exploratory discussion is more possible in an intimate group; talking with strangers in this way would be intolerable. Quite a small group is difficult to face if a person feels its members are critical and unfriendly. For a teacher it is hard to achieve effective classroom discussion in those classes where there are antagonistic cliques and where people are very much on the defensive. Audiences thus vary in their effects according to their degree of intimacy or formality. Any audience can be placed at some point on a scale from the most intimate to the most distant. If a teacher wishes pupils to grope their way into new understandings this is more likely to happen in a small intimate group. If he believes that they have mastered a piece of work sufficiently to be able to organise it explicitly he may best encourage them to do this for a larger and more distant audience. A similar range can be found in written communication, from scribbled notes for oneself to writing for publication. This can be shown clearly on a diagram (Fig. 2).

Variable	Intimate	Distant
Size	Small group	Full class or larger
Source of authority	The group	The teacher
Social relationships	Intimate	Public
Ordering of thought	Inexplicit	Explicit
Speech	Hesitant	Pre-planned
Functions	Explanatory	"Final draft"

Fig. 2. Audience effect on "communicator" and communication.
(From Barnes, D. (1973) *Language in the Classroom*, The Open University Press.)

In talking with others it is possible for people to learn strategies to use in their thinking: this happens slowly over a long period of time. The overt use of speech is a model of how pupils approach learning tasks when they are alone. It is also the readiest way of changing those approaches. Studying the speech of learners helps both to understand what cognitive strategies they are using and also to see how they might be helped to improve them.

Language performs two functions at once. It conveys an overt message and simultaneously sets up or confirms the relationships of the people who are communicating with one another. In education language provides the main means by which teacher and taught organise their relationship and by which they construct shared meanings. The public and shared meanings of the classroom are not the only ones. Education is concerned with whatever meanings a student takes away with him. Language functions for the individual: it is one means by which he makes his own sense of whatever is presented to him, thus making it part of his own thinking and feeling.

3. MODELS AND IMITATIVE LEARNING

Suggestion, imitation and identification play an important part in learning: this tends to decrease with age and maturity in the learner. The process of imitation or the taking over of behaviour characteristics of a group probably operates when student doctors, for example, acquire professional attitudes (Beard, 1972). An important point about these processes is that they can speed up learning considerably. Bandura and Walters (1963) define imitative learning as the tendency to reproduce the behaviour of living or symbolic models. The use of models is very ubiquitous and in many countries the word for teach is the same as the word for show. Problem-solving in monkeys and men is often observational learning. The subject looks at a situation, perhaps makes implicit trial-and-error attempts to deal with it, and then achieves a solution. Through the ability to learn by observing instead of only through action, such animals may be helped by observing the performances of others. Monkeys have solved problems, without overt trial and error, by watching others solve them. Mowrer (1960) explains imitation in terms of secondary reinforcement. The sounds made by a parrot's owner become secondarily reinforcing for the parrot by virtue of their association with the owner who provides direct reinforcement such as food. If later the parrot makes a similar sound by accident this will have reinforcing properties and will tend to be repeated. A baby learns to imitate its own sounds and then sounds made by other. But imitation by children, and imitation of parents in particular, may be reinforcing for children regardless of the act being imitated. Perhaps no single psychological theory will explain all examples of imitation. Since it can be expected that imitative responses will generalise, imitation is important not only for learning in childhood. There is a considerable degree of uniformity in behaviour; if people imitate or copy the actions, thoughts and feelings of others they will "keep in step" with one another. This facilitates co-operation in groups. Deliberate requests for information are basic in learning; also ideas or suggestions are picked up from other people without being aware of this. As far as communication in general is concerned, experience and practice are necessary for increasing efficiency. This comes from observing and copying people such as parents and other family members. Later, school teachers and friends play more important parts. Attitudes, prejudices, values and interests are communicated by them and provide standards for judgements of self and others. To state this briefly not all communication is in the form of language. People are influenced by others when they copy their actions (imitation), their thoughts (suggestion), or their feelings (sympathy) (Miller and Dollard, 1941).

Some suggestions about the possible influence of the academic setting on social work students' learning were discussed in an article in 1966. While teaching social work principles and methods and administrative theory training courses give demonstrations of these in the way the training is organised. The Younghusband Report pointed out the need for this: "The reason for training is that it can equip people who, because they have a common body of knowledge and skill, are able to do a better job in range and depth than the untrained. But this will only happen if the training itself is so planned and run as to achieve the aim in view . . . The whole course should also be planned to develop and deepen those attitudes of respect and concern for people in trouble and the realistic desire to help them, on which social work is based" (Ministry of Health, 1959). Some reasons why this seemed important were illustrated by Day (1965) and Edom (1965). The argument went as follows.

I asked how far those concerned with the study of human relationships applied their knowledge relevantly in planning organisations and whether we paid more than lip service to the adoption or development of new administrative techniques in the social services and other industries. In another Case Conference article Edom raised the question in another way, and suggested that we should take another serious look at the question whether people really matter in a situation where high theoretical sophistication and practical inadequacy exist side by side. Similar anxiety was expressed in an anonymous letter which appeared in *New Society* in July 1965. The writer said that the idea was rapidly spreading that children were produced solely to be pushed around by elected laymen or anonymous officials in the interest of plans, in which human rights and dignity were totally lost. There seemed to be a danger that schools were becoming processing establishments and not places in which human relationships were fostered.

There seems to be a growing awareness of our widespread failure in the social services and elsewhere to develop methods of administration appropriate to twentieth-century conditions and of our tendency to rely on rigid hierarchical arrangements and the inflexible application of regulations, to take two examples, in situations where they are no longer thought to be helpful or appropriate. The growth of the administrative machine causes anxiety and sometimes the insensitiveness of power-conscious officials produces disquieting results. There is concern about their apparent failure to distinguish the different administrative functions involved in dealing with things and dealing with people; the needs of the individuals the machine is supposed to serve may become subordinated or overlooked. If the individual refuses to allow himself to be overlooked he may be regarded as an administrative anomaly or a nuisance. Tendencies like these are inimical to the principles of democracy and those indicated in the quotation from the Younghusband Report above.

In social work training we are trying to prepare students to administer services for people. In doing this a social work school is providing a service for people and is therefore providing a model. This model, whatever its imperfections and inadequacies, represents an . attempt to express certain values and to embody "good" administrative practices and this attempt may be adapted and improved on in other situations. A social work course attempts to express casework principles but it does not exist in isolation and the extent to which it can move towards higher standards depends to a great extent on the objectives and resources of the institution of which it is a part and the support it can secure within this framework. Examples provide students with the opportunity to test the theories with which they are being presented. The explicit use of a social work school as an example could provide both staff and students with the opportunity for continual evaluation and sharpen their awareness of behaviour in organisations. In any educational programme it appears to be fundamental to avoid the charge of advocating things other people should practise in their work while failing to practise these oneself. It seems important that relevant social science theories should be applied and that this should be evident to students and others associated with a course. In many institutions the development of this idea is not necessarily easy, since it depends on changes in their social structure and on the recognition that its educational value justifies the discomfort and anxiety to which it gives rise, among other things. Since social work students are encouraged during training to study organisations and are aware of and affected by the institution which is responsible for their education, it would seem to be a logical development.

The explicit use of a school for studying behaviour is a complicated issue which cannot be dealt with briefly and without reference to real-life examples. As far as social work training is concerned, however, it is possible to mention some goals at which we aim in trying to give an implicit demonstration of good administrative practice and the expression of social work principles in the way a course is run. It is necessary to be clear about the values underlying a training programme at the outset; they are not easily summarised and raise many further issues but it seems reasonable to begin by saying that the educational and social values underlying a course are related to those of the social work profession. This means that the experience of students and other people associated with a course gives indications that individuals are respected, that their differences and limited democratic rights are recognised and supported and that the professional and personal integrity of the social worker is valued. It means that attention is paid to those aspects of the training which will help the student to examine and modify his attitudes, with the aim of providing a climate which is stimulating and which helps rather than hinders him in acquiring knowledge and developing skill. Fundamentally the attempt is to create an atmosphere in which the application of casework principles is demonstrated with the aim of helping students and others associated with a course to feel that their contribution is appreciated and that this is a "good" course, association with which will be congenial and purposeful. These general aims affect the teaching methods used, the personal relationships between students and teachers, the thinking about planning and content, and relationships between staff. The social work teacher tries to demonstrate "good" aspects of practice and this begins from the time an application for training is being considered. In applying for social work training applicants are asked to give a fair amount of personal information, and this has to be discussed during their interviews in an attempt to understand why they would like to enter social work and what personal experiences have contributed to their wish to train. It is possible to demonstrate that the information the applicant gives is treated responsibly and that his right to privacy is recognised, in the way the selection interviews are conducted. As the course proceeds it is possible to pursue the general aims in ways like these, thus providing learning experiences which will complement and reinforce the theoretical and practical work.

Administrative arrangements give a great deal of support to the partial realisation of these aims and ensure that people associated with a course are treated with courtesy and consideration. Adequate consultation and communication between all the people involved in a course ensures this, helps to minimise the impact of problems and prevents difficulties, such as the duplication of external contacts, which might occur if communication was absent or defective. Revans (1965) has discussed the fact that institutions in which subordinates feel free to discuss questions with their superiors are those that adapt to new circumstances best. Where, for example, school teachers feel that the outside directors of a school are aware of their internal problems, or feel that they have a contribution to make to internal organisation, they tend to be both liked by their pupils and to be seen as effective teachers. If the teachers see their superiors as remote and dictatorial they, in their turn, are seen as unfriendly and ineffective.

"Once lack of opportunity to ask questions has engendered resentment to authority its coercive responses can only deny that lack more strongly, for the capacity to learn by working with authority has died." The freer communication is between fieldwork supervisors and social work tutors the more likely it is that attempts will be made to cope with difficulties at an early stage. This is another essential aid to the smooth running of a course and helps to meet the needs of those engaged in teaching and therefore the needs of the students themselves if these are perceived correctly.

New responses can be learned by reproducing a model's behaviour. In addition to transmitting new responses imitation can inhibit or disinhibit responses which the learner already possesses. Jehu (1967) cites experimental evidence supporting these points and a third effect of imitative learning which is to elicit existing responses of a kind which do not involve inhibition. A native returning to a district after prolonged absence recovers the local dialect more quickly than a stranger could acquire them. The model's behaviour serves to release similar behaviour in the observer. It is helpful to distinguish personal and positional models. A personal model is followed for the sake of his personal attributes. A positional model is imitated for the sake of the attributes pertaining to his social position. In imitating a positional model a person enacts a social role and not a personal style (Winch, 1962). It is also helpful to think of children in connection with imitation and the conditions governing the two kinds of modelling. Familiarity, based on previous experience of interaction with the model, may well be crucial for personal models but not for positional models. A person's capacity for threatening a child by punishment may help to establish him as a personal rather than as a positional model. However, it is difficult to produce experimental evidence for the occurrence of imitation as a defensive reaction, although the claim that modelling may fulfil defensive functions is very plausible.

I now quote a case which has been used for teaching purposes and which has also been written up elsewhere (Day, 1972). The probation officer here facilitated the clients' learning in ways which are discussed later. I suggest too that he provided a personal model for Mr. Brown, in some respects, for example, giving him fatherly care.

Mr. Brown was 24 years old. It was alleged that he had committed an assault on a girl, who denied in court that the incident had occurred. Other evidence against Mr. Brown was, however, fairly conclusive, and he was placed on probation for two years with a special requirement that he should not associate with the girl. Mr. Brown lived with his younger sister, two younger brothers and parents in a council house. Since leaving secondary modern school he worked at a hotel and then as an agricultural worker.

Mr. Green, the probation officer, in his report said that his client had not liked his work at an hotel and had returned home after six months. The family had moved around in their locality quite a lot. Mr. Brown was virtually a non-reader and non-writer when he left school; of limited intelligence, easy-going and casual, and taking life as it came; he was very dependent and easily led. He seemed to like his home and parents, talking mostly about his father and rarely referring to his mother. Father's work habits were irregular and he had been a scrap dealer for many years. Mr. Brown senior was very much on the defensive where his family was concerned and seemed to be rather a tough, brusque man. The son seemed to Mr. Green to be slow in thought and speech and "not at all sure what all the fuss was about". He maintained that all that had happened was that he had kissed and cuddled the girl and did not think this wrong. He had been thoroughly frightened by the court appearance.

When he was interviewed after the hearing it was some time before Mr. Brown understood the requirements of probation, although these were explained in simple terms. It seemed he had some difficulties in social adaptation, partly because of low intelligence, and that his home circumstances were unlikely to help him to come to terms with this to any great extent. He seemed to be emotionally insecure and lonely. The problems perceived by Mr. Green were of rather a general nature, whereas from the client's point of view, one of his problems was his lack of understanding of "what all the fuss was about". His main idea appeared to be to avoid further involvement with the police.

The early interviews with Mr. Brown seemed to Mr. Green to be fairly friendly. He encouraged Mr. Brown to tell him about his motor cycle which he was keen to maintain and repair himself, but Mr. Brown seemed to be extremely slow and deliberately on guard. A turning-point came when Mr. Green showed ignorance about his client's work. Mr. Brown derived obvious satisfaction from explaining it and it seemed to help him to feel that he was competent in an area where Mr. Green was not. The probation officer asserted his authority later in the interview by reminding his client of the requirements of probation. This pattern was repeated in later interviews, the client being encouraged to assert himself while Mr. Green showed that he too could be assertive while remaining friendly.

At an early stage Mr. Green visited the home and saw his client's father. The probation officer was not invited into the house and the interview with the father, who did most of the talking, took place outside in a cold wind. Father had given his son clear guidance about relationships with girls.

As the relationship with the probation officer developed Mr. Brown made good progress in his ability to talk. He appreciated having a good listener. Mr. Brown appeared to be growing in confidence and although his limited intellectual ability was a handicap his capacity to put his thoughts into words increased. Mr. Brown showed no anger about further hear-say allegations about a continuing association between himself and the girl. That he did not show anger or indignation may have been because of his limited ability to express himself, although it might have been because there was some foundation for them. But Mr. Green noted that his client's verbal ability "did not run to the art of being indignant or angry in words".

A further development which was thought to be significant occurred about seven months after the order was made. Mr. Brown told the probation officer about one of his friends who changed jobs frequently. He was critical of this and said that it was time that his friend settled down. The way in which Mr. Brown discussed this seemed to indicate a marked improvement in his capacity for self-expression and reasoning. Seven months earlier the client would not have thought about the behaviour of another person or about his own behaviour in this way. By this time Mr. Brown "obviously enjoyed himself just chatting". He gave Mr. Green a lucid description of how he had decarbonised his motor cycle. They discussed Mr. Green's suggestion that the maximum benefit could be obtained from the motor cycle by making longer runs, and what Mr. Brown had been doing at work.

At the beginning of the contact Mr. Brown had been lonely. After seven or eight months he seemed to have a number of male friends in a nearby town. He responded to the probation officer's encouragement to take more interest in his personal appearance. Mr. Green thought that his appearance was "rather off-putting" and suggested that "the time had come for a hair do". During later interviews the probation officer noted improvements in his client's appearance.

The probation officer quickly noted Mr. Brown's slowness in thought and speech and geared his own behaviour to this assessment. To some extent Mr. Green saw his role as playing "adult friend" to his client. He had to identify areas where he would have to be authoritative (for example in relation to Mr. Brown's association with girls) and those where he would encourage Mr. Brown to exercise more independence and assertiveness. Mr. Green showed willingness to learn from his client about agricultural techniques and motor bikes.

The early structuring of roles appeared to be important to Mr. Brown, who seemed to gain confidence in Mr. Green as someone who respected him as well as being someone who could be firm in exercising authority. It also seemed to be important that Mr. Green encouraged his client to think for himself about the definition of roles. Mr. Green tried to help his client to feel less anxious about their relationship at the same time discussing his situation in ways which were not too emotionally threatening. He did this by using simple language and by repeating what he had said until Mr. Brown indicated that he had grasped what the words were intended to convey.

It seemed that Mr. Brown developed a greater capacity for self-direction and self-control and his confidence and self-esteem appeared also to be enhanced. It seems quite possible that improved communicative capacity was a significant contributory factor. He discussed with Mr. Green days he had spent at the seaside when he had avoided involvement with gangs of teenagers "who were looking for trouble". He did this on at least two occasions. Previously he had been easily led and very likely to become temporarily involved with gangs.

Mr. Brown's comments about his friends' employment changes appear to show a developing capacity to identify significant aspects of behaviour and to look at consequences by making inferences about behaviour. It may also be reasonable to suggest that this comment reflected Mr. Brown's developing ideas about self-control. Mr. Green was impressed by his client's capacity to put this in words.

Mr. Green's technique in listening and responding to his client tended to reinforce certain behaviour. Mr. Green's responses appeared to be aimed at helping his client to organise his thoughts through verbal discussion. It seemed that Mr. Brown's improved communicative capacity contributed to an ability to generalise and conceptualise. It seemed also that he developed a greater capacity for self-direction and self-control and his confidence and self-esteem appeared also to be enhanced. It seems quite possible that improved communicative capacity was a significant contributory factor.

A number of features of this case are common to many situations in which social workers are involved. These features suggest some questions about ways of helping and about the part which communication plays in this. Theories of learning and communication help us to clarify some aspects of the complex processes involved.

In the normal course of development a child becomes more and more able to recognise relationships between different pieces of information. This growing ability is due to accumulated experience of perceiving the environment and often also to the use of language in symbolising the information. As they grow, children acquire ways of representing recurrent regularities in their environment (food and bed are common examples). They develop ways of linking past, present and future. To progress to symbolic thinking they have to assimilate linguistic skills from their culture.

Intellectual and linguistic development are important keys to social development. As the child learns to subordinate himself to language it begins to act as a regulator of behaviour. This is the beginning of a long chain in the formation of complex aspects of his conscious and voluntary activity. These developments introduce essential changes in the child's perception of environmental influences. He becomes able to isolate verbally the immediate and final aims of his behaviour, to indicate the means of achieving these aims, and to subordinate them to verbal formulation.

Language also makes a progressive contribution to the child's awareness of himself. It relates him as an individual to others and helps to transmit group values to him and thus influences his attitudes.

Deficiency in language development may thus cause difficulty in the mastery of complex systems of thought and in the control of behaviour and may also affect a person's self-image and capacity for self-awareness. Inadequate stimulation of a child by illiterate or semi-literate parents is an important factor in class differences of ability and achievement. Linguistic disability impairs the person's ability to cope effectively with his environment. The physical and psychological effects interact and are mutually reinforcing. Cultural deprivation may also occur in middle-class homes where the parents are preoccupied with their own activities and neglect their children.

Mr. Brown's difficulties in many of these areas were identified by the probation officer. Abstract thinking was not easily undertaken: there were problems of behaviour control and Mr. Brown felt lack of confidence in his capacity to cope with many social situations.

Jehu has distinguished two aspects of casework treatment: (1) the reduction of excessive environmental pressures on the client and (2) the modification of his behaviour (including perception, emotion and thought) so that maladaptive responses are eliminated and adaptive responses are strengthened.

In addition to the activities described in the summary of Mr. Brown's case which fall under the second heading the probation officer worked with his family and involved them in helping the client.

The work of Jehu (1967), Picardie (1967) and Holder (1969) demonstrated how learning processes produce adaptive changes in the behaviour of clients either in direct treatment with a social worker, or, indirectly through changes promoted by the social worker in the client's environment. The reduction of environmental stress may be achieved in ways which strengthen the client's adaptive behaviour. The stressful behaviour of people in the client's environment may be modified by similar techniques.

The role of verbalisation in social adaptation and problem-solving provides important suggestions for social work practice. We may develop further insight into how clients may be effectively helped to analyse their situations so that new behaviour could result from new ways of perceiving. Such learning normally occurs gradually, ways of dealing with a problem being worked out slowly and laboriously, but it may also occur suddenly, the client becoming more aware of logical connections and new ways of interpreting difficulties.

To sum up, in the case of Mr. Brown it seemed that the social worker was concerned to stimulate his client's use of language (1) in describing experience, (2) in learning and organising responses by structuring information and making inferences and (3) in making generalisations as an aid in coping with his situation and weighing the actual or possible consequences of different actions.

4. SOCIAL SKILLS AND HUMAN RELATIONSHIPS

Some elements of social skill are required in all social situations. The most popular or influential members of groups have more accurate perceptions than other members. In a study of children at a summer camp it was found that popular children made more highly organised descriptions of others. Their perceptions were richer and more complex and they discriminated between people more sharply (Campbell and Yarrow, 1961). In another study it was found that while emotional meanings were interpreted more accurately from facial expressions than from speech the same people were best at interpreting both (Davitz, 1964). This suggests a general factor of sensitivity. Successful therapists and teachers are able to establish contact with a wide range of people and to offer secure relationships. The ability to establish rapport may be partly an ability to respond rapidly to the social techniques of others and partly a matter of learned techniques. Rapport involves at least three things. There must be a clear channel of communication between two people. There must be some degree of trust and acceptance of each other. There must be a relatively smooth pattern of interaction between them so that both feel comfortable and there are few interruptions. The social worker or therapist may invest quite a lot of time in the early stages of contact without trying to influence a client at all but simply in trying to build rapport and in strengthening the relationship. (See, for illustration, the case of Mrs. Mead in Day, 1972.) Studies of psychotherapy, teaching and other social skills show that without establishing the warm secure personal relationship the teacher or counsellor can do nothing. Experience suggests a number of actions which contribute to establishing rapport. These include a warm and friendly manner with eye contact and smiles at suitable times, the reduction of social barriers and the establishment of an easy pattern of interaction. It is also helpful to discover bonds such as mutual interests, and to show interest in the other person, giving him full attention and listening to him carefully. For different purposes different degrees of rapport may be required and if an interviewer is not careful an interviewee may withdraw from a situation or may become sullen and unco-operative. Argyle (1967) refers to the "need to keep the other person in play" and to ways of doing this from simply being agreeable and acting as the other person wishes to using alternative rewards such as showing approval, smiling, or being persuasive. The social skill operator must be able to arouse motivation relevant to the job in hand. In the case of teaching, for example, a lecturer may raise questions which he assumes are of interest to the audience, point out that they do not know the answers and then say that he will provide the answers in the lecture. Argyle refers also to the need to reduce anxiety and defensiveness (in the interviewee or the audience sometimes) and to the social performer's concern about the impression he is making on the client. The performer should be sensitive to feedback; the teacher, for example, should concentrate on relevant feedback such as the signs of learning and comprehension in pupils. "It is no good having a sensitive receptor system without the capacity to make the appropriate responses. The skilled performer has command of a wide range of social techniques, together with an efficient set of translation processes to tell him which ones to use." Some studies indicate attitudes on the part of a helper which contribute to a relationship being growth promoting or growth inhibiting. Baldwin and colleagues (1945) studied clusters of parental attitudes towards children. What they called the "acceptant-democratic" seemed most conducive to growth. These parents had warm egalitarian attitudes and the children showed accelerated intellectual development, more originality, more emotional security and control and less excitability than children from other types of homes. "Actively rejecting" parents' children showed slowed intellectual development, lack of originality, quarrelsomeness and emotional instability. Whitehorn and Betz (1954) studied seven young doctors who had been outstandingly helpful (the A group of patients) and seven whose schizophrenic patients had shown the least degree of improvement (the B group). The doctors in the A group tended to see their schizophrenics in terms of the personal meaning various behaviours had to the patients rather than seeing them as case histories or descriptive diagnoses. They tended to work towards goals oriented to the personality of the patients rather than such goals as reducing the symptoms or curing the disease. The helpful doctors primarily had person to person relationships and made less use of procedures classed as "passive permissive". They were even less likely to use such procedures as interpretation or advice. They were much more likely than the B group to develop a relationship in which the patient felt confidence and trust in the doctor. A number of chronic schizophrenic patients were greatly helped through operant conditioning by a vending machine. This was set to reward some kinds of behaviour. For example, if the patients pressed the lever in certain ways the machine would produce rewards such as sweets or cigarettes. It was also possible to set it so that pulling the lever would provide a hungry cat (which the patient could see in a separate enclosure) with milk. In this case a patient is rewarded for altruistic behaviour. The machine was also used to study extinction. No matter how many times the lever was pressed no reward was produced. This led a patient to become untidy, more childish in his behaviour and uncommunicative. This indicated that in the helping relationship to the machine trustworthiness was important if the relationship was to be helpful (Lindsley, 1956).

A comparison of theoretical approaches to therapeutic communications indicates the need for empirical work towards providing a comprehensive account (Staines, 1969). In the Rogerian account "empathy" or "accurate empathy" is one of the important aspects of therapeutic communications. At first this notion was the counsellor's reflection, by way of restatement, of the client's feelings (Rogers, 1942). Later the notion embraced the counsellor telling the client something different from what the client had previously told the counsellor. The later position thus stressed that counsellors introduced clients to new points of view (Rogers, 1959). If for Rogers the key word in therapist communications is "empathy" (or AE) the Freudian account's key concept is "interpretation". The difference between the two approaches is that the Rogerian's responses are less deep than the Freudian's. The Rogerian account (with the Freudian equivalent in brackets) would be that the counsellor (therapist) via his empathic responses (interpretations) brings to awareness (makes conscious) the feelings (strivings) of the experiencing organism (unconscious). In his paper Staines also reviews operant theory. Therapist communications can be regarded as reinforcing stimuli (Truax, 1966). The method is to measure changes in the frequency of response classes. For example, self-exploration may be altered by reinforcing client self-exploration and not reinforcing (or punishing) client resistance to self-exploration. A study of one long-term case handled by Rogers (Truax, 1966) found a non-random relationship between three reinforcers, empathy (positive), non-possessive warmth and acceptance (positive) and directiveness (negative) and five out of nine predicted classes of client verbal behaviour. The study showed that important reinforcement effects are found in client-centred therapy. The basic assumption of cognitive dissonance is that individuals try to maintain consistency among their cognitions. The existence of non-fitting cognitive elements produces tension which a person tries to reduce. The theory predicts the conditions under which attitude change will occur and to some extent what the changes will be. Both Rogerians and Freudians confront their clients with assertions from the client's verbalisations. Discrepancy is created. Rogerians make their comments more tentatively than Freudians and their interpretations are less deep. For these reasons they create less discrepancy than Freudians. The operant theory accounts for non-attitudinal change. Dissonance theory deals explicitly with attitude change. A combination of operant and dissonance models provides a theoretical account of the effects of a variety of therapeutic communications. Linking operant and dissonance theories and Rogerian and Freudian therapies points to substantial agreement of predictions based on the operant approach to therapeutic communications.

In one very limited study of psychotherapy it was hypothesised that there would be a significant relationship between the extent of constructive personality change in the client and four therapist variables. (1) The degree of empathic understanding of the client shown by the therapist, (2) the degree of acceptance (or unconditional positive regard) shown by the therapist, (3) the extent to which the therapist responded to the client's expressive communications. It was found that the quality of therapist-client interaction could be judged satisfactorily on the basis of a very small sample of this behaviour. Second, if the therapist's words were congruent with his feelings and if he understood the client's essential feelings as they seemed to the client there was a strong possibility that it would be an effective helping relationship (Halkides, 1958).

Heine (1950) studied the way in which persons in psychotherapy perceived the relationship. Regardless of the type of therapy clients reported similar changes in themselves. They gave some different explanations depending on the orientations of their therapists. But they agreed on what they found helpful. They said that these attitudes in the relationship had been helpful: the trust they felt in the therapist; being understood by the therapist and the feeling of independence they had had in making choices and decisions. They found it helpful when therapists clarified and openly stated feelings which they had been hazy about or hesitant in expressing. There was also high agreement on what had been unhelpful, again regardless of the therapist's orientation.

Therapist attitudes such as lack of interest, remoteness, distance, and too much sympathy were perceived as unhelpful. They found it unhelpful when therapists gave direct specific advice about decisions or had emphasised past history rather than present problems. Fiedler (1953) also found that therapists of differing orientations formed similar relationships with their clients. The relationships regarded as being composed of more constructive elements were characterised as involving an ability to understand the clients' meanings, feelings and attitudes, and a warm interest without emotional over-involvement. Importance is attached by clients to the desire to understand on the part of the helper. "Understanding" of the clients' meanings is essentially seen as communicating an attitude of desiring to understand. It was found in one study that judges presented only with the communications of therapists could assess the degree of understanding equally as well from this as from listening to the response in context. It seemed that it was an attitude of wanting to understand which was communicated by the therapists (Quinn, 1950). It was also found that success in psychotherapy is closely associated with strong and mutual liking and respect between therapist and client (Seeman, 1954).

5.   COMMUNICATION SKILLS:
A COMMON CORE OF PROCESSES

Although the studies have shown differences in orientation, design, and analysis there has been close correspondence between them in findings about helpful interviewer communications. In view of the similarity between profiles of worker communications it seems that counselling consists of a common core of processes (Hollis, 1968; Reid, 1967; Pinkus, 1968). These studies have been of empirical descriptions of the counselling process based on existing concepts or theoretical systems. An important aspect of recent work has been the making of qualitative distinctions among different kinds of verbal communication such as distinguishing a supportive comment and an interpretation. There are qualitative differences between a directive comment and one concerned with clarification. Mullen (1968) analysed half of the dialogue between counsellor and client — the counsellor's communications. He used a well-defined typology of casework procedures with the aim of contributing to a validated theory of casework practice. He asked (1) what treatment procedures are used by experienced caseworkers, (2) to what degree do these procedures vary in their occurrence and (3) what variables account for the variation that is found? Social workers' remarks were tape recorded and then coded according to six major types of treatment procedure (Hollis, 1967). These procedures are considered to be basic to casework by most therapists.

1. *Sustainment:* "I understand how you feel."
2. *Direct influence:* "You should go to the clinic."
3. *Exploration, Description, Ventilation:* "How did you feel about it?" "How old were you then?"
4. *Person — situation — reflection:* "Your reaction to him was unexpected."
5. *Reflection concerning personality patterns or dynamics:* "You expect others to distrust you."
6. *Reflection concerning early life:* "You and your father avoided each other."

The first three procedures rely on the strength of the counsellor-client relationship to achieve their effectiveness. The effectiveness of the other procedures, it is assumed, rely on the client's achieving knowledge or understanding; they rely primarily on the intellect as the source of change. The last two major procedures are commonly thought to be at the core of counselling concerned with development of self-understanding. Psychological insight, concerned with the understanding of psychological processes, is related to self-knowledge and may also be concerned with understanding of relationships with other people. When the term is used psychodynamically it refers to the appreciation of feelings by experiencing them and is not a predominantly intellectual process. This emotional insight is held to distinguish insight from other forms of understanding. This distinction and the relationship between insight and empathy is discussed by Yelloly (in Jehu *et al.*, 1972).

One of the basic elements in counselling or interviewing is attending to or listening to the client both verbally and non-verbally. A basic task in training is to help the trainee interviewer to pay attention to what the client is communicating and to refrain from jumping suddenly from one topic to another in an interview. The interviewer has to learn to be attentive and to communicate his attentiveness to the client. This learning involves a number of components; verbal attention means responding to the client's last statement without necessarily introducing a new topic. Attentiveness is also communicated non-verbally, for example by posture, movements, gestures and eye contact. These components can be practised. Showing empathy and the communication of warmth and genuineness involve the skill of reflection of feelings. This may be treated as another aspect of the skill of attending. The interviewer pays special attention to certain aspects of his interaction with the client, such as a particular emotional state. Taking a broader class of stimuli the interviewer has to attend to diverse elements of interaction simultaneously. He requires skill in bringing them together, and communicating their significance and relationship to a central theme. This involves summarising what the client says and commenting on it.

6. LEARNING EXPERIENCES AND THE DEVELOPMENT OF COMMUNICATION SKILLS

The work of teaching and learning involves (a) developing the students' ability to control his thinking so that (b) the student can develop the ability to think critically. Instruction begins with an intention to reach a conclusion or to arrive somewhere. (This is in contrast to the kind of conversation which meanders according to the whims of the people concerned.) It consists of a course of study which aims at reaching conclusions and at showing the steps or reasons leading to the conclusions. In such a process detours, blind alleys, and false steps have to be recognised and avoided. The teacher attempts to demonstrate that a conclusion is warranted by using a chain of ideas. In learning, attention is drawn to something that is uncertain or problematic and attention is sustained until the problem is resolved or clarification is achieved. Curiosity is satisfied and this is rewarding. But what motivates and satisfies curiosity is unknown although it seems to be inherent in the expression of curiosity. The child seems to be sorting out his impressions of the environment and storing of them and apparently searching for recurrent regularities. In order to do this he has to direct his curiosity and master it. One capacity which assists this is literally talking to himself. A course of instruction involves operations such as definition, interpretation, explanation and justification. These operations are carried out with language tools — words, sentences and statements. In justifying an action, for example, or in explaining an event, reasons are given or a form of classification or the application of a law or rule is demonstrated. In defining a term the rules for its use are stated. These teaching operations thus involve the systematic manipulation of words and statements, their meanings and relations, signs· and symbols. They should be distinguished from the psychological processes of perceiving, conceiving, feeling and judging.

"Good" teaching is sometimes thought of as avoiding talking to or telling students facts or opinions. Instead of these particular verbal operations the teacher involves students in problem-solving activities where they learn by planning and working out things together. It might be suggested that the involving of students in these activities requires no special knowledge on the part of the teacher apart from suitable knowledge of human relations and skill in the techniques of group organisation. However this description seems to be unsound and unrealistic. To say that "a good teacher uses these methods" is circular (as "all black birds are black birds"). The description is unrealistic because teaching operations are not exclusively group work and problem-solving. When these methods are used the learning does not result solely from peer group instruction. The teacher's role would then become only that of a psychologist to activate and support this process. In practice the teacher using these methods is involved in the processes of communication that go on, in other ways too. His work with the group and its members is to help them clarify meanings, analyse ideas, evaluate reasons and arguments, and judge or assess hypotheses and plans of action. This means helping in making and checking factual statements, and controlling his discussion of linguistic operations. Logic is an inherent part of instruction as well as being necessary in teaching the student control of his thinking. Teaching or instructing at the beginning has the aim of arriving at a conclusion: it is not supposed to be a form of sociable discourse which is undirected. An instructor carries out logical operations by using language tools. Explaining events, demonstrating laws, proving propositions, giving reasons for actions or defining terms are all logical processes. Although this may seem to be an old-fashioned style of pedagogy in fact the instructor still requires logical rules in student-centred problem-solving work, that is, in talking with the learners. Conceptual systems are functional only to the extent that they are attuned to the subtle nuances of change. The jump from theory to practice is a large one. Whether one begins theoretically with constructs from previous experience or atheoretically with generalisations from the here and now the learning process involves interaction between the raw material of human experience and the meanings attached to it. We learn from one experience, whether experiential or experimental, and generalise to other experiences that have common ingredients. We seek a system that orders these generalisations conceptually. Such systems are continually evolving and changing.

A person's performance before training has often been influenced by models. The imitation of models is a method of teaching social skills, for example in demonstrating techniques of interviewing or using one-way screens in studying play therapy methods. Sitting in with a more experienced practitioner or watching filmed performances are other methods: with all of them there is usually a verbal commentary explaining the reasons for what is being done. It has been found that people are more likely to imitate models under certain conditions. These include a good relationship with the model, when the model is similar but more successful than the imitator, when the imitator is rewarded (e.g. praised) for imitating the model, and when the model is seen to be rewarded for his behaviour (Bandura, 1962). However, a great deal has to be learned about the conditions under which an observer will vicariously practice the role of another person. The idea of identification has developed from clinical findings about apparently unconscious phenomena such as a person's guilt feelings towards his parents. A child thus learns to be like a parent without receiving any apparent reward. According to another theory everyone wants to be like the person he envies and covertly practices their roles. It may be that people are included who normally provide for his wants and establish his values although they are not necessarily envied. It seems likely that a model who has demonstrated his power to withold resources will become the object of covert learning (Whiting, 1960).

Carkhuff (1969) emphasises the utility of employing a variety of learning experiences and the need for providing a structure for trainees. The helping field has existed for too long with the artificial dichotomy of didactic or experiential learning. Both are desirable. In addition to providing an appropriately lifelike experiential base, with its punishments as well as its rewards, the trainer is responsible for teaching the trainee in a structured and didactic fashion the components of both intra- and interpersonal communications. Like the effective parent the effective helper teaches the products of his own experience while providing the experiential base within which the trainee can come to appreciate his own experience. It has been found that student-centred teaching produces higher scores on tests of reasoning ability and creativity (Smith and Johnson, 1952). Social adjustment and social skills also appear to be improved by student centred methods. This was found in experimental situations outside the classroom (Gibb, L. and Gibb, J., 1952; Asch, 1951; Fau, 1949). Also an increase of empathy occurred in classes taught by student-centred methods (Kelley and Pepitone, 1952). Another study found that students preferred a directive method of teaching. It seemed that the group in which the tutor is non-directive may increase the student's feeling of helplessness because he does not know what to do in order to do well in his course. It might be predicted that an effect of tutor permissiveness would depend on whether or not a group possessed the skills necessary to achieve their goals. In a new group it could depend on the presence or absence of individuals in the groups who had had previous experience of working in democratic groups (McKeachie, 1954). Such speculations need to be tested. To make research productive theories and methods need sharpening.

The plan of this book which follows takes up the theories which I have discussed in this chapter. It seems that we do have suggestive evidence about how to make learning effective but it would be foolish to assert that in the present state of knowledge there are verified rules. One guideline, however, is that learning requires organisation. To organise learning experiences is a challenging problem which requires acquaintance with the learners and their needs. The teacher-learner relationship, like other relationships, constantly changes and each group of trainees, and each individual, develop their own ways of working. People aiming to facilitate learning have to be knowledgeable about their subject-matter in order to make decisions about what the learning objectives are, and possible ways in which they might need to be modified. The organisation of learning experiences is also based on information about how learning takes place. These topics are taken up again therefore in Chapter 2. The following chapter is concerned with the variety of ways information is presented and discussed, and some ways in which communication skills (particularly verbal skills) may be developed. Chapter 4 is concerned with learning about influences on communication and is followed by discussion of learning about interviewing (Chapter 5). Carkhuff (1969) said that perhaps the key means for developing effective communication of helping is role playing. It enables the trainee to be involved in lifelike experiences and to experience being the person in need of help as well as the helper. Role playing and other kinds of simulation exercise have been used in social work training (as well as in other professional trainings) for some time but in recent years the process seems to have accelerated. Chapter 6 discusses and illustrates simulation exercises. In Chapter 7 the learning which may take place in unstructured groups is considered. Evidence about the effectiveness of various approaches is complex and sometimes conflicting conclusions or competing claims make it difficult to assess different methods. As with topics raised earlier there is room for different opinions and argumentation which this section provokes. Carkhuff, referred to above, said that the most effective training programmes appear to be those that integrate the didactic, experiential, and modelling sources of learning. Human-relations training focuses upon the core facilitative and action-oriented dimensions, particularly those that use role-playing techniques as an introduction to skilful constructive communication. Illustrations of combined methods are included in this section. In a further section of Chapter 7 supervised field experience is discussed.

CHAPTER 2

The Organisation of Learning

1. BASIC PROCESSES IN LEARNING

Learning is defined (Hilgard and Bower, 1966) as the process by which an activity originates or is changed through reacting to an encountered situation, provided that the characteristics of the change in activity cannot be explained on the basis of native response tendencies, maturation or temporary states of the organism (for example, fatigue or drugs). An essential feature of learning therefore is the experience which leads to changed behaviour: learning occurs whenever the activity of an organism brings about a relatively permanent change in its behaviour. In discussing learning it is necessary to distinguish the kinds of changes which are included and related changes which are not regarded as learning. Different kinds of change may be identified and, perhaps, described as different forms of learning. There is the acquisition, understanding and retention of new information or knowledge. There is a change in motivation such as coming to like doing something that you previously disliked. There are changes in deep-seated attitudes or beliefs, for example changes in political or philosophical views. Fourthly, there are developments in acquiring skills.

The unconditioned and conditioned reflexes are two of the mechanisms which regulate behaviour. Conditioning is a process by which a response comes to be elicited by a stimulus or, more generally, a situation, other than that to which it is the natural or normal response. The original use of the term was where a reflex action, normally following one stimulus, came to be elicited by a different stimulus. Pavlov measured salivation in dogs. The presentation of food was called the unconditioned stimulus. It produced salivation, called the unconditioned response. Where food was presented at the same time as a bell rang this turned the originally neutral stimulus (the presentation of food) into a conditioned stimulus which now elicited salivation as a conditioned response. The neutral stimulus, after repeated presentations of food, came to elicit salivation in the dog when it occurred on its own. But, although the natural response of salivation to food in the mouth was found not to change the acquired response to a previously neutral stimulus (the ringing of the bell) was liable to die away after a time if it was not followed by presentation of food. Extinction is the term for the abolition of a conditioned reflex by repeated stimulation without being accompanied by the unconditioned stimulus. Having consistently followed the sound of the bell with food and having established a conditioned response (salivation) the situation is changed so that food no longer follows the bell. As the bell is repeatedly rung but no food is given the conditioned response eventually disappears. A hungry cat is put into a cage. Food is available outside the cage and can be seen through the bars. The cage is built in such a way that an operation like pulling a string or pressing a lever opens the cage door. At first the cat reaches out towards the food, tries to get out of the cage and so on. At some stage it operates the escape device by accident and is able to leave the cage and eat the food. This behaviour is repeated and the cat more and more often and more quickly shifts towards the cage-opening device. The period between being put in the cage and getting out becomes progressively shorter. These results are summarised as follows: acts followed by a state of affairs which the individual (or animal) does not avoid and which he often tries to preserve or attain are selected or fixated. In other words, behaviour which is followed by reward or success will tend to be repeated whereas behaviour which is not rewarded will tend to die away. Activity which results in the reduction of a need is said to be reinforced. Reinforcement is the individual's reaction to the results of his own activity. Thus it refers to food for the dog coming after the ringing of the bell. The conditioned stimulus is followed by the unconditioned stimulus. The sound of the bell associated with food (primary reinforcement) may come to have reward value in itself. It may come to serve as a secondary reinforcer. This is reinforcement through something which, while it does not satisfy a need directly, has been associated with this satisfaction. This learning process is at first one of trial and error, and it is known as instrumental learning. In instrumental learning or operant conditioning the learner is active in the sense that he has to make a specific move or perform a particular act. In both conditioning and instrumental learning A is followed by B. In conditioning A is an external event. In instrumental learning A is an act of the learner. In instrumental learning and in conditioning the learning of a sequence is involved. A stimulus becomes a signal or a cue indicating what is going to happen next or what can be obtained as the result of a particular action.

If a particular learning situation does not occur again for a long time the effect of the first learning will probably be lost or forgotten. It is important for repetitions to be spaced properly for any task that is being learned. Much of the effectiveness of reward learning is lost if its administration is delayed for too long. In order to obtain food the animal in the experiment has to discriminate among the stimuli in the test situation. If the animal acts on anything except the piece of string or the lever it receives no reinforcement. It has to discriminate between behaviour which enables it to reach the food and behaviour which does not. In fact animals can learn to discriminate accurately among various stimuli; this process of stimulus discrimination is important in survival. Stimulus generalisation is complementary. It is simply illustrated by a child who was conditioned to fear a white rat and also become afraid of a man with a white beard and a white rabbit. Fear was generalised from the original stimulus to other stimuli which resembled it. This represents a departure from the original learning situation. As well as fearing the white rat the child came to fear objects which differed from it in various respects. Feedback or knowledge of results is another important factor in learning. This enables a person to correct his mistakes and then by continuing to practice he can go on in developing skill.

An account of learning processes which failed to refer to cognitive theories, even briefly, would be inadequate. Cognitive theories emphasise behaviour in complex circumstances which might be described as insightful. Behaviour appropriate to the circumstances appears comparatively suddenly. Problems arise, however, in the attempt to explain how cognitive maps lead to appropriate behaviour.

We lack models of how understanding or purpose work. Gestalt means form or configuration. The term Holistic is also applied to Gestalt psychology, because of the emphasis on the whole person or the whole situation with which he copes. Gestalt psychologists argue that perception is more than the sum of sensations derived from introspection. They argue that wholes come first and parts have little or no meaning except when considered with respect to their place in the whole. Whereas behaviourists regard habits as chains of conditioned reflexes Gestaltists have demonstrated that some learning defies piecemeal analysis. There are two basic ideas in Gestalt psychology. The Gestalt view was developed from the study of perception. Perception, it is said, is organised and the organisation tends to be as good as the stimulus conditions permit. It was suggested that since wholeness and organisation are essential features of psychological processes they cannot be analysed (Kohler, 1957). Kohler stressed that learning occurs through the perception of essential relationships. He devised problems for apes in which the direct path to a goal was not open but where another indirect but visible path was available. In his experiments he suspended bananas from the top of a cage out of the apes' reach but provided them with sticks or boxes with which they could reach the food. Kohler found that generally the apes would sit for some time looking at the problem. Often, it seemed that a solution would suddenly occur to them and they would follow the indirect method in dealing with the problem. The ability to see relationships between parts of a problem and suddenly coming to a solution without previous trial-and-error approaches is called insight. Kohler suggested that insight was used whenever possible in problem-solving, trial and error being used only in the last resort.

Objections have been made to the use of insight as an explanatory concept. For example, it does not show how reorganisation of a perceptual field occurs. The term seems to be ambiguous: it is used in two senses, first as a description of a pattern of behaviour observed in some problem-solving situations and second as the name of a psychological process which controls behaviour. Another difficulty involved in the concept of insight is the part played by previous experience. In some experiments apes showed insightful learning only after quite a lot of preliminary training in simpler tasks (Harlow and

Harlow, 1949). However, the fact that under experimental conditions animals or humans start new learning at the trial-and-error level does not mean that they must all go through this stage whenever they learn something new. Short cuts may be found to reduce the random searches in the early stages of learning: teaching may assist this process. Although the concept of insight involves difficulties it is used in practice to describe a kind of understanding which involves the appreciation of previously unrecognised patterns and links between events. It is a useful concept of relevance to discussion of problems of behaviour change (Yelloly in Jehu *et al*, 1972). It is helpful to regard insight as a cognitive process involving the recognition and labelling of behavioural events or sequences. The nature of human and animal learning is controversial; no one theory explains all the evidence. Broadly speaking there are two approaches: (a) the association view of learning as stimuli response chains produced to reduce needs and strengthened by use; (b) the field theorist approach considering learning as a purposeful attempt to interpret and construct a mental image of a problem situation. Put crudely, for teaching the implications of the two approaches are a choice between habit-forming procedures or meaningful explanations. That this is a crude dichotomy is obvious: learning experiences utilise both approaches. It seems that insightful learning does not occur without previous experience and the quality of learning depends on what has gone before.

2. EMOTIONAL FACTORS AND MOTIVATION

Basic needs or drives which are innate lead to activity aimed at ensuring physical survival. They lead to the avoidance of painful experiences, to the reduction of feelings of hunger and thirst and so on. An important basic need of animals is that of knowing the environment which involves the investigation of novel situations. This orienting reflex is thus evoked when new stimuli enter the environment, in order to maintain equilibrium or reach a new equilibrium. An unknown stimulus may appear to be dangerous. Once it has been investigated and found to be harmless equilibrium is restored. The tendency towards the maintenance of equilibrium as motivating behaviour is seen in the new baby. Activities which restore equilibrium are found to be pleasant and are likely to be repeated. The young baby in addition to basic needs for food and warmth needs to have physical contact with the mother or mother substitute. Experiments with monkeys have shown that this need for contact comfort is not dependent on the need for food. Monkeys developed attachments to a substitute mother made of wire covered with towelling but not to wire frames which held food. The attachment to the towelling mother was very similar to that usually made to the natural mother. Characteristically people try to achieve equilibrium and to maintain their stability with the minimum effort that is necessary. A principle of learning is derived from this — the principle of economy. Learning takes place through experience: as well as trying to achieve equilibrium with minimum effort people learn actively — by doing things — by trying things out. The fundamental needs are related to simple patterns of behaviour. Human behaviour is complex, but to a large extent it develops on the basis of primitive impulses through learning. It is naive to suggest that a particular need can be simply related to any piece of behaviour, but biological motives are important, partly because of the feelings with which they are associated. As children develop the need for affection or for approval gradually becomes differentiated from the more basic physical needs with which they are associated. Parental approval may be a powerful influence on a child's capacity to co-operate with other people. The orienting reflex can be a strong reinforcement of feelings of satisfaction in solving problems.

In addition to the basic needs much human behaviour is controlled by acquired motives. These motives are acquired in the course of development from personal experience and learning. These acquired motives can often be traced back to early learning experiences and they gain strength and persistence with reinforcement. Two illustrations have just been given. We can extend them by observing how most people want praise and credit for their achievements and for what they attempt to do. They also want to feel that they belong in groups of other people who think of them with respect and who have feelings of warmth towards them. They derive satisfaction from participating with others in group activities such as making decisions and taking action. The need to have a feeling of security, shown in a wide variety of ways, seems to be a universal and deep need. It is often considered in relation to people's needs to feel self-respect, to acquire material things or psychological qualities, or to be creative in very many different ways.

Inevitably accounts of motivation carry the danger of over-simplification. It is necessary not to overlook hierarchies of needs and the complexity of motivation. There are further complications. For example, people learn how to satisfy their needs and wants but they also develop new needs through the learning process. Motives are purposeful but once the aim of survival is satisfied other experiences associated with that satisfaction may become motives themselves independent of their original association. For example, behaviour rooted in childhood may later become independent of its "cause" and yet the response may persist. A person may be unaware of his motivation: unconscious motives govern much behaviour. A young child who had to fight for his nourishment may develop an aggressive adult. He may behave as if always threatened by hunger. This response may well become generalised so that as well as grabbing for his food he grabs for many other things — such as status, or other peoples' ideas. He might even feel driven to control or dominate others as a mode of "possession".

Human behaviour cannot be adequately described solely in deterministic terms. A person can be thought of as being guided by rules and so aiming his behaviour at certain objectives. This description too has to take learning into account. Rules and objectives are derived from experience: they are learned. To recapitulate briefly homeostasis is the term for the processes of maintaining constant physical and chemical conditions within an organism despite external change. It is the primary function of most organs of the body. Feedback means the return of impulses to a control centre where they play a part in further control. An example is that of impulses produced by muscular activity returning to the brain, informing it of the posture of the muscles and thus contributing to further control of these muscles. It is comparable with the functions of a governor on a steam engine which feeds back the information that more or less steam is needed. Feedback is fundamental in the maintenance of homeostasis. Learning involves adopting patterns of behaviour which further this adaptive process. Motivation refers to whatever it is that causes behaviour. It refers to the tendency of the organism to seek a state of equilibrium (homeostasis).

An animal deprived of but requiring food is motivated to search for food (Bowlby, 1971).

Many kinds of motivation affect learning. Sufficient drive to learn must be present but if there is too much internal pressure, i.e. if the student is too highly motivated, this can lead to a high degree of anxiety. Too high a degree of anxiety interferes with learning. There is clinical and experimental evidence of the importance of emotion in learning (Freud, 1966; McGeoch and Irion, 1952). Emotional factors affect what is remembered or forgotten. At school liking for a teacher usually correlates highly with interest in the subject he teaches and therefore the capacity to learn and retain the subject. There is a tendency to remember material which fits in with existing attitudes and beliefs and a corresponding tendency to forget evidence which appears to threaten them. Recall is selective, especially of controversial or emotionally changed subjects. The problem is that the student cannot normally neglect the study of topics which he finds distasteful or of evidence which he finds it hard to accept. He cannot usually present one-sided arguments without also giving the evidence for the other side. It is not surprising that emotional difficulties are sometimes reasons for educational failure or drop out both at school and college. Learning about social and psychological problems involves thinking which is emotionally often highly charged. This means that prejudices and value judgements which are involved have to be subjected as far as possible to impartial scrutiny. The learner has to develop understanding or insight into his own emotionally determined views about problems or his attitudes towards certain kinds of behaviour. Some subject matter arouses old emotional conflicts or bears on a student's current life situation and it may appear to challenge or in fact conflict with a learner's cultural values.

In the previous chapter I said that identification and imitation are important in learning. The attitudes of the teacher or facilitator help to shape those of group members both towards each other and towards what they are learning. Certain expectations will be communicated subtly or explicitly by the leader's behaviour. The ability to listen attentively, to control resistance or negative feelings towards a speaker, and to support or encourage clear thinking in problem-solving can be learned in part through demonstration. Imitative learning is defined as the tendency to reproduce the behaviour of living or symbolic models. Children learn skills through the use of toys which are smaller versions of adult equipment; often they accurately reproduce the appropriate adult behaviour without any direct instruction. They also learn from human examples, for example, real or fictional characters who are used by their parents to show what behaviour is desirable or undesirable. Symbolic models may be in the form of pictures or writing or they may be communicated orally. In some cases it is difficult to see how learning could occur without models to imitate; imitation often speeds up learning (Jehu, 1967). Imitative learning can occur by observing a model's behaviour without actually reproducing it. Learning a language without the opportunity to hear and imitate speech might be impossible. It is suggested, for these reasons, that imitation cannot be explained as a situation in which a learner's responses are reinforced or not reinforced, according to whether or not they match those of the model. A further reason for distinguishing imitative learning and operant conditioning is that it is doubtful if some kinds of behaviour could be acquired only by the method of successive approximation and reinforcement of appropriate responses. Psycho-dynamic learning theories consider thought processes as affected by an individual's perceptions. The positive and negative values placed on his perceptions derive from the person's cultural conditioning and from his inner needs and drives. New ideas are seen as good or bad according to past experience. From this perspective the emotional elements in learning are thus underlined.

The traditional view of motivation in learning described above has, until recently, been expressed in terms of a theory of drives and reinforcement. Learning occurred because a response produced by a stimulus was followed by a reduction in a primary drive. The notion of secondary reinforcement indicated that any state even remotely associated with the reduction of a primary drive could also produce learning. Bruner (1961) does not accept this view; he maintains that a person's full intellectual capacities are developed by much more complex strategies of thinking. In his active involvement in what he learns the learner organises information into forms that are meaningful and useful to him. Bruner writes of effective interaction with the environment as competence (i.e. proficiency or skill). Competence describes such actions as exploring, crawling, walking, perceiving and thinking. It is necessary to make competence a motivational concept. He suggests that there are activities that develop the competence motive in children and make it a driving force behind behaviour. The exercise of competence motives strengthens the degree to which they gain control over behaviour and reduce the effects of extrinoic rewards. In the end this development frees the learner from immediate stimulus control. Thinking is characterised as starting with a dialogue of speech and gesture between child and parent. Autonomous thinking begins when the child is first able to internalise these conversations and "talk to himself". This is a typical sequence in the development of competence. Bruner then argues that teaching also can be done in this way. The narrative of teaching is of the order of the conversation. Competence develops with the internalisation of the narrative and its rules of generation; the child becomes capable of running off the narrative on his own. Success and failure are experienced now, not as reward and punishment but as information. He can regard success as indicating he is on the right track and failure as indicating he is on the wrong one. The hypothesis is advanced that emphasis on discovery in learning leads to the learner organising what he meets in such a way as to discover regularity and relatedness and avoids failure to keep account of the uses to which information might have to be put. It is a necessary condition for learning a variety of problem-solving techniques, of transforming information for better use, of learning how to learn. A further hypothesis is that if learning is approached as a task of discovery (rather than "learning about *x*") there will be a tendency for learning to become autonomous, discovery itself being rewarding.

Curiosity, then, is one motive for learning. Another is the drive to achieve mastery or competence, capacity, or skill. These words describe activities such as crawling, walking, exploring, attending and perceiving. Complex accomplishments like skilful manipulation and speech promote effective interaction with the environment. As well as this kind of achieved capacity there is competence motivation, an intrinsic need to deal with the environment. Behaviour which leads to competence is not random, and continues because it satisfies an intrinsic need. It seems that an activity that is socially approved requires a meaningful structure if it requires skill a little beyond what the person possesses: effort is needed to learn it. Social approval is of great importance. A person wants to have the respect of his reference group and tends to model himself on another person. Pleasure comes from the feeling of success in being like the model; it is painful to feel that one has let him down. The model is a certain kind of person, belonging to a particular group and loyalty is extended to include this group. Identification appears to be a self-sustaining process because it passes to the learner the control of punishment and reward. The child achieves some independence of external rewards and punishments when he internalises his own standards. In the process of teaching a skill a parent or teacher serves as a competence model. In learning language from the parent the trial and error, correction and revision process continues until the child learns the rules for generating and transforming sentences. A set of productive habits enable him to be his own sentence matter and his own controller. He learns the rules of the language, and language skills, by interaction with his teacher-parent. The teacher or parent also teaches more than this. He passes on attitudes towards a subject and toward learning itself. It has already been indicated that the teacher is more than someone to imitate. Potentially he is a competence model, or a working model, with whom to interact. In becoming a language speaker the language of interaction with the model becomes part of the learner. He wants the model's respect and to share the model's values. The teacher becomes part of the student's inner dialogue. This seems to mean that the teacher is now not just a model to imitate: he is someone with whom to interact.

There seems to be a human need to respond to others and to work jointly with them towards objectives. This reciprocity seems to be important for survival. It should not be confused with a motive to conform. Barker (1963) said that the best way he found to predict children's behaviour was to know their situations. Situations have a demand value that seem to have little to do with motives like that of conformity. Where reciprocity or joint action is needed for a group to reach an objective it seems that there are processes which carry an individual along into learning or acquiring a competence required by the situation. Although little seems to be known about the motive to reciprocate it seems to be a motive to learn as well. Children learn their roles in families and schools through reciprocal learning. This reciprocal learning may be seen in complicated games. A more specific example is the way a young child learns to use the pronouns "I" and "you" correctly. The mother says to the child "you go to bed now". The child says "No, you go to bed". The mother is amused. "Not me but you". At first the child feels confused but then learns that "you" refers to himself when another uses it and to another person when he uses it, and the other way round with "I". Reciprocity occurs in the give and take of discussion. But if reciprocally working groups are to give support to learning by stimulating each member to take an active part there will be a need for tolerance for the specialised roles that develop, such as the experimenter and the critic. From the cultivation of these interlocking roles members get the sense of operating reciprocally in a group. The emergence of the role of auxiliary teacher can be encouraged, thus getting away from the oversimplified view of "teachers and experts" higher in the hierarchy than "students and laymen".

3.   SYMBOLS AND HUMAN LEARNING

The stimulus response theories of learning involve the notion that thinking is produced by chains of responses and that what is learned may be thought of as habit. Habits are conditioned responses which in their highest form become smoothly operating skills. If the learned habits prove to be inappropriate in a particular situation the person attempts to solve the problem, at least at first, by trial-and-error activity. However, it is also important to recognise that human learning is only partly a matter of associating responses acquired as a result of conditioning. These cannot be regarded as comprehensive accounts of learning, because the acquisition of new skills and the capacity for abstract thinking are too complex. Insight learning involves solving new problems by combining previous experiences together so as to produce a novel solution. Learning may thus be a far more complicated process than conditioning schemes suggest. Nevertheless all the different forms of learning have elements of reinforcement and association in them. Conditioning processes in human beings are similar to those of other animals. In human beings the more complex forms of learning are built on conditioning but it is very different from that of other animals. They develop a highly complex pattern of reactions determined both by their physical environment and by psychological processes of abstraction and generalisation. Language is the medium used in dealing with concepts. It has a profound influence on the processes of conditioning. Instead of responding only to the physical aspect of stimulation most of the human being's behaviour is influenced by its symbolic aspects. Human beings have obtained a high degree of control of their physical environment (the social environment appears to raise complicated questions) because of their capacity to manipulate symbols. Language represents aspects of the environment symbolically and permits the linking of signs and stimuli which could not otherwise be associated or related. Complex stimulation can lead to correspondingly complex behaviour patterns. For this reason human learning is more complicated than the learning of other animals.

It is suggested that understanding or insight develops through studying a complete set of relations or a whole subject or the whole of a problem rather than just through analysing its parts. The learner tries to organise what he sees or studies in such a way that it "makes sense" to him. Experiments were mounted which showed that animals could recognise knowledge and thus solve problems (Kohler, 1925). This kind of learning, usually referred to as insight learning, involves a perception of the relationships between the elements of a problem and the solution. The whole situation is restructured so that it is seen in a new way. The most important step in human reasoning, therefore, is the making of inferences concerning the solutions of problems. Where they have to face problems which cannot be met in a mature way inferences are made about the solutions of problems. They are made, as we have said, on the basis of past experience. Inferences are usually elaborated either by further implicit activity or by checking on their application. Insight learning seems to require a perception of the relationships between the elements of a problem and its solution. The whole situation, including the present and past experiences of the learner, is reorganised so that it is perceived in a new way leading to a solution. Possessing the necessary previous experience is not itself sufficient to find a solution: the learner has to be able to reorganise the situation and then relate earlier experience to it. Also, associational processes in reasoning are linked to the way the learner perceives the problem. This "set" facilitates recall of some items and inhibits the recall of others. Despite this tendency to search in particular directions, certain limitations on thinking, for example, accepting the first inference that comes to mind, can hinder the search for a solution. The reasoning process is more efficient when there are frequent changes of direction and new searches for fresh inferences. Problems may often remain unsolved because they have not been properly defined: sometimes it is not even clear what a problem consists of or if it really exists. Thus cognitive theories of learning regard thinking as being related to certain processes in the brain involving memories and expectations and as involving goal-seeking behaviour. Instead of (or as well as?) learning habits the person assembles evidence and makes decisions about alternative kinds of activity. Instead of trial-and-error learning there is problem solving by insight. Thinking is a kind of perceptual structuring of the problem; decision-making and action are based on perception. Learning is regarded as being based on generalisation, i.e. applying principles to specific situations. The generalisation theory, then, regards learning as the development of generalised methods of dealing with various categories of situations or problems. Many types of learning occur because of the learner's perceiving general principles that might be used or developing a general attitude towards certain situations. Adherents of this theory view objectives in general terms. They tend to view objectives as general modes of reaction to be developed rather than highly specific habits to be acquired.

4.   SOME IMPLICATIONS FOR PLANNING TRAINING PROGRAMMES

The brief survey above shows that learning involves the development of mental and/or physical powers and personal character. It involves change. It occurs whenever modifications take place in people whether they result from influences exerted by individuals or groups or other individuals later in life or from social pressures such as those involved in the upbringing of children. Modifications in states of knowledge or information involve processes like observing, memorising, recalling and reasoning. Changes in skill may also be illustrated by child development. Everyday living also involves changing attitudes, and values and in developing interests. What are the implications in considering objectives in training or education? It was said earlier that the orienting reflex was a fundamental factor in behaviour and it seems to be very important in learning. This suggests that orienting activity should be related to current learning and new stimulation should be introduced before habituation occurs. In other words, new learning experiences need to be available so that interest is maintained. A person's interest in and receptivity to new material is enhanced while orienting activity continues. The most important points about the study of conditioning are (a) that essentially learning depends on making connections and (b) that the establishment of these connections depends on their occurring near to each other in time and space. Remembering depends on the building up of associations. One thing reminds a person of another thing because they occurred simultaneously at some time in the past or because they are linked in some other way (for example, they have certain properties in common). Reference to stimulus generalisation shows that learning a response to one stimulus will produce similar responses to similar stimuli. This is called transfer of learning. Positive transfer refers to building appropriately on earlier learning. Negative transfer involves that the learning of an earlier skill interferes with the learning of a second skill. Only where there is quite close similarity between stimulus situations can transfer be expected. It cannot be expected that training in one subject will improve performance in subjects which are very different. Learning one method of tackling a problem and then later learning a completely different method of dealing with the same problem, involving activities antagonistic to those previously learned, makes learning the second method far more difficult than if the first method had never been employed.

Too much concentration on trying to master detail may involve the student in failing to understand the overall outline of a subject or topic. Getting an idea of total content makes it possible to select relevant material; this involves asking specific questions. The principle of surveying the whole before learning a particular part may be illustrated by reference to reading. It is necessary to select relevant information from books and from case records. First, however, obtaining a general view of the material, e.g. by studying the list of topics covered, summaries of sections and so on, enables the reader to find what is particularly relevant or of interest to him. The general reading may indicate a need for a second reading or, as stated above, what sections require detailed work. Further questions arise on second reading about the topic and this leads to a more critical or more sharply focused study of the evidence or the arguments. Notes, which may refer to other work, are profitably made next. The student then proceeds to other work altogether with periodic revision of this detailed work. Effort and time can be saved if reading can be speeded up. But there are obviously dangers if one's work becomes too superficial. A general survey can be a safeguard against too severe skimming of the surface. There is less forgetting when new facts can be linked to existing knowledge. There are several ways that this can be done, e.g. discussion with other people, formulating meaningful analogies (although it will be remembered that these can be dangerous tools) and thinking of concrete examples from one's own experience. The more that this can be done the better will be the student's retention. His existing insight in the field of study constitutes background to which his new learning can be related. This connects with evidence that learnings which are consistent with each other, which are in that sense integrated and coherent, reinforce each other. But pieces of learning which are inconsistent with each other require more time to disentangle and may interfere with learning.

Reinforcements do not necessarily have to take place each time a trainee or student responds. Partial or occasional reinforcement can sometimes be more effective than constant reinforcement. This is the basic principle of learning. It is preferable to learn under the incentive of rewards. Incentives, however, will only be effective if they are important to the student. The reward must be wanted and the material or skill to be learned must have meaning to the student. When he does something that leads to success he is more likely to repeat it. Earlier learning tends to be extinguished both by lapse of time and by activities intervening between learning and recall. It is advisable therefore to make arrangements for periodic revision. It means, for example, that after reading each important part of a book the student should put the book aside and attempt to remember the important points he has read. This is an application of the principle of learning by using information and by active response to material. Early revision of lecture notes, or early recording of an interview, while the initial imprinting is still fresh, helps to guard against the danger that these initial impressions cannot be amplified. This makes it impossible to expand them later or to organise them systematically for later repetition or linking with new evidence. Failure to understand is often due to failure to link new to existing information or because of inability to organise it. Such failures occur, for example, if a great deal of attention is given to a secondary activity like trying to make verbatim notes instead of giving attention to the speaker, noting the important points and the gist of what he is saying. Once the general scope of a curriculum has been worked out the subject of the course is divided into different homogeneous parts. The problem is that in making this division the curriculum can be changed into many separate courses unconnected with the others. It is not easy to retain the central units or teaching on some subjects for purposes of preparation but at the same time interrelating them. The effectiveness of the unit method of course planning depends on how skilfully the different parts are related. Tyler (1949) reviews the problems faced in developing an effective organisation of learning experiences and suggests principles useful in dealing with them. He suggests the following steps: (1) Agreeing on the general scheme of organisation. (2) Agreeing on the general organising principles to be followed (for example, using a chronological sequence; proceeding from the concrete to the more abstract; starting from smaller social units to larger ones and so on). (3) Agreeing on whether units will be daily lessons or sequences of topics. (4) Developing "source units" or flexible plans. The purpose of these is to provide a great deal of possible material from which a selection can be made for use with any particular group of students. These plans are flexible so that they can be modified in the light of the needs, interests and abilities of any group. A typical source unit includes a statement of major objectives expected to be obtained from the kinds of learning experiences outlined, a description of a variety of experiences that can be used in attaining the objectives, an outline of the cumulating experiences that can be used to help the student at the end to integrate and organise what he has derived from the unit and a list of source materials. Tyler found that it was difficult to suggest possible schemes that may serve to organise source units but in the main the more successful ones have been organised around problems.

Table 1. Plan for instruction: basic psychological needs

Learning outcome	Tutor's behaviour	Trainees' behaviour
Understanding the nature of basic psychological needs and implications for social work.	Discusses the concept of psychological need and describes basic needs. Asks for illustration of the relation between needs and behaviour, and of effects of satisfying or frustrating needs.	Relate the ideas to their experience. Give illustrations.
People want recognition: as individuals, of their worth, of their views and ideas.	Recognition involves acknowledging individual's dignity and worth. Asks for examples. Leads discussion of examples	Take notes and relate to experience. Recall examples. Interpret and generalise.
People want opportunity: to exercise initiative to assure responsibility and to feel worthwhile.	Discusses the concept of opportunity and its relation to freedom of action and initiative. Raises questions about how people can be given more satisfying opportunities.	Take notes and begin to broaden idea of opportunity. Discuss own experiences and get a wider perspective on needs.
People want to feel they belong, that they are making a contribution to a group, and to feel they are accepted and know what is going on.	Explains concept of affiliation and sociability and implications. Asks how the need to belong may be frustrated. Asks how feelings of belonging may be promoted.	Take notes. Recall feelings of need to belong. Perceive signs of feeling isolated. Comment on ways of helping.
People need to feel secure (and to maintain "equilibrium") against unexpected change, that they can depend on others and not feel "threatened".	Discusses relationship between concepts of "belonging", and needs for opportunity and recognition. Asks trainees to elaborate and discuss implications.	Thinks about application in helping: how security may be threatened and how feeling of personal equilibrium may be restored.
Recall and review the work.	Summarise main points.	Summarise and note main points.

Plan for instruction: basic psychological needs (see Table 1)
Sources
Munn, N. (1961) *Psychology*. Harrap.
Towle, C. (1957) *Common Human Needs*. National Association of Social Workers, New York.

Aim

The aim is to introduce the idea of basic psychological needs and their significance for individuals and their behaviour and to raise questions about implications for social-work practice. Each psychological need will be discussed and trainees will be involved in giving examples and discussing them.

The plan for instruction in basic psychological needs consists of five steps. The lecture or lecture-discussion begins with the tutor introducing the concept of need and of what will be covered in the period. Then he asks questions of the students and in this way alerts them to points to watch for. He draws attention to the interpretation and application of the material in experiences students have had in practice. The tutor explains or analyses each element as the programme proceeds and finally recapitulates or summarises the main points. Table 2 analyses these stages for different learning methods. The factors in this table should be found in all learning programmes, ideally. This system, in ideal form, ensures that the principles of effective learning are built in to any particular programme. Most teaching periods usually involve combinations of methods rather than only lecture, simulation exercise, or group discussion. Often, however, in any one period one method will be the principal one.

Table 2. Different learning experiences analysed in stages

Stage	Lecture	Simulation-exercises	Group discussion
1.	Outline of ground to be covered.	Outline of exercise, e.g. what roles are to be played.	Agenda and objective of discussion.
2.	Important questions to be dealt with.	What are the crucial elements in situations of the type to be demonstrated?	Important questions to be dealt with.
3.	Main lecture.	Conduct the exercise.	Conduct the discussion.
4.	Trainees give summary of what was said.	Trainees analyse what happened.	Trainees summarise result of discussion.
5.	Recapitulation later: abridged version of lecture.	Trainees recall and interpret important elements of exercise.	Follow up discussion or provide written summary of discussion.

5. PROBLEMS IN ORGANISING LEARNING EXPERIENCES

The problems involved in defining educational objectives are ones of identifying the knowledge, skills and attitudes required for the present and future performance of a number of tasks. Education has to take account both of the students' interests and needs and of contemporary social change. Thus social work, in common with other professions, demands of its entrants a more broadly based training, and flexibility in using training to respond to new situations. Rapid changes in knowledge and techniques mean that trainees need to develop skills in acquiring and mastering new information, and the ability to co-operate effectively in teams. The emphasis is more on such things as how to obtain information and apply it to new situations in contrast to "acquiring a body of knowledge". Perhaps it should be pointed out that this is a matter of relative emphasis. That this is a current tendency in education in no way implies a devaluation of acquiring information or of research in general. Research in social work practice and education is badly needed.

Supposing that objectives have been defined a new set of problems faces the educator. These problems arise in attempting to translate the objectives into appropriate academic and field learning experiences (including content and method) and organising them in ways which build on and reinforce each other. This is the problem of devising a course of learning which forms a whole integrated system. There are further problems in deciding on the degree of generality or specificity to be desired in formulations both of the behavioural and content aspects of objectives. As far as the behavioural aspect is concerned the problem is one of obtaining a level of generality in keeping with what is known about the psychology of learning. More general objectives are usually desirable. To identify appropriate learning experiences it is helpful to attempt to differentiate the characteristics of the behaviour desired, for example, the acquisition of information (through memorising) and the ability to apply principles to new problems, primarily involving the interpretation and use of facts and principles (memorising is still implied here, but, in addition, ability to indicate meaning, to provide illustrations, and the ability to apply facts and principles to other situations).

Learning takes place through the student's experience, that is, through his reactions to the environment in which he is placed. In planning a course it is therefore necessary to decide on the educational experiences which should be provided. It is through participation in them that learning will take place. To a large extent emotions determine thinking and action: students have strong feelings about the process of learning and about the process of helping people. Towle sees learning as having the effect of reducing anxiety for some people and of increasing anxiety for others, as ways of achieving stability or equilibrium. In developing training programmes the major problems include (1) the objectives a course should try to attain, (2) the learning experiences that can be provided that are likely to bring about the objectives, (3) the effective organisation of the learning experiences (a) to help provide continuity and sequence for the learner and (b) to help him in integrating what could appear to be isolated learning experiences, and (4) the testing of how effective the learning experiences are. Information which is important in thinking about objectives is what is available about the students. It is not always easy to define their present level of development and their needs. Their interests need to be considered, what activities they will be expected to perform, and the problems they are likely to encounter. Suggestions for objectives come from the subject to be learned and from the opinions of specialists in that particular field. This involves thinking about the contribution the subject can make to the students' education and the kinds of learning that can come from study of the subject, and its contribution to other subjects. The learning experiences in a training programme are not the same as the content of the programme. They are the interactions between the learner and the situations to which he can react. Learning experiences appropriate for attaining objectives will vary with the kind of objectives aimed at. But there are some general principles that apply to the selection of learning experiences. They are as follows.

First, for an objective to be attained a student must have experiences that give him the opportunity to practice the kind of behaviour implied by the objective.

Learning experiences must give the student satisfaction from carrying on the kind of behaviour implied by the objectives. It follows, thirdly, that the reactions desired in the experience are within the range of possibility for the student concerned. This is the principle of "starting where the student is". There are many particular experiences that can be used to reach the same objectives. The fifth principle is that the same learning experience will usually bring about several outcomes. For example, students who study aspects of communication in social work may acquire information about the psychology of perception and attitudes, about the nature of complex administrative structures, conflict in families and so on and on. The process of planning learning experiences needs to be flexible. Tyler (1949) points this out: it is not a mechanical method of setting down definitely prescribed experiences for each particular objective. It involves consideration of a range of possibilities. The teacher thinks about the objectives and the kinds of experiences that he has heard of; as his ideas develop he may produce a more detailed outline. It needs to be ascertained (as far as this is possible) whether or not the proposed experiences give the student an opportunity to apply in practice what he learns, and whether the experiences suggested will be likely to be satisfying. Do the proposed learning experiences require actions that students are not yet ready or able to carry out? If certain reactions are to result from an experience these must be within the range of possibility for the students involved. It is likely that one learning experience will bring about more than one learning objective.

These points may be effectively illustrated by looking at some objectives of field work training and at some criteria for evaluation. The topics of assessment, evaluation and feedback will be discussed again later. They are highly controversial subjects; this is well-known territory for most students and teachers but it is none the less a very difficult area to negotiate. Further research is needed in this subject as well as all the others included in this book! The objectives of supervised field work placements are often stated in general terms: they are illustrated by the following excerpts drawn from material prepared by training courses and from courses on student supervision.

An eight-week introductory placement

1. To help students acquire knowledge about the framework and functioning of the social services, statutory and voluntary.

2. To give students some knowledge of the structure and functioning of the department and its place in the community.

3. To develop students' understanding of human behaviour and motivation and to promote in them an attitude of compassion and concern towards people in trouble.

4. To introduce students to casework practice and to develop their understanding of what is involved in it, and in behaving as a professional person.

Some criteria relating to development of skill in casework

1. Evidence of warmth and empathy shown for clients. Ability to appreciate expressed feelings in addition to verbal communication.

2. Ability to form a helpful relationship involving sensitivity and detachment. (Mention people to whom trainee relates well and those with whom he experiences difficulty.)

3. Evidence of realistic appreciation of material and financial needs.

4. Evidence of capacity to give advice and information in a helpful way when necessary.

5. Evidence of use of theoretical knowledge in the interview situation and the capacity to perceive the significance of client's past experience when it contributes to or effects current behaviour.

6. Evidence that the student or trainee attempts to work in a purposeful way and tries to make an objective assessment of the client and his situation. Evidence of an attempt to formulate a realistic plan of action while remaining flexible in carrying it through.

Outlines produced by courses for the evaluation of students' field work always refer in one way or another to the development of communication skills. Here are some examples.

1. "The student's capacity to produce records, reports, letters etc."

"The student's development in the conduct of professional relationships (a) with clients, (b) with the supervisor and (c) with other workers and students."

2. "Recording"

(1) Process records.

Do they contain the information necessary both for the purposes of the agency's service to clients and for facilitating teaching and learning?

(2) Departmental records.

Are they appropriate to the requirements of the agency?

Do they convey concisely a picture of the process, a statement of the social work task (related to agency function) and the client's understanding of the situation?

Are they on time, up to date, and easy to read?

Are they used as a tool in practice?

(3) Letters and referrals.

Is the content related to the purpose and appropriate to the person addressed?

(4) "Ability to use the English language in all aspects of recording."

3. A measuring rod is difficult but things to assess are:

. . . .

Ability to interview and relate the information gained.

. . . .

How the student makes relationships and gains information and how he uses these to help the client. Ability to communicate to others what he is doing.

Summary

Report could cover:

. . . .

4. Communication — reports, process recordings, letters, discussions, conferences, etc.

. . . .

4. "During his first fieldwork placement the student should have begun to judge what is appropriate for various types of records and reports, of the practical aspects, the feeling content, and the assessment of the client-worker situation . . . The student should be able to write

adequate letters on practical matters but he may still require some help. He should have learned the value of agency records, and be able to use them in order to help the client, understanding their confidential nature." "The student should be aware that interviewing does not consist purely of giving advice, directing, or arranging to do concrete things. He should appreciate that it involves concentrated listening, in order to hear what the client is really trying to say, and responsive questioning in order to help a client express his feelings and clarify his ideas. He should be aware of the process of giving support and of clarifying confused facts and attitudes. The student should be able to show his respect and caring for the client both verbally and non-verbally and have a capacity for good observation and clear perception."

Some objectives in training in communication skills are now set out. A student could work towards these in both his theoretical and in his field work. The reader will see that they are stated in general terms: some of the theoretical assumptions behind them and training implications are to be spelled out.

(1)   To develop the ability to communicate purposefully, for example in providing information and expressing ideas in ways that enable a variety of people to understand the information and ideas as intended by the sender.

(2)   To develop ability in recognising some of the many factors which make this process difficult, in understanding when they may be modified and developing skill in using this understanding to modify difficulties.

(3)   To develop these abilities through using various media and to gain confidence in, for example, the use of oral and written forms of communication and in non verbal forms of communication.

(4)   To apply these capacities in helping individuals and groups by means of social work methods, i.e. by establishing constructive relationships governed by professional standards.

(5)   To apply these capacities in relations with members of organisations or other groups associated with the client or social worker or who may become associated with them.

(6)   To develop comparable or parallel abilities in receiving and

interpreting verbal and non-verbal messages sent by other people in various situations.

(7)   To recognise some of the many factors which may make this process difficult.

(8)   To apply these capacities in trying to help individuals and groups.

(9)   To develop skill in making decisions and in encouraging trainees to feel competent in attempts to help, on the basis of effective straightforward communications.

(10)   To recognise problems in relationships, e.g. in family situations or in interviews represented by communications which are paradoxical. To learn how to deal as effectively as possible with the emotional problems which such communications represent.

The content, form and development of these objectives and some implications for organising learning experiences and their relations with other parts of a course could be critically assessed. Alternatively communication could be seen as a core subject and the problems of curriculum development could then be considered, e.g. what psychological and sociological knowledge should be integrated and in what ways? The objectives above should be analysed in terms of knowledge, attitudes and skills. A "smaller" unit, e.g. training in interviewing in field work might then be discussed in relation to the general objectives.

CHAPTER 3

Some Tools of Learning

1. LECTURES

A lecture is a process of verbal communication between one person and a group of others: the lecturer has the responsibility for one-way communication. It is a way of imparting knowledge and of helping students to organise and pattern it so that they perceive relationships between various pieces of information. A lecture may also aim to further understanding and to interpret knowledge which a student possesses but has not necessarily mastered. Training for social work aims to help the student to learn ways in which he can search for knowledge and understanding, and to organise, test and use it for the benefit of other people. This means learning through application in field practice and in discussions of theoretical and professional questions. Thinking has to be about something; it has to be based on knowledge of certain facts, situations or theories. Sometimes, however, the information which is required for thought, discussion and action is not readily available or finding it is an uneconomic use of a student's time. On other occasions the actual search for information may in itself be an important part of learning. A lecture may serve to provide basic information which is not readily accessible. Much informative material about social work, for example, is diffused in journal articles rather than concentrated in textbooks. Some of the knowledge used in practice may never have been formulated at all; some of this may be required only in outline form. Facts or theories used in other professions, for example in medicine, may be required by the social worker but not in the detail required by the doctor. Knowledge has to be structured and general theories have to be related to the basic evidence if it is to be used in practice. The lecture which has the purpose of organising or structuring knowledge has to clearly identify significant principles or theories and relationships between them. This does not involve presenting new ideas but what the students have already learned and thought about is presented systematically. In doing this the lecture may demonstrate ways in which what has been perceived and thought about may be understood and used in further study. There are various ways in which the lecture may make this contribution. Examples are relating the general to the specific, relating part to whole, using previous learning in working on current problems, and presenting a logical outline of a field of study. These are some ways in which a student who sees a need for a pattern to make sense of new ideas and experiences, and to make practical use of his knowledge may be helped towards new perspectives by a "structuring" lecture. The lecture which is used for interpretation is a presentation of ideas, opinions or beliefs. It presents points for the group to consider, to accept or reject. It is a way by which the tutor shares his thinking and imaginative ideas about a topic as a way of stimulating students' thinking and feeling.

What a lecture means to its learners can only be gauged by their reaction to its content whether this is by way of a discussion about it or a response in writing as in an essay. Discussions may indicate a need for a lecture in interpreting or summarising material which may not have been fully digested or analysed. Brief lectures held at intervals may help a group to pause and take stock: to see where they are in the course and what directions to take to pursue the objectives, or how to revise them. Such lectures have to fill in some gaps not covered in discussion and they always have to pull in various pieces and form them into a whole. The pieces might be details of particular cases which were raised in discussion and which the student tries to relate to general theories or conceptual schemes. An efficient learner must develop the capacity to organise his knowledge through perceiving relationships and digesting and integrating facts and ideas. Both discussions and lectures can be used to develop these abilities. Discussions provide continuing practice in studying significant relationships, analysing areas of knowledge, and understanding or reviewing possible applications.

2. GROUP DISCUSSION

Rogers (1973) has pointed out the vagueness about the purpose and value of "discussion" in education. It is fashionable to have so-called seminar or discussion groups although these descriptions may be misleading and the value to students may be small. Rogers gives examples of comments reflecting a range of opinions about the widely varying activities of some adult classes. One person said, "I dislike the discussion part of the class because some members (not me) always lose their tempers." Another said, "I encourage them to be frank. The content of the course (psychology) is less important than the business of learning to work as a group and getting to know yourself. I say virtually nothing. They do all the talking." These and other comments lead to the conclusion that "discussion" can mean anything from a few questions tossed to a class at the end of a gruelling lecture session to a solemn group therapy session. None of these processes, however, is authentic discussion. This may be roughly defined as a situation where students and teacher can and do make an open, equal and personal response to a book, a theory, or any other subject which requires interpretation to take it beyond a factual statement. This implies that in controversial areas the adult student has as much right to articulate and expect respect for his point of view as the teacher. (1) When two people discuss some information they are engaged in a common search for meanings. (2) This is justified educationally in that it consolidates knowledge, improves the social atmosphere of the groups, allows people to test themselves and is, in itself, a supremely valuable process. Many discussions in adult education are far from free or equal because the teacher, often quite unconsciously, guides, manipulates, and dominates proceedings, where it is inappropriate for him to do so. He may feel obliged to follow every comment from a student with a larger one of his own. Under this system communication may be brisk and lively but it will be in several sets of two-way traffic, student to teacher, teacher to student. In this kind of system the danger is that the teacher talks too much.

Discussions may become stilted and abortive for a variety of reasons. There are dangers in too rigid or inflexible planning. If the tutor tries to drive a group to reach the goals he had in mind in his preparation this, can kill discussion. It may mean that a group's energy and interest is not allowed to follow up important topics which were not part of the preliminary plan. There are also dangers in trying to lead discussions without having prepared a plan. It may well be that an outline is not used immediately, because a discussion turns towards other topics. But without an outline the tutor or group leader will not be able to remain clear about where the discussion should be leading and when certain conclusions have been reached. The outline which is not used is still valuable because it provides reassurance which in turn helps the leader to be able to listen attentively to group members and to follow and remember their arguments. This will be used to follow through logical connections. A group becomes persuaded of the need for logical thinking as it works on disentangling irrelevancies and complex arguments. Again some group discussions demand too little from some members who may have the more energetic or more able people to "carry" or dominate the group. It may be helpful sometimes for members to be asked to write down some of their ideas before the start of the discussion. They might then feel more confident in contributing and if they did focusing on written notes may have been helpful in itself. Some teachers try to control a discussion by drawing up very detailed plans for it in advance. Control can become manipulation where a teacher also tries to anticipate the content of the students' answers. Preparation for a class means that a teacher has to have a rough plan in mind and to have information available to explore the questions that may be expected to arise. But he should be prepared to abandon this plan if the interest of the class points clearly in another direction. It is a mistake for a teacher to have too many rigid expectations about the length, content and likely conclusions of a discussion.

In a discussion then, a great deal depends on relationships between the participants. Taking some school situations for illustration we can see how the classroom relationships set up by a teacher are likely to be related to the way he sees communication being carried on in his lessons. The classroom relationships tend to determine the speech roles open to the pupils and the kinds of learning which they are able to engage in. If teachers are asked about the talk that goes on in their lessons and the writing that they ask their pupils to do there is likely to be a considerable degree of consistency in the replies of each one of them. The assumptions which they make about the part played by language in learning will fall somewhere on a continuum. To explain the nature of this continuum its two extremes can be described. An imaginary teacher at the transmission end sees language as a kind of speaking tube. He sends knowledge along the tube and his pupils receive it or fail to do so. His main object in questioning his pupils or telling them to write is to test whether they have received the knowledge he transmitted. The language tube is now operating in reverse as a source of feedback. He does not see writing as connected with his pupil's thinking or understanding. He does not see talking or writing about something alters the way in which a person knows it. If he mentions learning in connection with language he will be referring to the accumulating or memorizing of information. At the other extreme is the teacher who emphasises language as a means of interpretation. He will see discussion and writing as ways of helping pupils to think more effectively and will credit them with the ability to make sense of experience for themselves by talking and writing about it. For him knowledge is something which each person has to make for himself, and he tends to be very aware of his pupil's attitudes to the work that he gives them. He is careful to be a good audience to his pupils and writes comments on their work; he often reads it aloud or displays it, and uses it as a springboard into the next piece of work. It will be seen that what is called language overlaps with (a) curriculum and (b) classroom interaction. This is because "language" refers to behaviour and the meanings which are negotiated in the course of behaviour.

Language, then, conveys information overtly and at the same time sets up or confirms the social identity and relationships of the people who are speaking or writing to one another. At the same time as teachers and pupils are talking and writing about their subject matter they are also negotiating their relationships. If a teacher is trying to impose his wishes on an unwilling class this will inevitably affect the way language is being used by pupils and therefore the kind of learning going on. Consideration of language as a means of learning and as a way of negotiating classroom relationships cannot be separated. In the following passage Dr. William Budd of Bristol wrote about the spread of typhoid in polluted drinking water.

On October 24th, 1866, my friend Dr. Grace told me that if I had half an hour to spare he would show me a striking illustration of my views on the spread of typhoid fever.

The temptation was too great to be resisted; so: jumping into his dogcart, we presently pulled up in front of two labourers' cottages built in a single block by the roadside. These cottages may be called, for convenience sake, Nos. 1 and 2. In the form of a lean-to against the gable end of No. 2 was a privy, which served the inmates of both dwellings. Through this privy there flowed a small stream, named the Wayne Brook, which formed a natural drain for it. Having already performed the same office for some twenty or thirty other houses, higher up its course, this stream had acquired all the characteristics of a common sewer, before reaching the cottages in question. From this point it passed into a field, and crossing, now as an uncovered drain, some three or four meadows, the stream came into the open again in a large court occupied by two other labourers' cottages and some farm buildings. These cottages, which may be conveniently called Nos. 3 and 4, had the same sanitary arrangements as the other two cottages.

The outbreak began in the person of the father of the family living in No. 1. Having a horse and cart, he plied a small trade in Bristol, partly as a hawker and partly as a huckster. His chief business in the city lay in the filthy back slums of St. Philip's, where, for some time immediately before his illness, typhoid fever was epidemic. That his disease was contracted there was indicated by the fact that when he was stricken all the other inmates of the two cottages were, and indeed, continued for some time after, to be in their usual health.

His attack proved to be severe and protracted, and for a considerable time was attended by profuse diarrhoea. As a matter of course, all the discharges were thrown into the common privy. In this way, the stream was fed for more than a fortnight with the excreta of the diseased patient. Four weeks later, several persons were simultaneously attacked with the same fever in all of the four cottages.

Within a space of a few days, Dr. Grace was attending quite a cluster of cases in each of the four, and before long, the majority of the persons living in them were in bed with the fever. One more fact must be recorded to render the history complete. From first to last, the outbreak was confined to these four cottages, and there was no other case of typhoid fever at the time in that neighbourhood.

These facts speak for themselves. The little stream laden with the poison-fever cast off by the intestinal disease of the man who had been stricken with the same fever some weeks before, was the only bond between them.

The teacher read this passage with the class and had suggested some lines of action which could have been taken to stop the spread of infection. He had then left the group to consider this from the point of view of the people involved. The group is of 13-year-old girls in a second-year comprehensive school class.

Transcription of the discussion

(1) *Anne:* Well, first of all, we'd have to have the streams drained out and cleaned . . . and um . . . we'd have to have better toilets than what there were already.

(2) *Beverley:* While the drainage were going on I think . . . they er they should . . . make . . . new drainlines so so they should go . . . so the sewage should go to the places instead of back in the stream and then they would . . . and if it went back into the stream again with it being . . . drained out, I think they . . . they'd get typhoid again wouldn't they? So . . . they'd have to make a new drainage.

(3) *Carol:* I think they should've made little wooden bins to clip on the end of the . . . wood and then . . . everday they should take it out and empty it somewhere convenient and if it would they could burn it.

(4) *Beverley:* Er, I think that's quite a good idea and . . . em, they'd have to tell the people first . . . about how they're catching this disease . . . and em, . . .

(5) *Carol:* But would the people understand because they're only common people and not educational jobs or anything?

(6) *Anne:* I know, but they could explain it in a . . . in a simplified, yeah, a simplified manner.

(7) *Carol:* I don't think they'd listen to you.

(8) *Beverley:* Ah, but would . . . would, em, would they believe you when they said they were contact . . . contract . . . contracting it from the stream?

(9) *Anne:* Well, they'd probably would believe you after, after they'd being seen all these people with the disease. They'd have to, they'd have to be aware of getting this disease so they must listen.

(10) *Carol:* How would the . . . drain . . . the stream?

(11) *Beverley:* I think if they dug a channel into ground but . . . the sewage would probably soak into the ground wouldn't it really, and then if they started . . . then later in the later years if they started ploughing an that . . . grou' . . . well, they'd em, they'd probably contract the typhoid again.

(12) *Anne:* Well, they could probably drain all the water out. They could probably drain all the water out of the stream and then clean it thoroughly all inside and they could have . . . and then the water will be filled up again.

(13) *Carol:* How could they get rid of the em, . . . sewage . . . you know, could they burn it? Or . . .?

(14) *Beverley:* Oh, I doubt if they could burn sewage.

Laughter

(15) *Carol:* Could they dig it under ground, you know dig a right big ditch and then pre . . . in this right big ditch and then dig it all over, you know, cover over . . . dirt all over it?

(16) *Anne:* Oh, I don't know because the disease could prob . . . may be it would spread again . . . underground.

(17) *Beverley:* Well, what can you do to prevent it? Is there any way how we can prevent it or just prevent it stopping. It would be better than letting it spread.

Speech can function as an active part of learning. For example, it is possible to follow Beverley (No. 2) as she sorts out for herself why the sewage system should be built separately from the stream. She seems to "know" this in an informed intuitive way. The need to put it to someone else makes her clarify the message. The three girls suggest other ways of disposing of sewage, and for them, these ideas are new and unexplored. The pupils control the direction of the discussion. Carol's question (No. 5) turns their attention towards public understanding of infection. Carol's question (No. 15) is different again. By putting her suggestion as a question she implicitly invites the others to take up her idea and modify it which Anne does. None of these questions is a simple request for information. They all play their part — the complex give and take through which the three girls approach a common viewpoint. In this, collaboration is very important. Most suggestions are taken up by following speakers and extended, modified or called into question. This means the group carries the thinking further than any one of the girls is likely to have reached alone. Improvisation is characteristic of the exploratory function of language. The girls set up hypotheses about methods of preventing infection. No teacher was there to act as an authority and the girls thus had to go to their own existing knowledge of methods of sanitation to test these hypotheses using knowledge of the present to make sense of the past.

These exploratory discussions differ from what usually occurs when a teacher faces a whole class. The children are using a far wider range of speech roles than full class discussion usually allows — questioning, encouraging, surmising, challenging, and so on. The children are virtually in control of the learning activity. They have to co-operate with each other to do this; they have to draw one another in and to use each others' ideas. The signals they exchange include the ideas they want to put forward and also invitation, encouragement, acceptance, and disagreement. They have to set up an appropriate mode of communication as well as deal with the task in hand. Language is serving cognitive and social functions simultaneously. If the members of the group do not find the right social mode of communication they will not get far with their task. Every group must have some devices by which members can signal the strategies they are adopting and devices for accepting, rejecting or modifying these. For the group members the social negotiation goes on unnoticed at the same time as they discuss the task in hand.

The following transcription of part of a geography lesson begins after some minutes of the lesson have passed. This is a second-year class in a comprehensive school.

Transcription of part of a geography lesson (T=Teacher)

(1) *T.* It's mainly around London. London is in the south-east. It's not only around there, though, is it? Is it further, yes, Philip?

(2) *B.* It's, um, further up in Scotland.

(3) *T.* There's some further up in Scotland. What about that bit in the middle? Can I borrow Susan's a minute? What about this bit? That's not around London in the south-east, is it? Philip?

(4) *B.* It's in Yorkshire. Somewhere, some parts of Yorkshire.

(5) *T.* Think perhaps your directions are a bit out, but

(6) *B.* In the north.

(7) *T.* In the north . . .?

(8) *G.* Liverpool.

(9) *T.* Around Liverpool. Yes, around there. Not quite the north, the Midlands and just a little bit further north than that. So generally, it's in the south-east and just going up a little bit further north than that and as Philip said a bit in Scotland as well. Now look at the map you've got open in your atlases on page 10. Now remember it's just Great Britain, it's not

Ireland as well. Compare the two maps. The brown area is higher land, the green area is lower land. Is there any relationship? Are the two roughly the same? Let's have someone else apart from Philip. Can you see any . . . any similarity between the two? Look hard. Theresa.

(10) *G.* There's not many people living in the high land.

(11) *T.* Good. So what's the opposite to that? Not many people living in the high-land, so . . .?

(12) *B.* There's a lot of people living

(13) *T.* In the . . .?

(14) *B.* Lowlands.

(15) *T.* That's it. Yes. Yes. Not many people live in the high lands, so more people live in the low land. Can you say absolutely in every single bit of low land more people live there than in the high land? Can you compare it as absolutely as that?

(16) *G.* Yes.

(17) *B.* Yes.

(18) *T.* Paul says yes, other people say yes? Philip says no. Have a careful look Philip. Are there any areas of high land there where there are lots of people living? Any areas of high land which is brown on your atlas map, which aren't white on your worksheet map? Can anybody find any areas like that? Any brown areas on atlas that aren't white on worksheet?

(19) *B.* Up in Scotland it's mostly brown and rocky, and on this map it's plain white. So . . .

(20) *T.* So that's the same isn't it, that's what you said before. Yeh. In fact we can almost say that in almost all those highland areas there's very very little people living. Why is this? Why don't they live in the highland areas?

(21) *G.* Is it cold?

(22) *T.* Colder, yes. Stephen, another word?

(23) *B.* And you can't grow things up there.

(24) *T.* Yes, the same thing as we got yesterday. Remember all that land that couldn't be used for farming yesterday?

The teacher had given out copies of a map of Britain with population densities marked on it. When the extract begins the teacher had asked her pupils to say where in the country the areas of high density were. The main purpose of the teacher's questioning was to find whether the children could read the map and accepted what she said about the relationship between population distribution and physical geography. The children responded to this demand; their replies tended to be short; there was no expectation that they should think aloud. The teacher's questions performed a variety of functions including instructions to search further, asking for more precise explanation, requiring the children to specify relationships and asking for words to complete a ready-made structure. The teacher leads the pupils through a ready-made sequence and she retains control of the process. The role of the pupils is to follow this lead and therefore the teacher's line of thought. Speech is a means of providing the teacher with feedback indicating that they are following. They are not expected to formulate knowledge in speech, except in that sense. It is necessary for children (and adults) to be given information directly sometimes or to be taken step by step through a process.

The next small group discussion is by the three girls who previously talked about ways of dealing with a polluted stream. Here they are talking about a small water creature, *Daphnia,* which they had studied under the microscope. The teacher's aim was that the girls should feel encouraged to reason out answers from what they had seen and from what they already knew. His questions encouraged the girls to find evidence to support their statements and to consider other ideas. His undogmatic manner encourages the children to use language at length for exploratory thinking.

Transcription of group discussion with teacher

Carol: How do you think that this . . . will survive . . . from . . . one year to the next?

Beverley: Well, as I said before I think it's going to live in mud, you know, mud that's left behind when the water kind of soaks into it.

Carol: But what if it dries up completely?

Beverley: I don't really know.

Carol: It might live on the reeds around it.

Beverley: I think it can only live when when while there is water round it but when that dries up the animal will dry up as well so I don't think it can live . . . alone.

Carol: I think it must be producing something else.

The teacher now enters.

Teacher: You're quiet. What have you found out up to now?

Anne: Well, we've come to the conclusion . . . that when the pond dries up . . . the animal will dry up as well because the animal's made of water. Largely of water.

Teacher: Now if that happens it'll be rather strange because if that creature lives in that pond and the pond dries up . . . and then the pond fills up again the next year, where will the new generation of creatures come from? You see if your little creature's dried up as well . . . with the pond, does that mean it's died?

Beverley: Well I think er . . . it'll kind of bree . . . breed when it's when it's when there's plenty of water and . . . then while it's . . . stuck kind of thing kind of half-alive and half-dead in dried mud it will then . . .

Carol: It might lay its eggs (yeah, yeah) or something . . . and then . . .

Teacher: That's a good idea, you mean it lays its eggs when it's wet?

Beverley: And keeps them in a shell and then when water comes again they crack open.

Teacher: That could be one idea. Yes. Have you found any other way studying other animals in which they can . . . get through a hard time, you know, get through the winter or get through a time when there's no food? What other things can other animals do?

Anne: Hibernate?

Teacher: Yes, well what does that mean?

Anne: Is it . . . they sort of . . .

Carol: Get ready for the winter, don't they?

Anne: Yeah it collects its food for the winter . . . then . . . then sort of hides away . . . where it's warm.

Beverley: Warm, yes.

Teacher: And you were suggesting before that this animal might go down into the mud . . . and live down there. Which do you think is the better idea of the two that you've suggested? One idea saying that it laid its eggs and it was the egg that stayed over the dry period, or the second one that it hibernated and stored food in the mud?

Beverley: I think the one with the egg.

Carol: It lays an egg.

Teacher: Why?

Anne: Because it seems more possible.

Beverley: Yes it seems more natural.

Teacher: It is a tiny creature to sort of survive a dry time isn't it? (Yes I think it's . . .) It's not like a squirrel that could curl up in its fur and keep warm.

(These illustrations are taken from Barnes, 1973).

A constructive discussion is a reasoned verbal communication between two or more individuals. Emotions are engaged and expressed in the reasoning but an effort is made to hold them in check. This effort is to control feelings by intellectual processes: if feelings get out of hand rational communication breaks down. Discussions start from some accepted premises or from a factual basis, or from differences of opinion or judgement or interpretation. The starting-point is one of agreement about the facts or issues that are to be the focus. These form the frame of reference. In a discussion people explore, analyse, and evaluate issues or topics and try to reach conclusions about them. It may be that they cannot arrive at a final judgement as a group and that each person has to form his own opinion. These are the elements which appear to be common to all discussions. The value of constructive discussion in learning is that it provides practice in clear thinking and clear communication. However, this assumption will only hold under certain conditions. Whether or not it is a useful means of learning depends partly on the tutors' understanding of his role and the purpose of the discussion, and partly on how it relates to specified educational objectives. As leader and monitor the tutor has to work out how to facilitate communication in discussion so that learning will be promoted. The role of monitor means that the leader of a purposeful discussion must help the group keep aware of where it is going and whether it is moving in the right direction. If the discussion is to promote effective learning questions which will be thought provoking should be formulated in advance. Possible responses and reactions to the material and to the questions about it and possible further questions can be considered by the tutor in preparation for the discussion. Frequently such "focusing questions" are given to students in advance with the case record or other discussion material. What is important is that the tutor should imagine and think about the possible issues which may emerge from the discussion, and what ideas he hopes will be considered. This may enable him to see how possible stalemate may be avoided and how speculation may be stimulated. He may then be able to think about possible conclusions to which the discussion may lead.

An important preliminary to group discussion is to help members to come prepared. One way in which this happens is that a learning task is set at the first meeting. The learner is engaged actively from the beginning. Theoretical work may be suggested. A case study may be given for reading and an outline of questions "for discussion" or consideration may be suggested. A task may be agreed at the end of a discussion; this may simply be that "we can continue to discuss a, b, and c next time". It is helpful to the learner if he has these positive ideas about where he is going. He is able to think about problems more selectively and economically. Instead of reading a book or an article as a general kind of job to be done, it will be read for information which can be put to use to illuminate the subjects to which attention has been drawn. A case record will be read with a similar aim: to explore particular points and questions. It will not then be seen just as another anecdote. It is not necessarily easy to find ways of stimulating interest, providing perspective, or helping to focus or formulate questions. But if the tutor can attempt to do this it helps the student to come ready to participate and share in discussion. He has the chance to mull over material beforehand and it is to be hoped that stimulation and focus has been provided. Classroom discussions need to be controlled if they are to achieve their aims, viz. that students should gain certain information, develop habits of thought of particular kinds, and learn certain skills or methods of work. The considerations which it seems advisable to bear in mind are the amount of time that is available, students' previous experience and knowledge and their pace of learning, as well as the content to be communicated.

The next illustration is of social-work teaching. The subject is an interview with an unemployed man, Mr. Brian Thomas. The field work teacher, Mrs. Ann Hall, has a preliminary session with the student social worker, Mr. Jim Blake. This gives him information about the referral and the student and teacher discuss the aims of the first interview. The session has the purpose of helping the student to learn about preparing for an interview or home visit. Following his report on the visit student and teacher study the interview. These three episodes are in the form of conversations involving the three people and the reader will need to remember their names and positions or to refer back to this passage. After each episode I have added brief comments of my own by way of invitation to the reader to agree or disagree and to consider the learning process described. Only the verbal communications are given here; this widens the scope for speculation about what went on. I hope that where there is lack of information this will act as a stimulus.

Illustration

First Teaching Session: Mrs. Ann Hall, *Field Teacher,* and
   Mr. Jim Blake, *Student*

Mrs. Ann Hall: We have had this referral which I think you could deal with. It came from the Assistant Director who is on the Disablement Advisory Committee of the DEP. It concerns Mr. Brian Thomas who has been out of work for the past two years. There is a difference of opinion about his disability although they are not fully documented. This makes it more difficult of course. But Mr. Thomas' family doctor says he can see no reason why Mr. Thomas should not get a job. Mr. Thomas himself says that he cannot stay in work because of his bad nerves. He has agreed to a suggestion by the advisory committee that we should visit. So this will be one of your first cases. What do you think you should bear in mind in approaching Mr. Thomas in view of the circumstances of the referral?

Mr. Jim Blake: As far as I can see my own position is a bit problematic I'm not quite sure about explaining the reason for seeing him and what I can offer in the way of help.

A. H.: Well, in the first place you are representing the department and if he asks you, you say that you are one of our social workers. This is our position on student placements. What other problems do you see? I agree that this is not a straightforward request for help.

J. B.: I think he will be suspicious about me seeing him. He's been to see the committee. He might now be worried about his situation with the DEP. He might think I'm someone who is going to try to get him back to work. Perhaps he'll think I'm siding with his doctor against him. The difference of opinion between him and his doctor is a problem. Somehow I've got to get to know Mr. Thomas and get him to tell me how he sees things. I think I've also got to try to offer him services and advice.

A. H.: So what do you think you'll have to do to make things clear at the beginning of the interview?

J. B.: I'll have to say where I'm from.

A. H.: And that you're not from the Department of Employment.

J. B.: Yes, and not from National Insurance and I'm seeing him because he agreed to this. I'm wanting to see if I can be of help.

A. H.: He's been off work for two years, and he's been seeing them at the DEP. He doesn't agree with his doctor. What do you think his point of view could be?

J. B.: As I said I think he's likely to be suspicious. But he might be very much wanting to be able to hold a job down. He's been off sick for a long time. He seems to have been a responsible kind of man in employment before, looking at these notes. He was in the Forces and had a good record there and in his other jobs. I think he might be wanting rehabilitation for himself. One thing I'm not sure about is whether to go to see him at home or invite him here.

A. H.: How do you see the pro's and con's then?

J. B.: I'd write and make an appointment in any case. I think I'd prefer to go and see him at home. He might like it if someone went to see him for a change. And he'd be on his home ground, that might help.

A. H.: That seems alright. He's married with three sons and people are saying he ought to be at work. It makes me wonder if his family or other people might regard him as being a malingerer. I wonder what relationships might be like in the family and how Mr. Thomas feels about them all. Do you think you've got to get across to him that you can understand how he feels?

J. B.: I ought to give him some sympathy and show him I can understand something of his circumstances. It could be that his doctor isn't too keen about Mr. Thomas. It could be a personality clash I suppose. We'll have to contact the doctor at some point.

A. H.: We'll need to have Mr. Thomas' agreement and do it when we think its the right time. Then there's the question of the family.

J. B.: Do you think I should see his wife do you mean?

A. H.: We don't know very much about how Mr. Thomas is feeling about it do we?

J. B.: There could be some strain in the marriage. He might just want me to see him and no one else.

A. H.: I agree with you. I think you need to wait to see how the first interview goes and from that decide about the possibility of seeing his wife. She must be concerned about the situation. The members of the family could well have ideas about how things have reached this point. As far as Mr. Thomas is concerned do you think one of our main tasks will be to do with his employment?

J. B.: Not unless this is what he wants. I think it would be wrong to go along and offer to help get him a job just like that. Anyway I'll write to him about a visit.

A. H.: If he writes or phones to say he does not want to see you we should discuss it again. For the moment we'll have to assume that he'll be willing to see you. We're hoping that your seeing him may help him to say how he sees things and feel reassured about your understanding this.

J. B.: So I've got to go and see him and listen to what he says about how he sees the future. I'll offer to help and . . .

A. H.: Let him tell you about the problem as he sees it and possibly express his feelings.

J. B.: I've got to bear in mind that we might want to get more medical information later on. We might suggest he sees a psychiatrist if he feels his nerves are bad and they won't allow him to work.

A. H.: Certainly this is something we might need to consult with the general practitioner about. If you were thinking of obtaining information relevant to that you would probably want to explore his experience in his last job and what it was that led to him losing it. You'd probably want to know more about his health at the time and how things were in the family. Were there any stresses at that time which reduced his capacity to cope? This is necessary in order to try and understand the anxieties Mr. Thomas has had. Its in this area of anxiety that he is complaining: he says it's his nerves and he is anxious and lacks self-confidence. Do you think there is anything else we need to discuss now?

J. B.: No, I don't think so. I'll see how it goes.

A. H.: I'll be interested to hear.

Comment on the first teaching session

In this first session the field teacher gives the student additional information verbally and the written notes about the referral. She underlines some important points about the referral, in particular the conflict between Mr. Thomas and his doctor, and the fact that Mr. Thomas agreed to seeing a social worker. The student has the opportunity to discuss things, like his own position, which he sees as problematic. He expresses uncertainty about explaining to Mr. Thomas why he is seeing him and what help he can offer. The field teacher is authoritative and supports the student by giving clear guidelines about the departments' policy on the position of students. The field teacher also stimulates Mr. Blake's thinking by raising questions in a way which encourages the student to look at the coming interview and at "where the client is". This could be regarded as one of the main teaching themes in this session. Mrs. Hall tries to encourage Mr. Blake to put forward his own ideas about the referral and is also concerned to ensure that as far as possible they discuss important basic points about interviewing: sometimes she reiterates points already made. For example, she agrees that they should wait to see how the first interview goes before approaching other members of the family. This reinforces the recurring point about going at Mr. Thomas' pace. Jim Blake seems to be well engaged in the discussion: he takes a full part in it and seems to use his teacher's help. We have little information about the non-verbal communications in the three interviews and this limits the validity of these interpretations. Mrs. Hall presents the facts about the case and comments on them in ways which enable Mr. Blake to examine different possibilities and to test his own ideas. The discussion seems to be a fairly free-flowing exchange of ideas: the two people seem to have a commitment to their task and their shared assumptions about their roles seem to contribute to this constructive discussion. In reading these conversations it is advisable to study hesitations and changes of subject and to speculate about what they might mean.

Home visit to Mr. Brian Thomas

Mr. Jim Blake, social worker, called to see Mr. Thomas having sent a letter saying that he would be going to see him if it was convenient. He tells Mr. Thomas who he is and that he is from the Social Services Department. Mr. Thomas invites him into the house, "Oh yes, you'd better come in and sit down", in a rather flat tone of voice. He looks questioningly at the social worker.

Jim Blake: I suppose it's a bit of a problem getting letters from people about coming to see you or asking you to go to see them.

Brian Thomas: I suppose so.

J. B.: The department has had some brief information from the disablement section of the DEP saying you had been to see them and asking us if we could be of help.

B. T.: I don't know what you could do. All I want is a good job.

J. B.: I noticed that you've been out of work for two years now.

B. T. Briefly: Correct.

J. B.: Before that you had a good job with the bus company.

B. T.: I was a storekeeper in the workshop.

J. B.: Did you like the job?

B. T.: Yes, it was a good job. But I was off sick and they made me redundant and another man, younger than me and without stores experience, got the job. It makes you fed up. It's got me down all right.

J. B.: I see. Do you still have treatment at the hospital or from your doctor?

B. T.: I'm finished treatment. I'm all right now.

J. B.: So it's just the job problem is it?

B. T.: It is.

J. B.: It's possible we could help I suppose. You'd want something like the last one; something responsible would you?

B. T.: I want some money. I don't care what kind of job as long as I get paid regularly at a decent rate. The Employment people aren't much good. They just shuffle through the vacancies and offer something really low paid. I'm just not interested: I'm as well off on the dole.

J. B.: But you wouldn't be satisfied with a routine job even if it was well paid would you?

B. T.: I'd have no choice. I want a bit more money don't I?

J. B.: I thought you liked responsibility. You were in the Forces weren't you?

B. T.: That was years ago.

J. B.: Would you be willing to move to another part of the country if . . .?

B. T.: All my friends are here.

J. B.: Yes, I see. I don't expect your wife would want to move either.

B. T.: No. She doesn't want to change her job.

J. B.: Your sons are at work are they? Do they mind where you live?

B. T.: One doesn't bother. We don't see much of him. But none of them come into this. It's my business.

J. B.: Yes, I can see it's a problem.

B. T.: I get fed up in the house with the wife being out all day. Time goes slowly. I've got no choice.

J. B.: I don't like shopping and all that myself.

B. T.: I think men are better at it than some women I know. I'm careful. I compare the prices but I don't take long to make up my mind.

J. B.: Do you see many friends?

B. T.: I see one or two at the pub but I haven't got many friends left. People don't want to know you when you're broke as I am.

J. B.: Well, do you think there is anything I can do to help where the job is concerned?

B. T.: Well, there just doesn't seem to be anything available at the moment. We've tried everywhere.

J. B.: Well, I don't want to waste your time . . .

B. T.: That's one thing I've got plenty of.

J. B.: I'll make some inquiries.

B. T.: No harm in trying I suppose. I wouldn't mind going round seeing people like you do.

J. B.: Well as I said I'll make some enquiries.

B. T.: That's it then. OK.

J. B.: Well, thank you Mr. Thomas. I'll see you again as soon as I can.

B. T.: Cheers.

Comment on the home visit

In assessing the nature of communication between Mr. Thomas and Mr. Blake it may be helpful to focus on the use Mr. Blake is able to make of the preliminary briefing and to what extent the interview moves towards the objectives discussed with Mrs. Hall. How far has the student's discussion of his position in relation to Mr. Thomas been useful, for example? I think that this conversation is strained in contrast to the student's session with his field teacher which I see as more relaxed. Mr. Thomas is clearly not entirely convinced that Mr. Blake's help is for him: he says clearly that he does not know what Jim Blake can do. The student does not deal with the challenge this implies and comments instead on the length of time Mr. Thomas has been unemployed. When Mr. Thomas indicates that he is fed up (saying "it's got me down all right") the student again does not deal with that message by helping Mr. Thomas to say more about it. He closes the subject by saying "I see" and moves on to the state of his client's health. This is a relevant enquiry but it might appropriately have been set aside for the moment in order to discover a little more about Mr. Thomas' miserable feeling and his attitude towards his redundancy. It is now the client's turn to close the subject. The reader is reminded of Jim Blake's anxiety about whether or not he can be helpful first observed in the preliminary briefing, in this interview. He seems almost half-hearted, or at least very cautious, about this. Mr. Thomas' frustration is seen again in what he says about being financially as well off on the dole. Jim Blake has some preconceived ideas about Mr. Thomas needing to have a "responsible" job and he seems to hold on to these preconceptions. He does not seem to receive the message about his client's frustration and his strongly expressed desire for any job which will provide him with more money. Again we observe a change of subject when the client appears to make it clear that he is not inclined to talk about his experience in the Forces. This change of topic brings further negative responses which provide useful information about factors limiting choice of future courses of action (or, at least, the client's perceptions of limitations). There is evidence of family tensions in the lack of contact between the parents and one son, but it is made clear that Mr. Thomas is reluctant to discuss this. He sends a further message, however, about feeling fed up but Mr. Blake's response about his own attitudes ("I don't like shopping . . .") is followed by a further attempt by Mr. Thomas to try to maintain some area of self-esteem. But Mr. Thomas' feeling of pessimism returns and the student seems almost apologetic about taking up his time. The end of the interview seems scarcely more hopeful than its beginning. Jim Blake again does not follow up cues he is given at this point.

Teaching session on the home visit

Mrs. Ann Hall: How did you get on with Mr. Thomas? I know you told me you'd been to see him but we did not have time then to talk about it.

Mr. Jim Blake: Yes. I'm sorry that I was not able to write it up earlier but I think I have the main points in that record now.

A. H.: I haven't read it thoroughly this morning so perhaps we could go through the interview.

J. B.: When I arrived he was quiet and did not seem particularly keen to talk very much. But we started talking about his old job. I asked him whether he was still having treatment. He told me he had been made redundant and had not given up his job because of being ill. He said someone else younger than him had been given his job even though he was inexperienced. He was fed up about it: that's what he said.

A. H.: Could you give me an idea about how Mr. Thomas seemed when he was telling you this? It all happened some time ago.

J. B.: I thought he was still rather uncommunicative and, sort of flat in a way. He seemed kind of indifferent . . .

A. H.: How would you have expected him to feel about losing his job? Do you think he sees it differently now than he did at the time?

J. B.: I'd expect someone to feel unhappy about losing a job they liked although plenty of others are only too happy to have finished with the graft. But I suppose I'd have felt unhappy at the time and that would have made me want to get things sorted out. He doesn't seem to operate quite that way.

A. H.: What about finding someone else had been given your job?

J. B.: He did talk as if he did not like the younger man much and him being made redundant.

A. H.: You are describing the way he told you about it really. It is really the way he said things and the clues you could pick up from his tone of voice, his facial expression and so on. Do you think he felt angry about all this?

J. B.: Not really.

A. H.: So the passage of time had changed things a bit? Or do you think he did not want to show his feelings too directly because he wasn't sure about your reaction.

J. B.: I don't think he was entirely genuine. It wasn't the whole truth so he couldn't have expressed anger as he could have done if his story had been entirely true.

A. H.: I don't quite understand you about this. Are you saying that Mr. Thomas was trying to justify himself in being out of work?

J. B.: Yes, that's my opinion. We went on to talk about how he'd feel about moving to another area to find work. He said he did not want to leave: he said all his friends were there.

A. H.: How did you get on to this?

J. B.: It came up in talking about the difficulties of getting a job. He said at the beginning that all he wanted was a good job. He said he did not know what I could do. Later on he said all he wanted was a bit more money, and did not care about what kind of job it was. He didn't think much of the DEP either. He didn't want to be offered poorly paid jobs. He said he'd be as well off staying on the dole. I must say I thought he wanted an interesting responsible job but he didn't agree about this at all. Then I asked if he'd be prepared to leave the area to get work. I was trying to discover what he really wanted. But he said quite definitely he did not want to leave the area and anyway what he wanted was more money. He said if he went for a job either it was too badly paid or it had gone before he got there!

A. H.: Well, don't you think this sums up how things are with him quite well? Jobs are hard to find now and the ones that are vacant are low paid. There really isn't much incentive for him, is there?

J. B.: No and he's aware of it. He said he was better off staying at home. His wife and sons go to work and probably bring in a reasonable income. This must limit his benefit.

A. H.: Right. This information is helpful in understanding his situation isn't it? Does his wife work full-time?

J. B.: No. He said she does six hours a day. He does all the shopping. He reckons men are better at it anyway. I think he was defending his position. He seemed to do some housework but didn't go into details. I asked about the family's ideas about them leaving the area. He would not discuss whether his sons would be prepared for them to leave. He said they had nothing to do with all this. He didn't really want to discuss his sons.

A. H.: It's a difficult relationship.

J. B.: Yes. I think that he has a particularly difficult relationship with his married son. There's little love lost there I guess. The son got married about two years ago.

A. H.: Would that be around the time Mr. Thomas was ill or losing his job?

J. B.: I'm not sure about that. He told me he went to the nearby pub. I suggested that he probably met his friends there. You remember earlier he'd told me about his friends in there. You remember earlier he'd told me about his friends in the area?

A. H.: Yes.

J. B.: Well, he went back on it at this point. He said he hadn't got many friends really. He couldn't buy drinks for people at the pub.

A. H.: Did the interview get any easier as you went on? Do you think Mr. Thomas relaxed more?

J. B.: I don't think he felt much more relaxed: I'm not sure how tense he was really.

A. H.: Do you think he sensed that you had some understanding of how he might be feeling?

J. B.: Its difficult this.

A. H.: Yes it isn't easy to put into words.

J. B.: Well, I think . . . I did say to him how difficult I thought things must be for him at the beginning of the visit. I sort of hinted that I did not want to be a nuisance to him or intrude on his time. I said my reason for going to see him was because we wanted to offer to help if we could. He went on about wanting a job and that was all . . . I tried to say that we might be able to help. He said he had already explained all the possibilities. I said that as long as it was all right with him there might be something we could do. I wanted to keep the door open but he only agreed half-heartedly I thought.

A. H.: Perhaps it would be helpful to us both now to review the interview as a whole. One point is what feelings you think Mr Thomas was expressing and what you might have done in the situation to try to cope with them. Do you think you'd have done anything different if you had to make the home visit again?

J. B.: No. I wouldn't because this was only a first visit. What I was trying to do was to establish contact and get an opportunity to go back again. I was trying to get a foot in the door so to speak, so that we could go back without starting all over again from the beginning.

A. H.: One difficulty with a man like Mr. Thomas is that he has seen so many people that this foot in the door is important in reviewing the case. For this reason we need to establish contact quickly and to show our understanding about why he is feeling on the defensive and that we appreciate this is to do with the real stresses in his life at present.

J. B.: He must be very unhappy. He is in conflict with his family — his sons anyway; we don't know very much about how he gets on with his wife.

A. H.: Yes, I think you're right about that. Whether he is emotionalising or not if this is how he sees the situation we have to understand his point of view. It's important to him.

J. B.: Yes.

A. H.: And we do have some ideas about the kind of person Mr. Thomas is. I notice that he said he'd like a job where you go round seeing people like social workers do. Did you consider that he must be very fed up about people who just come and talk and that that was the underlying message? Should you have put this to him?

J. B.: Well . . . I sympathised with him.

A. H.: But he was angry or fed up with you.

J. B.: Oh yes, I think you're right. I think he was really angry and then I went on to talk about us wanting to try to help him if we could.

A. H.: It was not an easy interview for you.

J. B.: I suppose it was quite difficult. I can see that more clearly having talked it over and thought about it more.

Comment on the second teaching session

One constraint on discussion is the teacher's not having been able to read the student's account of the home visit beforehand, but they go through the report together. In comparing Jim Blake's report and what he says about the visit you might observe points that he omits and those to which he gives greater attention. You thus obtain some ideas about how he thinks his interview went and what he saw as important or as requiring discussion. Ann Hall, as in the first teaching session, aims to encourage Jim Blake to express his ideas within a structure for learning. Her comments are important components of this structure. They provide the frame in which the pieces of information are arranged. Again she uses direct questions: "How would you have expected him to feel about losing his job?" She asks further questions which seem to be to encourage the student to develop his ideas about certain topics which the teacher sees as important and which she is drawing to the student's attention. She "stays with" this point about Mr. Thomas' supposed resentment or anger about being made redundant. I have the impression that Jim Blake tends to have attached less importance to this and I relate this to my earlier impression that he would not want to be "unpopular" with Mr. Thomas. In his briefing session, for example, I noted what he said as expressing his need to justify his intervention. Many readers might well feel rather similarly because of the peculiar circumstances of this referral for example. By asking for clarification the teacher here seems to be genuinely asking for information to help in understanding and evaluating the student's work in the interview. While learning herself she involves her student in the process with the aim of enabling him to clarify his ideas as a basis for developing fresh insights. These will form the basis for further thinking about the next step — the next interview or inquiries to be made for Mr Thomas. In parts of the discussion, as in other illustrations in this book, your reading may help you to share the participants' thinking.

Jim Blake is "thinking aloud" as he describes his home visit. He is thinking about his client and examining his ideas about his situation. He is reconsidering his own actions: "I was trying to . . ." and sharing all this with the teacher. The teacher remains encouraging and supportive. This emotional side of the interaction comes through in what the two people say. Ann Hall, it seems, recognises positive aspects of Jim Blake's work, pointing out information is relevant and helpful, and making it clear when she agrees with particular points he makes. There is a shared view of the difficulties encountered in the home visit: Ann Hall points out that these are not easy to put into words: this seems to provide a stimulus to make the attempt. This is followed by the explicit recommendation that they should evaluate the student's work: having carried out one difficult task they have to deal with another one. This setting of aims clearly illustrates my earlier point about the structure provided by the teacher; this is a particular requirement of a student at an early stage in a course or, as here, in discussing a subject such as an interview. In addition some didactic teaching will be found in this session: at several points Ann Hall provides information which the student requires. This session is quite a demanding one for both people. It is not easy to discuss the unsatisfactory aspects of a relationship. For a teacher it is quite demanding to keep in mind all the points you feel need to be covered and to draw attention to those which are a source of discomfort. As in social work false reassurance can easily be given, but is not helpful; at the same time as being critical and recognising the limitations of a situation (being realistic) one tries to communicate a degree of optimism or confidence without which further learning may be negative.

The concern with evidence and logical processes, with the distinction between factual information and what can be deduced from it, is an educational objective which discussion can help students to reach. Abercrombie, for example, summarised her aim in the course of unguided discussions as being "to make it possible for the student to relinquish the security of thinking in well defined given channels and to find a new kind of stability based on the recognition and acceptance of ambiguity, uncertainty, and open choice". Ideal discussion management therefore involves the rejection of loose statements and terms and of emotional bias in thinking if it is excessive. It involves clear focus on the topic and the rejection of irrelevant material. It thus requires agreement about terms and issues, the use of knowledge and reasoning processes in the making of judgements, and recognising ignorance and speculation when they occur. It has been said that discussion is valuable in providing practise in clear thinking and clear communication. But its use is also affected by the task to be accomplished: the content to be learned and the time available have to be taken into account as well. Because social work is concerned with helping people in problematic situations, it tends to arouse anxiety in the student involving him in a personal way and possibly leading to the making of impulsive assumptions. It may lead to emotionalised thinking and prejudice, and thus distract or blur the clarity of the student's perceptions and judgement, depending on his capacity for objective thought. What the student thinks and how he thinks is known and can be examined as he shares his ideas and communicates with his teachers or in group discussion.

The discussion should aim at providing certain opportunities and experience. It offers practice in the synthesis of thinking, in sharing and testing ideas, and in communication. The method offers opportunities to practice professional skills: it aims to develop certain kinds of behaviour in group members. Value is attached to the sharing of responsibility for dealing with problems in professional development. The main purpose is to learn by doing certain things in certain ways based on habits of sound thinking and in particular to learn about professional communication. The group leader (as well as the members) should prepare for discussion: he needs to define aims and make some predictions about content beforehand. He has to be active in the discussion as an authority, as guide or conductor, and as facilitator. He has to formulate questions and to encourage the group to think about them through understanding various points of view and feelings, and by providing resources of information or structure when they are required.

Discussions about the theoretical aspects of interviewing and group relations are frequently based on disguised case records. They vary in length and students usually read the record in preparation for discussion. The use of detailed accounts of interviews and, increasingly, of tape recordings of interviews, makes it possible to have more thorough and more realistic discussions about real-life situations.

Summary recordings and brief illustrations based on case records or invented by students or tutors may also be valuable in illustrating theoretical ideas. This use needs to be distinguished from the kind of analysis to which a record is subjected for detailed study purposes. The method is unsuitable for some teaching purposes and it is therefore necessary to recognise its limitations. Discussion of the best of case records is an artificial exercise, at least to some degree. The picture of individuals which it presents is inevitably distorted to some extent and it is incomplete. The most vivid record does not engage a trainee's interests and feelings in the way in which this happens in real life. This also has its advantages. It does offer the possibility of standing back from practice and studying situations systematically and in a detached way that is not possible, nor perhaps desirable, in the field situation. A social-work tutor can apply his social work skills in the teaching situation. For example, in the area of communication, he will listen attentively to both latent and manifest content, that is, not only to what is said but also to what may lie behind the words. He will also try to connect what one member says with what has been said previously and also to develop it further. The complex interplay of questions and responses needs to be related to the main themes of the discussion. This is not easy to do: it is comparable to the social worker's task of providing focus and continuity in an interview (or group session). In the same way it means that the discussion leader has to be able to focus the discussion so that its basic unity of theme is maintained: it means pulling the threads of the discussion together and bringing different parts into relationship with one another. This implies that members of a group can feel they are making progress; although diverse questions may have to be discussed and may appear not to be logically related, the discussion must move forward in a progressive way so that the subject-matter is clarified.

3. LEARNING FROM RECORDS

Discussion in social work training is often focused on a specific piece of suitably disguised material derived from practice. It can take the form of material drawn from current field experience and presented by a member of the group or it may be a fictitious case record prepared specially for teaching purposes. The study of data, however it is recorded, depends on a structure for analysis. Items of information have to be classified according to certain criteria in order to study relationships between them. In approaching case material, which may be more or less well organised it is helpful to have ideas about topics requiring special attention. One suggested structure for studying a case record is reproduced here to illustrate this. (I do not know the source of this material which seems to be transatlantic in origin).

A STRUCTURE FOR STUDYING A CASE RECORD

1. Referral

How does the client get to the agency? Does he have any control over the process? Is he pushed by family or community? Why does he come now? What does the S.W. know about him before he gets there? How can this information be used?

2. Agency

The function and auspices of the agency, what the community expects of it: its clientele: how it relates to other social agencies: how the setting affects casework service.

3. Person with problem(s):

Nature of the problem: Duration, severity, pervasiveness, persons affected.
Motivation: What has the client done about the problem and with what success? What does he want of the agency? Why now?
How much discomfort, and how much hope, does the client feel? What responsibility does he take in relation to the problem? Is this realistic, or does he assume or project blame?
Capacity: Ability of client to share his feelings, to perceive relationships and consider alternatives. Are the client's defences serving adaptive purposes or are they crippling? Can he relate himself to the helping person? What is his present and past functioning in significant areas of life?

The evaluation of capacity may include psychiatric diagnosis or consultation to understand personality structure more fully. Such an evaluation may include a survey of health, education, employment, group relationships, etc.

Opportunity. Finances, housing, recreation, community resources, persons in family or other groups who support or impede client's efforts, minority group status, etc.

The extent to which the case record is an accurate report of what happens in an interview is open to question. Even if it is dictated or written out as fully as possible afterwards there will very likely be a number of important omissions. A good memory is needed to be able to reproduce a long interview. Itzin (1960) refers to study which aimed at identifying the elements of communication between worker and client. When tapes and process records were compared more than half of the observations that were regarded as significant appeared only on the tapes. In using tape recorders the effects on clients have to be considered. For many people having a mechanical device recording their words is more threatening than having someone other than the interviewer present at the interview. But if its use is accepted listening to a tape record can help an interviewer obtain new insight into the client's and his own participation in the interview. Listening to a tape being played is a time-consuming business, however; more time is taken if a recording has to be transcribed and typed out as a documentary record.

The use of tape recording as a training aid has been studied by Itzin. He noted that although tape recordings had been used by many social workers as a way of studying their own practice and in supervision little or nothing had been written about this. Itzin reported on the use of the method by a field work supervisor in a neuropsychiatric hospital. Twelve out of thirteen students reported on their experience and they all expressed a positive attitude. One of them, for example, said "it invokes confidence in perfecting your ability. You can 'hear' the helping process and you don't feel as if you're stabbing so much in the dark."

The students felt that using tape records had several advantages. The supervisor could be more helpful if he obtained an objective picture of communication during the interview. This objectivity was thought to increase students' awareness of themselves and of their clients and studying their tapes helped them in overcoming defences such as evasion and distortion. One said, "I feel certain that the supervisor was able to pin down my problems quite early in the placement and understand me much better than he could have had I been able to hide behind process recording." Another said, "he could actually hear and get the feel of the interview without the distortion that consciously and unconsciously goes into written recording." Tapes can help to record non-verbal communications in interviews. Tone of voice, sighs, laughter and silences are examples of such phenomena. They are rarely mentioned in process records; they are difficult to detect except in tape recording. A great advantage is that the interview (the primary learning experience in field work) can be re-acted over and over again. In addition to helping the supervisor to discuss important parts or aspects of the interview with the student, the student is able to review his own work for himself. A particularly important advantage seen by students was that their incentive for developing skill in interviewing increased. They found it more stimulating than writing process records.

Special attention was given to how interviewees felt about the recordings but no negative reactions occurred: initial tensions evaporated as interviews progressed. As far as students were concerned the fear that their anxieties would be communicated to clients seemed to be unfounded. There was no evidence that students concentrated their attention on themselves rather than their clients. Tape recording does seem to focus attention on the details of communication and relationship in the interview. This carries the danger that some important factors can be overlooked, such as the client's posture and facial expression and some students' observations. These disadvantages are now being overcome with the increasing use of other apparatus such as films, television and videotapes and, perhaps, the one-way screen which enables students to watch an interview in progress. Again, ethical problems arise. At the present time the use of modern equipment is growing rapidly in social-work training but we may not yet have obtained enough experience to comment on their use. However, I refer to other visual aids shortly. We have to learn how to combine media in conveying information effectively and in facilitating the development of skills.

4. DIAGRAMS

In this book diagrams and line drawings are used to illustrate discussion of the process of perceiving and how misperceptions may occur. For many people "seeing" is an aid to understanding. In this presentation I have assumed that these visual aids will help readers in later discussions of factors affecting recall and memory distortions and observation of other people. The concept of the schema is of help in studying processes of adaptation. It could be discussed elsewhere in this book but I propose to use it here in relation to the use of diagrams, pictures, tables and so on as aids in learning. Perhaps what is important to remember is that schemas are expressed or represented in a variety of ways. Later in this book the way individuals deal with information is discussed further. Depending on their circumstances people do not react to their surroundings in their entirety but specifically to those features which are important for them. All experience is selective. The abstractions which are made from the environment constitute peoples' schemas: the appropriate language for describing schemas is thus abstract language. Each schema is the basis of part of the total knowledge of the person. No two things or events are ever quite identical so that people have to learn that causes which are alike in certain respects produce similar effects, and this involves learning to recognise recurring features in the environment which matter to them in some way. These significant features have to be separated from unimportant features; the irrelevant and variable features are eliminated and the constant feature in an experience is preserved. A schema becomes important only through repetition and is thus the result of a learning process. The formation of schemas thus starts at birth and continues as a necessity throughout life, because they provide inner models of the outer world as well as of a person's body. Thus schemas are functional and influence each other. They may be thought of as forming a hierarchy. In this hierarchy the body schema has an important place: it consists of a type of consolidated information report which is kept continuously up to date and which tells the brain exactly where every part of the body is and how it is moving at any moment.

Schemas thus represent abstractions made by the senses from the flow of energy impinging on the person from the surroundings. This energy consists, for example, of heat, light, sound and pressure and it is communicated to the brain by the sense organs. These sometimes act separately, and sometimes together. To illustrate, sometimes a person may be both seen and heard, or he may be only seen or only heard. In this way the brain can distinguish different qualities of experience. The recognition of a range of colours, apart from coloured objects, is one important series of learned abstractions. There are other series, for example sounds, smells, tastes and tactile sensations. Thus a large family of schemas representing the range of sensory experiences is built up. The environment has qualities of colour and sound and so on; it also has shape and pattern. Objects are round and square, rough and smooth, and are found in various positions and at different distances. During the early months of a child's life his store of schemas is built up as his senses transmit impressions of touch, taste, sight, sound and so on. At first the mother "is" a succession of gratifying experiences and the child does not distinguish his own body from his surroundings until he has begun to move arms and legs, to reach out and to explore. The two differentiating factors in experience appear to be the distinction between the pleasant and the unpleasant (which give value to his experience) and the distinction between "me" and "not me" (which give location to his experiences). At this stage in the child's life value and location seem to be the most important aspects of the formation of schemas. The normal child also learns a variety of sounds, including, of course, those which he makes himself. He experiments in gurgling and babbling and shouting and discovers that he can control the noises that he makes in these ways. In addition he comes to associate the sounds made by other people with certain experiences, for example, associating some sounds made by his mother with being fed or being cuddled. As a result of experimenting with sounds himself he tries to produce sounds which have a meaning, for example, if he calls to his mother in a certain way this indicates that he wants her to come to him. An outcome of these developments is that the child no longer depends only on his own discoveries and experiments; through language other peoples' schemas become available and can be added to his store, or used to modify his community of schemata. This implies that after about the first year the child's group of schemas dramatically expands; at first this is through learning what other people say. Later when he learns to read, and when he goes to school, other uses of language continue to facilitate this expansion; more new schemas take shape. In the course of the process of development the child's primary schemas which are primitive and non-verbal are modified by the later schemas. There is a tension between dreams and realities, between "me" and what is "not me", and an equilibrium has to be reached and maintained since the primary schemas continue to exert a powerful influence.

The ways of storing experiences vary widely from one person to another and from one experience to another. Some people are helped to acquire and later to recall stored experience more effectively through seeing, some through hearing, and some through feeling and action. Since schemas form a hierarchy and there are supposed to be only a few powerful ones, they exert control over the less powerful. It seems that people want to interpret their experience: if they are faced with apparently meaningless and disconnected objects or ideas they either reject their observation, or set to work to impose an interpretation. Spearman noted this tendency to search for relations between things experienced; Freud looked for unconscious motives which influenced conscious attempts to reduce tension. The Gestalt psychologists suggest that the individual tends to "organise" his experience in the smoothest or neatest patterns. All of these may be regarded as partial explanations of the essentially active process of interpretation. A system of knowledge is not just a collection of facts; it is a structure. It indicates relationships between the facts. The network of relationships has meaning and this enables a person to reason about the facts and their relationships and to argue about their significance. Schemas have qualities both of permanence and fluidity. The permanence is due to conditioning by which schemas are established while the fluidity is due to forces at work among the schemas, separating, condensing and joining them. The processes at work are termed thinking, imagining and dreaming. Because of the need to reduce tension and to obtain stability there is a tendency to use the more permanent schemas. Each person has characteristic strategies which he follows in dealing with his experience and in acquiring information. Conditioning can aid adaptation to the environment. The acquisition of knowledge involves the possession of an elaborate system of schemas all representing parts of the environment and capable of many recombinations. A schema, then, organises information: it selects items of information and arranges them in a systematic way. A symbolic diagram is a way of expressing the relationships in or between schemata. The first part of this process is the symbolising of the facts or ideas. The symbols used must either belong to a known language or they must be capable of communicating meaning visibly. Diagrams are powerful methods of communication: they can use a number of codes simultaneously and they can express meaning economically. One important way in which symbols are used in diagrams is simply their relative positions. For example, a diagram or chart of two dimensions facilitates the display of relations between different elements of meaning. The same information could be presented by using a series of sentences but this method would not enable it to be presented so explicitly or clearly.

The learning process often seems untidy. It does not always work that new knowledge is acquired in a systematic way. It has to be organised into a system. As new information is discovered it has to be found a place in the plan. Some diagrams make it easier to classify different pieces of information as they arrive. An example would be the figure showing the dynamics of communication which can also be described in a written commentary although the diagram can be followed easily and shows relationships clearly. This diagram can be constructed gradually as new ideas occur to the person. Another example of a similar kind is Shannon and Weaver's (1949) well-known communication model.

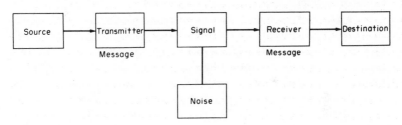

Fig. 3. Shannon and Weavers' communication model.

Another kind of diagram is one where the facts symbolised themselves impose a natural spatial arrangement. Some diagrams, for example those showing spatial arrangements of verbal information about complex process, almost speak for themselves. Arranging the ideas in a diagram has the advantages of economising words and of giving greater insight. A simple code of words and arrows may be all that is required to illustrate complicated relationships. It is helpful if such a diagram or table employs simple codes, say of words and arrows, so that it is straightforward, expressive and easily recalled. An example is the model of the relationship between communication and meaning. This is a fairly detailed figure which illustrates several concepts and relationships (see Chapter 1).

Tables and diagrams may make use of several codes and summarise many measurements or other facts and display them systematically. Some tables can present detailed information and enable a number of comparisons to be made and they can reveal systematic conclusions. The accompanying diagram showing balanced and imbalanced configurations of attitudes, requires understanding of attitude theory but it represents graphically the relationships described in the following written account. The accompanying figures spell out the attitude of a person P towards a source S, the person's attitude toward an issue I, and the perceived assertion of the source about the issue. Positive attitudes are shown by the $+$ sign and negative attitudes by the $-$ sign. Determining whether a particular configuration is balanced or unbalanced is by algebraic multiplication (e.g. minus $\times$ plus $\times$ minus = plus, i.e. a balanced state) (minus $\times$ minus $\times$ minus = minus, i.e. an unbalanced state).

If a person (P) has a positive or a negative attitude towards, say, the strict control of his children (1) and has a positive or negative attitude towards the legal system (S) and also thinks that legal authorities (S) have a positive or negative attitude he has a cognitive configuration relative to the issue of strict discipline for his children. If he also has a positive or negative attitude towards the legal system and also thinks that lawyers usually have a positive or negative attitude toward the control of children then P is said to have a cognitive configuration relative to the issue of the control of children and the legal system. The cognitive configuration is considered balanced, for example, if P has a positive attitude towards the strict control of children, towards the legal system and if he thinks the law courts also favour stricter control of children then P should feel comfortable about the whole situation. If P is for stricter control of children, but against the legal authorities, and if P thinks they too are against stricter control of children P should still feel comfortable about the situation. The attitude of the legal authorities toward the issue is expected by P given P's different attitudes towards the issue and towards the legal system. On the other hand, the cognitive configuration is said to be unbalanced if, for example, P is against stricter control of children, is for the legal system, and if he thinks the legal system is for stricter control of children. P is in a dilemma because given his different attitudes towards the issue and the legal authorities he should expect the legal authorities to argue with him and therefore to have a negative attitude toward the issue. In a situation where the configuration is not balanced the unit relations have to undergo a change either through action or through cognitive reorganisation in the person. A third kind of table consists of classification and summary of a large amount of detailed information which could not be absorbed and interpreted unless it was organised systematically. Such tables show the basic differences between different groups in ways which can be clearly understood. They can be dangerous if they lead a reader to assume that they comprehend all the aspects of a subject. They can appear to be static and it is necessary for the reader to look for underlying meanings and what new questions or ideas they may provoke.

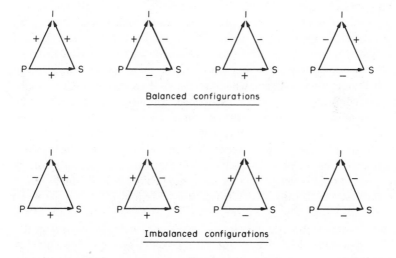

Fig. 4. Balanced and imbalanced configurations of attitudes.
(From Nan Lin (1973) *The Study of Human Communication*, Bobbs Merrill Co.)

5. EMPATHY AND CREATIVE ARTS

Empathy is an ability to project oneself into the other peoples' personalities, and leads to some understanding of their thoughts and feelings. In predicting how someone else will behave or in expecting certain behaviour a person makes assumptions about the other's internal psychological state. These assumptions may be based on observed behaviour: we perceive how other people behave. Ideas about the behaviour of others are related to ideas about oneself. The concept of self is developed through communication. The young child observes and imitates other peoples' behaviour and begins to act towards himself as others act towards him. Through this process he interprets his behaviour and the behaviour of others: he attributes meaning to it. At first he plays other people's roles without interpretation and he is rewarded for some role playing responses. As he develops, his role playing behaviour increases and so does his understanding of the roles he takes. This leads to his obtaining general ideas about how people behave, how they interpret, and how they act towards him. He relates his own behaviour symbolically to his internal psychological state. On the basis of these interpretations of himself he makes inferences about the internal states of others. It will be seen that this development of empathy is complex and may be analysed on different levels. In terms of communication the source and receiver of a message affect each other and are interdependent. At one level interdependence can be analysed as an action-reaction sequence. An initial message affects the response that is made to it, the response affects the next response and so on. Communications use responses as feedback: this information helps them to determine whether they are achieving the desired effect. At another level a person projects himself into another person's feelings or thoughts in order to predict how they will behave. A final level of interdependence may be described as interaction. If two people make inferences about their own roles and take the role of the other at the same time, and if their communication depends on the reciprocal taking of roles, they are communicating by interacting with each other. Interaction here is seen as the ideal or goal of communication (Asch, 1952; Mead, 1934).

Empathy has also been defined as "feeling oneself into, and losing one's identity in, a work of art, a characteristic of the essentially aesthetic attitude or emotion, used sometimes by psycho-analysts of the phenomena of identification; possibly more generally characteristic of perceptual experience of a situation than has generally been held" (Drever, 1952).

This definition implies an active kind of involvement in widening one's perceptions of other people's ideas and feelings. The sharing of other people's feelings appears to involve the representation and presentation of these feelings in oneself. Important elements in these processes seem to be creativity and imaginativeness. The empathic process may be stimulated by the arts in general and by imaginative literature. It is suggested that these are ways of widening a person's understanding, deepening his sensitivity for people, and also of improving the quality of life. Literature can provide an opportunity for a person to explore kinds of life and living beyond his power to participate in immediately. He can explore situations vicariously which he cannot explore in reality; it thus extends his experience through by-passing spatial and temporal limitations and permits insight into social groups other than one's own. The study of literature develops reading interests and habits. It can increase skill in interpreting literature, both in analysing the logical exposition of ideas and in deepening understanding of human motives and behaviour. In serving the function of appreciation literature offers opportunity for significant emotional reactions to literary forms and opportunities for critical appraisal of both form and content and a means of developing standards of taste in literature.

Literature (and other forms of emotive and artistic communication) performs a variety of functions. It can suggest new possibilities to people and can open up new areas of possible experience. It can suggest different strategies for dealing with situations. It can show us our own problems in a new perspective and if a person is feeling miserable it can make him feel that he is not alone in his misery. There is a sense in which the reading of literature may enable people to lead fuller lives than those who do not. It helps them to know how others have felt about life; this is because human life is "lived" or experienced at more than one level. In contemplating or enjoying a work of art deep enjoyment is found if the leading characters in the story symbolise members of the audience to some degree. In a novel events are organised into a sequence so that they may be related to one another. A story or play is an organisation of symbolic experiences in such a way that it will have an impact on the reader. The reader or audience has to imaginatively identify with the roles portrayed and he has to project himself into the situations described in the story. As an individual matures he steadily increases the range, sophistication and subtlety of his symbolic experiences. Hopefully, new symbolic experiences lead to an enrichment of his understanding of people and situations, and this increased insight provides new sympathy with other human beings everywhere. The arts enlarge people's sympathies thus making them more willing to co-operate and to become less suspicious of each other. The sharing of feelings is facilitated by literature because the expression of individual feeling is central to it. Literature can lead people to greater understanding of themselves and it can produce feelings of moral obligation; it can evoke attitudes towards other people. The feelings that are expressed may be subtle and complex. Literature gives expression to experiences or feelings that cannot be conveyed just by a few lines of verse or prose, but which may be the subjects of a complete work of art such as a novel or a poem.

The data of experience, when they are communicated, are found to be full of inconsistencies. This disorder leads to confusion so that a person is not sure what to do until he has "made sense" of experience so that things do not seem to be "meaningless" any more. Understanding involves the ordering of data in such a way that observations are related to each other into a workable system. These observations are at various levels of abstraction, from the descriptive to the hypothetical. The "understanding" conveyed by the novelist and the poet involves the organisation of his observations into a set of attitudes, and his observations will also range in level from the concrete to the very abstract. He is unlikely to present his system in a highly abstract way although he may describe a set of symbolic experiences which involve the audience emotionally. This symbolisation and organisation of experiences involves integrating data which may appear at first to have no coherence. From the point of view of the audience or the reader the ordering of experiences and attitudes which is accomplished linguistically by the writer leads to some organisation (or reorganisation) of his own experiences and attitudes (Diack, 1966). Jung (1936) said that to grasp the meaning of a great work of art it has to be allowed to act on us (the audience) as it acted on the artist; we have to let it shape us as it shaped the artist. Then we understand the nature of the artist's experience and how he has penetrated to the matrix of life which is common to all people and which gives a rhythm to human existence and allows the individual to communicate his feeling to others. Every great work of art is objective and impersonal but none the less is profoundly moving. Jung likens it to a dream: for all its apparent obviousness it does not explain itself and is never unequivocal. A dream never says "you ought" or "this is the truth".

Valk (1973) writes that the social worker needs to learn to sharpen his perceptions in order to select from and make appropriate connections with material presented by the creative artist. This can mean involving himself actively in creative processes so that works of art will come alive for him, rather than reading alone. A programme for this kind of learning needs to be formulated and taught. Valk said that students and teachers might decry literary or other artistic studies as not being an essential ingredient in learning about empathic processes if their aims were not explicit. An initiative is long overdue in experimenting with the possibilities of teaching about social work from imaginative literature. By acting poems and episodes from plays students can learn about feelings and how they are communicated. These methods seem appropriate for the subject matter of social work. It cannot be taken for granted that the majority of social workers would wish or be able to use imaginative literature unaided. Valk discussed the use of imaginative literature in social-work training. To her it is implicit in social-work education that people develop heightened sensitivity, perception and personal creativity which can help one to look outwards and to "tune in" to other people. She would like to see seminars based on imaginative literature in social-work courses and on other forms of communication, the basic touchstone of all art forms. These seminars could be interdisciplinary, involving lecturers from liberal arts, human growth and behaviour, sociology and social work. In her paper Valk referred to several literary works which could help in the integration of subjects across the curriculum. A. Alvarez's *The Savage God* is a study of suicide. One critic wrote of this book that the truest thing one can know about suicide is that we cannot know. But he added that after reading the book much more would be felt about suicide than could be hoped for from a dozen academic books. Stengel (1971) called the book the poetry of death. It was beautifully written, full of poetic truths and it presented the role of destructive tendencies in society through the mirror of poetry.

Classics such as *Anna Karenina* and *Madame Bovary* provide insights into marriage relationships as does a book called *Marriage In Life and Literature* by Robert Seidenberg, an American psychoanalyst. Although this made more use of case histories than literature Valk found it very readable. Reading William Faulkner's *The Sound and the Fury* helped in grasping how a subnormal boy might perceive the world; Faulkner communicated this through imagining the child's feelings and sensations. A hell created by a human system which bestowed absolute power on the ruling class is described in Solzhenitsyn's *The First Circle*. The system contained the seeds of its own destruction because those in power feared each other and became paranoid and finally turned on each other. The finest intellects (the "First Circle") were arrested and sent to prison where they perished in different ways or found the means to survive. Valk comments that this study of a bureaucratic system that evolved out of individual reactions to a closed system would make an excellent study for discussion by the sociologist and psychologist . . . and the group dynamics expert. How may students be encouraged towards realising their personal creativity? How may they be encouraged to bring to life inside themselves the symbolic processes necessary for personal integration? Valk (1973) suggests that they are many creative activities which students and teachers can invest for themselves. She quoted one in-service training course which contained a series of meetings called an experiment in Creative Art therapy. Using soap bubbles, photographs, light-sensitive paper, scissors and string, the lecturer gave demonstrations inspiring the students to feel creative themselves. The course was for senior staff of homes for the elderly. Changing the home environment could bring about changes in the drab lives of residents. The effect of different coloured walls, the relaxing nature of some colours and the stimulating effect of others were demonstrated to the group by using lamps, coloured bulbs and white emulsion-painted walls. The students carried out various activities with their residents, painting and flower-making, making miniature gardens. The students learned to express and enjoy their own creativeness (which some were unaccustomed to doing) through painting and making things as well as learning something relevant for elderly and handicapped people.

Empathising, the sharing of other people's feelings and the creative presentation of these feelings and similar feelings in himself enables the social worker to be less self-defensive. In order to widen one's understanding and feeling for people and to improve the quality of life, it is necessary for the social worker to feel creative and original. The empathic processes may be stimulated through immersion in imaginative literature and the arts in general. It is necessary to feel in command of living processes if one is to influence the aims of social policy and their application.

Lee (1974) discusses the place of literature in social-work education and in the study of the social sciences. He suggests that imaginative writing offers understanding of another kind and quality to that offered by disguised case records. He gives five quotations from fiction and autobiography, which he does not analyse, suggesting that students will attain various levels of understanding in studying the excerpts. In addition to the important assistance literary art may give in developing empathy it may also suggest social problems for study. Mental illness may be examined from the standpoints of psychiatry, psychology and sociology. In addition there is a rich fictional and autobiographical literature which can be drawn on. The social comment provided by the novels of Charles Dickens is illustrated by *Nicholas Nickleby*, on the theme of private education in the nineteenth century, *Oliver Twist* (poverty and the Poor Law), *Martin Chuzzlewit* (the Victorian sickroom — Mrs. Gamp) and *Little Dorrit* (bureaucracy; the circumlocution office). Lee observes that the novelists' own experiences inform his work: he refers to Dickens' unhappy marriage and miserable childhood. Jean Colin's autobiography *(You Never Had It So Good)* gives an idea of what it is like for a woman trying to bring up her children when her sole source of income is state benefit. This article contains several helpful suggestions, some of which are quoted above. The very moving book about her mother's last illness by Simone de Beauvoir *(A Very Easy Death)* is among others which are mentioned.

One author who has not been mentioned in the discussions of literature mentioned here is Georges Simenon. Much of his work, it seems to me, contains perceptive studies of relationships between people and how these influence communication. Maigret's interviewing techniques repay study. *The Man Who Watched the Trains Go By* is a sensitive portrait of an isolated man and gives a vivid account of the course of paranoid mental illness.

6. THE USE OF LANGUAGE IN WRITING

An outstanding feature of the study of literature is the emotive and figurative use of language. In prose, poetry and drama certain literary conventions are used and the reader or listener is challenged to use his imagination in understanding them. The content is supplied by the writer's imagination while it is in the imagination that the sometimes contradictory elements of experience and memory are joined together and interpreted. The distinctive character of literature is not in its relation to observable phenomena but that its material is assembled imaginatively and is expressed in artistic language. Not everyone reacts to literature and drama creations are not necessarily stirred by them and expressed in a symbolic way. This could be related to a prejudice against taking the arts seriously; this is particularly true of those social scientists and social workers who feel they must emulate natural scientists. However, when people do become emotionally involved they may be able to identify through pity and fear, for example, with characters in tragedy. Art forms, and drama in particular, provide means by which fears, problems and complexes may be modified by bringing them to consciousness and giving them expression. The person is involved and yet is able to stand back: a performance or role play is real and yet is not real: it has a life of its own. In addition to role playing in scenes chosen from novels or plays literary works can be chosen to integrate some aspects of the curriculum.

The inseparability of reading and writing and of reading and literature is because language is developed and invigorated through them. Reading and listening are the main means of command of language, and writing cannot be divorced from reading. The reading of great literature and poetry are basic aids to literacy. In schools "backward" children who have difficulties in reading and writing enjoy original simple stories of literature and poetry. The use of technical language is supported on the ground that ordinary language is not capable of conveying the precise meaning of contemporary thinking in a specialised field. This could mean that laymen could be excluded from discussion of particular subjects and that specialists could become increasingly incapable of communicating with each other. The use of technical language as a kind of shorthand may be necessary when specialists communicate with each other but it can be argued that there are few general ideas of importance that cannot be communicated in simple language.

Skills in speech and writing develop principally through practice. This practice needs to be carefully chosen, appropriate to the level the student has reached, and it should be interesting and realistic. As far as writing skills are concerned at least, this is the most important method of learning. Telephones and dictating machines and other mechanical aids may save time but they lead to increased dependence on speech and the typewriter. The use of jargon appears to come from people having to say and write more than they have the capacity to express in simple terms: to some extent it is produced by pressure of time. The debasement of language is an important factor in communication breakdown and therefore affects the effective carrying out of tasks.

In social work efficiency depends, among other things, on communication in speech and writing. Language is a very important vehicle of communication in professional work. Local authority social service departments and probation departments are large-scale organisations: their size alone has increased the importance of exact communication. The amount of work which is carried out and often the speed with which it is done means that communication failures are costly and troublesome; they can be dangerous too. Language is more than the means of conveying thoughts and feelings from one person to another. It is an instrument of thinking. It is a means for understanding what we are thinking and feeling as well as understanding what others have said or written. Powers of self-awareness are to a great extent affected by the ability to understand and use language. A person's ability to read and comprehend is not only a skill in a particular direction; it reflects his general level of emotional and intellectual development. Students learn from practice and from group interaction. They also learn by relating practical experience to principles and theory. This means learning about some factors in human interaction which may lead to poor relationships. For example, one may learn that the hostility of a group may be provoked further by some kinds of intervention or that poor interviewing methods lead to defensiveness and evasiveness on the part of interviewees. Students then have to go on to modify such mistakes and eliminate them by learning why the techniques were inappropriate. If the student sees that he obtains "better" results by using effective techniques he is more likely to continue to employ them.

A trainee needs to have opportunities to practice interviewing, to describe his successes and his mistakes and discuss them. He needs to be able to exchange ideas and to learn from the experiences of other trainees and more experienced interviewers. In order to do this as openly as possible he will need to feel that he will not be "blamed" or ridiculed for making mistakes and that, if he does make mistakes, he will help in dealing with them. This climate for learning is often emphasised. It appears to involve that everyone involved in training is willing to go on learning, that is, that they are sharing in the experience of trying to understand the complexities of behaviour. It is hoped that the trainee will perceive that the trainers want him to become proficient and want to learn from his experiences. Report writing involves a wide range of literary skills even if the subject is a special one such as a social-work interview. The general problems of purpose, definition, selection and arrangement all require training and experience. Skill is needed in structuring a report's paragraphs and sentences, in choosing a vocabulary of suitable range and appropriateness, and in communicating the writer's views on the evidence he is presenting. These learning tasks can be dealt with first of all by encouraging trainees to send messages to each other in writing (rather than doing written work on a larger scale). They can then be encouraged to criticise and help each other. By focusing on the purpose of the messages and their effects on the recipients it will be possible to suggest improvements to grammar and punctuation.

Some students have difficulty with recording because of never having been taught to write properly. The field work teacher does not expect to remedy such deficiencies in basic education but attempts to help his students reach minimum standards so that students are at least able to convey the work they have done for administrative purposes. If a student is handicapped in written work it may not be possible to use process records as a method of teaching. Other students have difficulty in recording, not because of an inability to write, but because of a reluctance to commit ideas to paper. The student may be quite open and relaxed in verbal discussion. A more general resistance to communicating with the field teacher is a more complicated matter. The more a field teacher can help a student to understand the variety of uses that are made of a record the easier it will be for the student to write appropriately. Thus a clear initial briefing about what is required and for what reasons will help a student to meet minimum standards. It may also be helpful to suggest a structure for the student to follow. Some departments have specific requirements while others leave it to individual social workers. The field teacher may then need to help the student to work out a structure to cover essential points in a way that is easy to follow (Pettes, 1967). A detailed recording of an interview (a process record) may not be a verbatim account but it attempts to show the way an interview has proceeded. It is useful as an aid in training: it gives a picture of the interview and stimulates thinking and discussion about what happened. A structure for recording, as well as for studying records, is often found to be useful, for example, stating the purpose of the interview first, giving a chronological account, and concluding with comments about what happened and possible next steps.

Frequently summaries rather than extended reports are required in social-work agencies. Some conventions govern the writing of summaries and these can now be discussed. Usually a summary is not written in the form of notes (for example, in the style sometimes used to précis lecture materials), but in continuous prose. The words of the original material may not be used, being replaced by the words of the person making the summary. Material which is summarised is likely to be reports or correspondence, that is material not already in continuous prose form. Practice in summary writing invariably involves reducing a written passage to a given proportion of its length (say a third or a quarter of its length). This involves a firm grasp of the original material and specifically the principal facts, themes or arguments. If this is to be undertaken successfully the person making the summary has to be able to understand the original passage in detail and to form an overall view of its main aim. This means that he has to exercise his skills as a receiver. Second, he must be able to divide the original writer's points into those which are relevant (and therefore must be included) and the irrelevant. The relevant points must be further divided into those which are essential and those which are relevant but not essential. He has to balance the proportion of relevant and less relevant points according to the priorities he allocates. He has to organise the material in a logical way. The next stage involves checking the length of the rough draft and reducing it to the limits required in the summary. As far as possible this should be achieved by rewording rather than by removing material. Usually this involves rewriting complete sentences rather than trying to remove or rearrange words or phrases. This process continues until the required number of words is reached. The revised draft is then read again to check that the sense is still clear, that it is grammatically correct, written in clear full sentences, properly punctuated and that it flows fairly smoothly. Contributions to this smooth flow include using connectives, and if possible avoiding very short sentences and excessive condensation of paragraphs. The final version of the summary is then written, further improvements being made if this can be achieved without using additional words.

The case record extract which follows consists of approximately 1200 words and it is followed by a summary version of just under half this length (500 words approximately).

FAIRBRIDGE PROBATION SERVICE   *CONFIDENTIAL*

    Name: Michael YOUNG.
    Age: 16 years.
    Religion: Church of England — nominal.
    Referred by:- His mother.

Summary of case at outset:

Michael is refusing to go to work, mother wants me to speak to him.

Any other information or comments:

Michael has only recently finished 2 years on probation (damage to lorry by throwing stones.)

Michael lives with his recently widowed mother and 8-year-old brother, Keith, in a small terraced house in a poor area of Fairbridge. Maternal grandparents also share the home, which is definitely overcrowded. Both father and mother were earnest and hardworking, and Michael was normally a good son to them.

4.9.62. Mrs. Fraser (a neighbour) telephoned on behalf of Mrs. Young
Could an officer please go and visit Michael Y. as his mother says he will not go to work and she has to depend on him working as she has no husband.

5.9.62. Home visit following telephone call:
The pattern of the interview was that when I arrived I was shown into a room full of people and Mrs. Young extended an arm and said "there he is mister". I then asked if I could have a word with her alone first of all, indicating the door through to the front; in the front was Grandpa but Mrs. Young soon managed to get him to understand that I was wanting a private talk with her. I then interviewed Mrs. Young, then Michael and then Mrs. Young again.

This story came out in odd bits, working generally backwards but definitely shunting around. I then put it together as best I could and checked that I had the right sequence of events.

About the time that Michael first went to school, either a little before or a little afterwards he was referred to the Highstone Children's Hospital by Dr. Price for severe temper tantrums coupled with banging his head on the floor. The doctor at Highstone is supposed to have told Mrs. Young — "What he wants is to be in a family of eleven or twelve". Mrs. Young thinks this meant he was spoiled, and she also thinks that at the time he was lonely. He still had occasional temper bouts until Keith was born when Michael was 8. He hadn't been told about Keith, and I thought Mrs. Young said "because I did not know anything about it". Anyway when Michael came from from school he looked at him rather queerly, and then for two or three weeks afterwards acted "all jealousified". From then until just before the father died Michael was alright, and "he thinks the world of Keith". "You would not think so sometimes to hear them in the house, but his mates say Michael thinks the world of Keith."

Michael has been working alright for a few months before he started getting big and answering back. He slept in the same room as his father and mother "but he had his own bed", although Mr. Young did not like him sleeping in the same room they could not do anything about it.

Michael's father went suddenly — coronary — he had been fit up to the time of his death. Michael was with his father when he was dying and Mrs. Young says that although he did not show much upset at the time I think it's upset him inside, because he is very quiet now, "he does not talk like he used to". Apparently Michael used to spend a lot of time with his father. A fortnight later the paternal grandmother died. Michael had some time off whilst they sorted out the premiums.

The start of Michael answering back coincided with them saying "no" to a motor bike — this was the first thing that he hadn't got, "because Mr. Land, we'd done everything for Michael."

Once Michael had restarted work after his father's death with the coach-painting firm he only worked for a couple of weeks, and then he started at Heaton's — bath makers. He had only been working a short time and he is refusing to go, and Mrs. Young feels "very dependent" on him.

In the house now there are maternal grandfather, maternal grandmother and mother,

Michael and Keith. Maternal grandfather and maternal grandmother have to sleep apart because maternal grandfather has a bad cough and maternal grandmother is ailing. Both are still ambulant. Michael and Keith sleep in the same bedroom, and mother sleeps downstairs on the couch. Michael, mother claims, wants privacy and he feels awkward now having his bath in the kitchen. (Mother is seeing Miss Boyd of the Housing Department at 3.30 p.m. today).

I then started to interview Michael. Not too easily, his attention would constantly stray, especially when he was being asked about reasons for not working or why he felt his mother should support him he did in fact start whistling.

Once he was talking he denied his refusal to go to work was anything to do with his father's death. "Everyone has to go sometime haven't they." He will not go to work because he does not want to tell them he does not want the job as he likes the two who are working with him; but he does not want the job because it is indoors. He got the job himself; he went to the Youth Employment Bureau for four months but they could not get him a job.

He wants an outside job where he can earn £4-£5 a week, even if this means working overtime, but he is not going to the Youth Employment Bureau again. He is hoping to get on as a builder's labourer or a gardener with the Parks Department. He is, however, making no attempt to find a job saying "there are none". Criticism falls on deaf ears, he merely switches his attention away from the interviewer. He feels his mother is too strict with him at nights — there are always rows when he comes in, he spends a lot of his time at his mate's (Barry's house) and feels his mother won't let him join in the activities of his mates to the extent that he wants to. He does not feel free to bring his mates into his home. He does not get on with his grandparents but does not want to say anything about them. When he is home from work he does not stay indoors, but works in the back garden, knocks around the street, sometimes goes to town, and goes up to his mate's with his guitar. At the moment his spending money is going on tattoos. I was with Michael for nearly an hour, I could not get him to give any definite intention of going out to find a job.

I then interviewed Mrs. Young again, and explained the position to her. I said I could not get Michael to go to work; she could help Michael best by helping him to face up to his problems and not worrying for him; that she should try to play down the rows when he comes in late at night, and encourage him to get a job rather than drive him. At this Mrs. Y. butted in. In the evenings when Michael comes in it is usually Grandma who starts on at him, and it is they who try to force Michael to go out to work: she can feel Michael pushing back against them, then she sides with Michael, and once she was so upset that she told Michael to get out of the house, but she does not want him to go. The grandparents want quiet and Michael is at an age when he wants noise, and they are always rowing. Just then there was an outburst from Grandpa. "He was in Middlewood", Mrs. Young explained. Apparently he was admitted about five years ago for loss of memory, "he's cured though but he still has an awful temper". Both grandparents are aged 75 years.

Mrs. Y. is really hoping to get something from Miss Boyd this afternoon. She also worries when Michael goes out in case he will get into trouble and she has to fill in his form because he never worries, she said she did not like being hard on Michael.

I explained that she was better to let Michael start thinking for himself now, and doing things for himself whilst he was 16, whilst she was still there in the background to keep an eye on things, than to find himself at 21 unable to do anything for himself.

Mrs. Y. seems to be in the centre of a home where all the members pull in different directions — should she please Michael she'll upset the grandparents, and if she please them Michael feels hard done by. Now that Michael is not working she will have a difficult time financially. She is on National Assistance and they have no allowance for Michael. Grandparents only pay 10/6 towards the rent, do their own cooking and have the use of the front room of the house and front bedroom.

Mother emphasised several times that Michael wants privacy, "he's a funny boy, some days he likes to have his meals without being disturbed, and if grandpa comes in there is a row and Michael jumps up".

Mrs. Y. said she'd get in touch with myself this week and let us know how she gets on with Miss Boyd.

Summary of Michael Young record

Michael Young, 16, had just completed two years on probation. He lived with his mother, recently widowed, his brother Keith, 8, and his maternal grandparents. The home was definitely overcrowded, and was a small terraced house in a poor area. A neighbour (Mrs. Fraser) telephoned on 4th September on behalf of his mother to ask if Michael could be visited; he was refusing to go to work and mother was financially dependent on him. I visited on 5th September. I made it clear to Mrs. Young that I wanted to see Michael and herself privately and separately.

In my interview with mother I learned that Michael had severe temper tantrums and head banging when he first went to school. He had been seen at the hospital about this (referred by Dr. Price). He continued to have occasional outbursts until Keith was born (Michael was 8). He was jealous of Keith at first but was alright then until his father died suddenly from a heart attack. Michael was with his father when he was dying. Mother thought that Michael missed his father: he, Michael, was very quiet. Two weeks after his father's death, paternal grandfather died and Michael had some time off from work then. Michael then started work again with a coach painting firm: after two weeks he started with another firm, has only been there for a short time and was now refusing to go. In the house now there are maternal grandfather, maternal grandmother, mother, Michael and Keith. The sleeping arrangements are awkward and mother thought that Michael wanted privacy. (She was going to the Housing Department to see Miss Boyd.)

I then tried to interview Michael whose attention constantly strayed especially when asked about reasons for not working. He said very little but denied that his refusal to go to work was anything to do with his father's death. He wanted an outside job but was not attempting to find one. He felt his mother was too strict and he did not feel free to bring friends home. He did not get on with his grandparents. The interview lasted for nearly an hour but Michael gave no indication that he would go to find a job. I saw Mrs. Young again and said that I could not get Michael to go to work; she could help him by encouraging him to face up to his problems and not worrying for him. Mrs. Young said the grandparents who are both 75 press him about work. Mother does not want him to go but once, when she was upset by grandmother pressing him, she told him to leave the house. Mrs. Young told me that grandfather had been in a psychiatric hospital for loss of memory; he still had an awful temper. Mrs. Young was hoping to have a successful interview at the Housing Department that afternoon.

I said that it was better to let Michael think and do things for himself now while she was still in the background than for him to find at the age of 21 unable to do anything for himself.

Mrs. Young seems to be a central person in the home but she is pulled in different directions by Michael and the grandparents, although the grandparents have their own room and cooking facilities. They pay only 50p towards the rent and mother would have a difficult time financially now that Michael was not working. Mrs. Young would contact me later this week.

The method used in report writing may be summarised as follows. First the passage, reports or letters are read through as a whole so that the *general* sense is understood. The material is then read again and the divisions of the subject-matter are noted. Sometimes it is preferable to do this by noting headings for the main sections. In some cases it may not be necessary to make actual written notes of headings: it may be possible to obtain a clear outline without writing anything down. Most passages or reports can be divided into three or four main sections representing stages in the writer's development of the theme. These sections are not necessarily indicated by paragraphs nor are they of uniform length. In the summary each section can be given a definite heading (where this is appropriate) and these headings will provide a framework for the summary. In examining each section the points which are essential to the theme are picked out. Illustrations and figurative expressions can be cut out or reduced to simple terms. As far as possible the chief points which must be included are written down in the summariser's own words.

The rough drafts of summaries should rely mainly on the rough notes that have been made previously but essential phrases from the original material can be retained if they are an aid to precision in bringing out the original writer's meaning. This may involve explaining how his ideas were expressed (for example, "the social worker light-heartedly suggests that . . .") but such explanations are only necessary occasionally: they should be used only to serve a definite purpose. The draft should be written in a single paragraph unless there is a distinct change in the sense of the original material. The draft should be compared with the original material to make sure that essential points have not been omitted. Alterations may be necessary if this has happened or, if the draft is still too long, some passages may need to be expressed more briefly. It should be assessed as a piece of prose which is readable and which can be understood by someone unfamiliar with the original material. A summary of a passage containing several sentences does not consist in a summary of each separate sentence. The substance of a whole sentence may be put in one or two words. A sentence normally has a central idea although in many sentences additional ideas are attached to the central one and are sometimes expressed in a large number of words. However, it should be possible to identify the central idea and state it briefly. It should be possible for the summariser to express the gist of the sentence briefly in his own words. But if the central idea is given in the actual wording of the sentence, appropriate words may be selected and the others discarded. It is advisable to read the report or other material thoroughly (if necessary two or three times) to be clear what it is about, and to note the main theme. This will be helpful later when the title is considered.

This chapter has surveyed a number of tools of learning and has illustrated the activity involved in terms of social interaction and communication between people. In Chapter 4 discussion of the interaction process continues. The main focus of that chapter will be on influences on communication and various illustrations of aids to learning about the topic will be included.

CHAPTER 4

Learning About Influences on Communication

1. INTERACTION BETWEEN PERSON AND SITUATION

We have seen earlier how in simple reflex behaviour the stimulus acts on the organism and a response follows. The organism does not play an active part in selecting or interpreting behaviour. Usually a person is exposed to a large number of stimuli; in any given situation he may react to a combination of them, depending on his state at that moment. Thus one of the things the person does to the situation is to select the stimuli. The individual not only partly determines what aspects of a situation will dominate but to a great extent he influences the nature of things to which he reacts. In other words, the individual organises or interprets the environment in which he lives. Among the influences on our interpretations of situations or problems is the information that is available to us. In attempts to solve problems trial and error may be used. In each case of error information about lack of success of the trial is fed back to influence further activity. If feedback is available trials and errors may proceed until a problem is resolved, or until the person's environment has been "mapped" and interpreted. It is possible to illustrate the effects of feedback of information.

To show how a person's perception of a verbal message is affected when feedback is reduced experiments can be devised to vary the feedback that is available. The task given to a person is to describe a diagram to a second person. The latter is then asked to reproduce it and the amount of feedback that is allowed is varied. One person is asked to describe the diagram to other people. The purpose of the exercise is explained to him and he is asked to become familiar with the diagrams. Also, he is told that he will have to describe the diagrams to other people under different conditions and that the experiment is aimed at getting people to reproduce the diagrams as accurately as possible. There are four sets of feedback conditions. The first is where feedback is minimal. The person who is to describe the diagram tells the other that he will be describing a complicated geometric shape which is to be reproduced as accurately as possible. He also says that the pencil ruler and compass that are provided can be used but "you may not ask any questions or say anything at all". The two people sit back to back while describing the diagram. In the second situation feedback is restricted. The subjects sit back to back again but this time the person drawing the diagram may ask the other questions that can be answered by "yes" or "no" only. No other responses are allowed. The third situation is one of free verbal feedback. The subjects face each other. They are allowed to talk to each other normally but the person giving instructions is not allowed to see the attempted reproduction of the diagram. The fourth kind of situation is like the third except that the person giving the instructions can also see the other's attempt while he is describing the diagram. But he must still not allow him to see the original diagram. Each person goes through the feedback situations in a different order as shown in the following table.

Subject
1
2
3
4

Order			
1	2	3	4
2	4	1	3
3	1	4	2
4	3	2	1

If the diagrams are used in this way they will serve for different conditions each time. The instructions given will vary depending on the order of conditions but they are kept as possible. The diagrams are in 4-inch squares. A 4-inch square grid can be constructed which divides the square into sixteen 1-inch squares. Each reproduction can be scored five points for each part which corresponds exactly to the original and between four points and nil if there is some discrepancy but some agreement. The maximum score for agreement is thus 80 and the minimum is 0. Discussion of the results could be about what differences might be expected with other kinds of material and about whether there was a progression in accuracy scores as feedback increased. This experiment was devised by Leavitt and Mueller (1951) and they formulated the method of scoring the results and suggested statistical procedures which could be applied. These were an analysis of variance which would compare all the groups with each other simultaneously and give an estimate of the difference between groups. It was sometimes necessary to follow an analysis of variance by t-tests to ascertain where the significant difference is to be found.

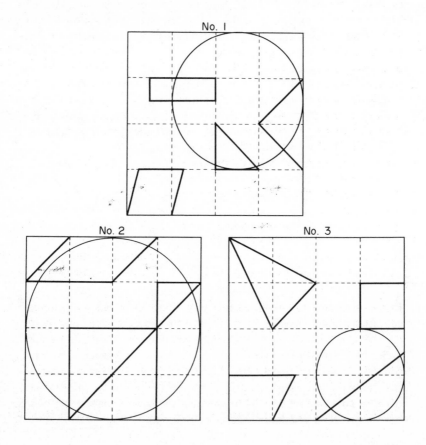

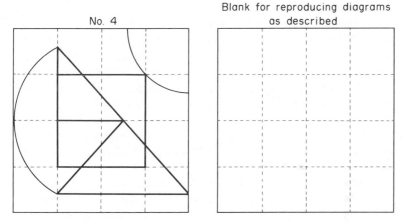

Fig. 5. Diagrams used in an experiment on feedback.
(From Liggett, J. and Cochrane, R. (1968) *Exercises in Social Science*, Constable.)

The fact that the same thing can be viewed in quite different ways can be effectively illustrated by diagrams and pictures and by using stories. In the diagram (Fig. 6) the lines may be seen as a pair of X's or as an upright and an inverted V.

If one person expected to see the X's he would be more likely to see them than another who expected to see the V's. There are more ways of seeing this figure. It could represent a W on top of an M. This piece of information helps the observer to see the figure in this way, as would the further suggestion that it might be a diamond with whiskers on its sides. Most people are able to see other viewpoints, such as these, when they are pointed out.

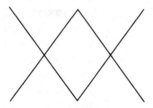

Fig. 6. X's or V's?

In the accompanying illustration (Fig. 7) the inner geometrical figures in (a) and (b) are the same but they are seen as a square and a diamond respectively because they are framed differently. In a sense an attitude is a frame of reference. Just as the frame gives specific meaning to the inner figures in the diagram so an attitude determines an opinion. A change in attitude may radically change opinions. If a person's attitude towards his job changes from an unfavourable to a favourable one his opinions about associated topics will become more favourable or positive.

Fig. 7. Frames of reference.
(From Abercrombie, M. (1969) *The Anatomy of Judgement.* Penguin Books.
By permission of Hutchinson Publishing Group Ltd.)

The next example shows how schemata may help people *not* to see certain things. The schema into which observers fit the new experience may be an inappropriate one. Most people read the statements in the triangles in the accompanying figure as "Paris in the spring"; "Once in a lifetime"; "Bird in the hand". They should then be asked to look again more carefully to find out what is wrong. After a period of concentration they will see the extra words. This illustrates how at first a person selects the words forming the familiar phrases, as if he is blind to the words which do not form part of the pattern, or as if he thought them irrelevant. Later he interprets the pattern in a different way. Some people see the actual pattern quite quickly: others reach it only with difficulty and quite a lot of effort.

Fig. 8. Schemata.

A group of people are shown the accompanying picture of a woman and asked what they think her age is, what are her outstanding physical characteristics, and whether she looks attractive or ugly. The picture is in fact ambiguous as continued inspection will reveal. In one version the woman is an ugly toothless old hag with a long nose. On the other hand, it may be interpreted as that of a reasonably attractive young girl with her head turned away so that an eyelash and part of her nose are visible. When people felt frustrated or uncomfortable about not being able to see one or the other versions which others can see this is a good illustration of the need to fill in the gap in their experience; they feel they are missing something which the others can see. The picture demonstrates the fact that different people see things differently. This can lead to questioning factors which may be responsible and discussion about how behaviour change may be affected by understanding an individual's perceptions. (The picture is from Leavitt, 1964).

Fig. 9. "Nice" or "nasty"?
(From Leavitt, H. J. (1964) *Managerial Psychology*. University of Chicago Press.)

Some medical students, in a set of experimental free discussions, were asked to compare two radiographs of a hand. The results showed how the students made a number of unjustifiable statements and how emotional factors coloured their judgements of the evidence. "The inferences the students had made were not arrived at as a result of a series of logical steps, but swiftly, almost unconsciously. The validity of the inferences was usually not inquired into, indeed the process was usually accompanied by a feeling of certainty of being right, and consequently the discussion of incompatible views sometimes became very heated. Frequently the correct inference had been made (as with the statement that A was a younger hand than B) and then discussion did not change the formulation of the end result, but only brought to light the processes involved in getting it" (Abercrombie, 1969). It is advisable to distinguish between the physical properties of a stimulus and the properties it has for the individual. It is a commonplace observation that the world is what people make it; different people see things differently. Their perceptions are determined by their needs and their picture of the world is distorted by their own tensions. So far this is an over-simplification. People may "see" what is important to their needs but this can mean that they see both what they want to and what they are afraid to see. Both wishes and fears are important to a person's needs.

The observer's role is an active one; he organises the information that is presented to him. In doing this he uses his past experience, i.e. he draws on his existing stock of information. Another experiment was with playing cards some of which had the colour changed, e.g. the six of clubs was coloured red instead of black. The cards were successively exposed for a very short time. Some people reported seeing normal cards and not anomalous cards; they reported the red six of clubs as either a black six of clubs or a red six of diamonds or hearts, for example. Others saw them as being purple- or brown-coloured six of clubs. It seemed that rather than see a red club the subjects saw what fitted their schema and changed the colour to what it ought to have been, black, or change the shape to a diamond or heart to fit in with the colour or compromise with brown or purple. A shorter time of exposure was necessary to allow people to name the normal cards than the abnormally coloured ones: people see what they expect to see. When the thing we look at is sufficiently like the thing we expect to see and easily fits our schema, our experience helps us to see when what we expect to see is not there our schemata lead us astray. A pattern is interpreted differently according to the state of the observer and therefore according to which of his schemata he uses.

2. ATTITUDES AND THE INTERPRETATION OF INFORMATION

Whether data will be observed or perceived accurately or not depends largely on whether emotions or attitudes interfere with the relationship between the observer and what is perceived. What is perceived is thought about and interpreted: inferences are made about the data and they are derived from the theoretical knowledge and previous experience of the observer. Inferences about the data are selected to form hypothesis or vaguer speculations. These hypotheses assign significance to the data and invest it with meaning. Such formulations are also affected by the person's feelings and attitudes and prejudices: this is unavoidable of course; the validity of these formulations can be tested. In the process of analysis account has to be taken of known facts, the inferences that are made, the suppositions that are put forward, what can be confirmed and what further information is needed. Finally the conclusions reached have to be evaluated as far as possible.

It has been noted that an attitude is a frame of reference. It can be thought of as a general background of feeling against which factual events are seen. Attitudes form frames of reference which supply the unique emotional loading to a person's perceptions of things and events. Attitudes are usually classed as favourable or unfavourable and are related to groups of people. There are favourable or unfavourable attitudes towards political parties, races, religious denominations, and work groups. We see members of such groups either in friendly or in unfriendly ways, or with feelings of superiority or inferiority. The interpretation of facts depends on more than the facts themselves because the interpretation organises them. The ambiguous diagrams can be seen in a number of ways because it is possible to group their lines or components differently. Words, thoughts and feelings also derive meanings from the way they are organised. In addition to organising facts an attitude affects their selection. For practical purposes in communication it is important not only to be able to recognise a biased selection of facts by another person but to be aware of this selectivity in oneself.

An attitude is a mental set and represents a predisposition to form certain opinions. An attitude has emotional components. For example, a father has certain feelings towards his child, such as affection. They persist and influence him to act in certain ways. In many situations you would expect to find the father doing things which will please his child and avoiding things which might displease him. An attitude is thus a predisposition to behave; it is a combination of feelings and motives connected with objects or people; it is characteristic of the individual and of substantial duration. Given a particular opinion this represents an interpretation of facts the nature of which depends on the person's attitude. If asked, a person will justify his opinion: the opinion causes the justification; the justification does not describe the "cause" of the opinion. The relative influence of facts and attitudes in shaping opinions may vary from one extreme to another. There may be little or no factual support of an interpretation: at the other extreme an opinion may be influenced almost entirely by facts. Such an opinion offers no problems. It will readily change when conditions or facts are altered. But because opinions are based on attitudes they can be problematic because unfavourable attitudes can continue after the facts have been corrected. Prejudices provide illustrations of attitudes that determine the meanings which facts may assume. The actual facts that conflict with the prejudice are rationalised to fit with the general attitude: the rationalisation protects the attitude from change. These relationships can be represented diagrammatically (see the accompanying figure) (Fig. 10).

From the point of view of psychology attempts to define meaning point to an important fact: meaning resides in people. A sign has no universal meaning until people agree about what it is associated with. A receiver must not only recognise symbols that are transmitted: he must also perceive the symbols as meaning the same thing as the sender intends them to mean. Unlike the measurement of information the measurement of meaning is a complex task which incorporates subjective evaluation of the symbols by participants in communication.

Shared meaning can be exchanged in many different ways. Spoken and written language are two of them; the movements of hands, bodies, facial expressions and varying vocal manipulations also contribute to the measurement problem. In attempting to measure meaning as contained in language it is assumed that when an incoming message is received the brain evaluates its meaning in terms of various dimensions. The result of this assessment is the meaning of the message for the individual. Osgood and Suci (1955) believed that measurement should contain three parts. It involved people finding the parts of a language that were generally used to assess meanings of things or ideas. People then had to give their preferences from among these responses relative to some eliciting stimulus. When asked to describe the idea of "mother", for example, they should be able to select from a range of responses. The third aspect of measurement had to be that the potential responses would include most of the symbols which adequately represent the major ways in which people attach meanings to things and ideas. Thus they tried to analyse the personal emotional meaning of words or concepts by asking individuals to consider each of several adjectives and decide the extent to which they really described the concept in question. Osgood used pairs of adjectives such as clean-dirty, good-bad, and asked his subjects to imagine a seven point scale with 'good' at one end and 'bad' at the other. By studying an individual's scores it would be possible to assess the strength of his attitudes to the concept being studied.

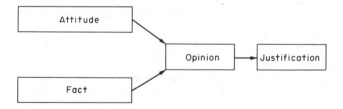

Fig. 10. The rationalisation of attitudes.

To use the Semantic Differential Scale the words to be used to define the concepts to be studied are decided. For example, interesting comparisons may be obtained by asking different groups to rate the same word or by comparing the profiles of different words given by the same person. For example, people could be asked to rate the concept "mother". If a person rates it "very good" he also tends to rate it towards "very pleasant" and "very positive". It is likely that similar consistencies will be found among strong-weak, heavy-light, hard-soft, active-passive, and excitable-calm semantic differentials. Profiles for "mother" and "father" could be compared, for example, or the concepts of "neurotic man" or "athlete" might be used.

The Semantic Differential Technique for plotting meaning in terms of a multi-dimensional space using subjects' judgements is to record them in seven-point scales as illustrated. The concept is printed at the head of the scaling sheet (e.g. "me", "neurotic man", "old man", "sex") together with the subject's name and other relevant information such as sex and age. Subjects are then asked to indicate rankings by a cross. The following illustration is of part of a scale:

Bad:	——:	——:	——:	——:	——: Good
Hard:	——:	——:	——:	——:	——: Soft
Active:	——:	——:	——:	——:	——: Passive
Worthless:	——:	——:	——:	——:	——: Valuable
Dirty:	——:	——:	——:	——:	——: Clean
Insincere:	——:	——:	——:	——:	——: Sincere
Foolish:	——:	——:	——:	——:	——: Wise
Dangerous:	——:	——:	——:	——:	——: Safe
Sad:	——:	——:	——:	——:	——: Happy

For each individual assessment of a concept a profile is produced simply by linking the crosses. A combined profile can then be drawn and compared visually with others — either of other people's profiles of the same concept or of other concepts. Osgood and his colleagues' technique of statistical measurement of meaning involved plotting meaning in terms of a multi-dimensional "semantic space". Speaker's judgements (as below) were recorded in terms of seven-point scales. Statistically they found that special significance seemed to lie in three major dimensions, those of evaluation (good-bad), potency (hard-soft) and activity (active-passive). The method can provide only a partial and approximate account of associative meaning. This is because it involves selecting from an indefinite number of possible scales and because a seven-point scale involves cutting up a continuous scale in seven parts.

No differentiation can be made in the seven parts. The Semantic Differential is thus a rather crude and insensitive technique but it seems that only by using crude tools of this kind that associative meaning can be studied systematically. Whereas conceptual meaning is largely part of the common system of language shared by members of a speech community associative meaning varies more with an individual's experience.

An interviewer-interviewee relationship can be characterised by such statements as "the interviewee has an attitude of trust (or suspicion) toward the interviewer": "the interviewer has attitudes of like (or dislike) or prejudice (or tolerance) toward the interviewee." Such attitudes influence the character of interaction and the content of interviews. The disguised record which follows is, I believe, frequently used in social work courses. It has been used to introduce several topics including the problems of the roles of grandchildren and grandparents, the reactions of an older person to a teenagers' behaviour, and ways of reacting to stress. It seems to be appropriate to introduce it at this point for another purpose. It may be useful to illustrate the relations between attitudes, opinions and communication. A group of students might also be able to learn from their own differences of opinion and their reactions to this situation. Finally, it may also be used to contrast the two interviews and to consider factors which may have led to Mrs. Bell's concluding remarks.

"Mrs. Bell"

Mrs. Bell had been referred by the clerk in the Collecting Office where she had called demanding money for her granddaughter Mary, for whom there was no court order in existence. The collecting officer thought that she was acting rather strangely and wondered if we should not see if the child was all right or in need of protection. As I had been delayed in court, she had waited in my office rather a long time, after refusing another appointment for the afternoon, offered by my secretary.

I noticed her and the granddaughter sitting on opposite sides of the waiting room as I passed through on my way back to the office. Mrs.

Bell is a rather tight-lipped, bony woman in her late fifties; Mary, who is 13, is rather thin and unattractive, with straight fairish hair. She wore a rather shapeless faded dress about 4 inches too long for her.

First interview: Wednesday morning

When I collected Mrs. Bell from the waiting room she turned to Mary and said "You stay still until I come for you. Mind you do then." Mary did not answer, look up or give any indication that she had heard her grandmother speak. I said to Mrs. Bell that she had had a long wait, and she replied rather belligerently, "I want some money for that child." She responded to the puzzled look on my face by explaining that a neighbour had told her that she collected 30s. a week from the court for her granddaughter. She had also been told that if the court made the arrangements you could get a pension book paid through the post office. She complained that the collecting officer at the court had thought that she was a fool and sent her to see me. "I want you to arrange for me to get some money for Mary"; she ended, "They say you help people." I said we tried to do that, and I would like to help her if I could, but I would have to know a little more about her circumstances. From what she told me it was clear that there was no financial hardship, and that in fact they were better off than they were seven years ago, when they first took Mary to live with them. At that time the husband was recovering from a long illness and was only in receipt of National Insurance sick benefits, and she had had to go out cleaning to "make ends meet". I explained about the court and why it could not help her with money. As I could see that she had no claim for National Assistance I also explained about the pension books. I said I could see how hard it must be for her to find that we could not help her in the way she had expected. She made it clear that it was not that she did not want the child (after saying this was all the thanks she got for caring for Mary), and of course she would do her best for her, but she could not see why she and her husband should have to support the child just because her daughter's husband was a "no good". She had warned her daughter about marrying him. He was Irish! With a great deal of feeling she described her row with her daughter shortly after the runaway marriage. She showed extreme bitterness over the whole incident, and hurt over some of the things her daughter had said.

I asked her why Mary came to live with her and her husband, and she told me that her son-in-law had died and that soon after that her daughter Anne had contracted T.B. and gone to a sanitorium. She talked about the hard times she had faced, and hoped that they would none of them have to go through times like that again. If she had not had Mary they could have taken a lodger to help out, but she believed in children having a room to themselves. Mary only thought of herself and was now staying out late, and this worried both Mr. and Mrs. Bell and it disturbed their rest. Normally they explained they went to bed early as they are early risers, "not like some people". She looked very fierce and grim at this and closed her mouth firmly.

I said it seemed to me that Mrs. Bell was feeling that things were near to breaking-point, and that perhaps she was seeking help because of Mary's behaviour, rather than help with Mary's expenses. She said "I told her that if she weren't in by 9 o'clock I'd have her grandfather take his belt to her, and I would too, only the little besom knows that she can twist her grandpa' round her little finger. He never raised his hands to either of our own girls. Nor did I. Though maybe I should have done, and maybe if I had things would have turned out different." She seemed unable to continue thinking aloud and stopped short saying "But why am I telling you all this?" I said maybe because she felt it was important for me to know. She said she couldn't see how it was, she had wanted money for Mary's keep but she could now see that she was not going to get any, so there was no point in staying here talking. I said although I could not help her in the way she had hoped, I thought it might help to talk about her difficulties with Mary and if she felt that it did, then we would always be glad to see her again. I told her the best times to call, and gave her my telephone number and said she could ring for an appointment if she wished, or just call, if she did not mind waiting. She said civilly "thank you" and made for the door. Mary was waiting and asked rather pathetically "Will they give you money to keep me?" but Mrs. Bell just hurried her away without answering.

On Friday of the second week after this interview Mrs. Bell telephoned for another appointment and this was arranged for Monday evening.

Second interview: Monday evening

Mrs. Bell seemed more grimly tight lipped than ever, but there was an air of anxiety about her, which betrayed itself by a quick red flush, when I greeted her in the waiting room. She started the interview by telling me she wanted to talk to me about Mary, who was proving very difficult and might be out of control. Last week she came in late after being warned to be in early, and Mrs. Bell had given her a "good hiding". The home had been in an uproar and Mr. Bell had made more fuss about it than Mary. He had cried more than Mrs. Bell herself had, "Like a baby he was". Mary had become worse, and was now threatening to leave home altogether and go to her mother. I said "To the sanitorium" but Mrs. Bell said that she had been discharged some two years ago, and was now living at the other end of the town with another man to whom she was not married, but fortunately she was unable to have any more children.

I said something about her feeling that her daughter ought not to have the care of children, and Mrs. Bell said she had always worried that Mary would go back to her mother and turn out like her. She had done her best to bring her up right to prevent this from happening, but now all her efforts seemed to be no good. Maybe Mary should be put away for her own protection. I asked her if she thought this was the solution to Mary's behaviour, and she said she would not like it to come to that, and would I talk to her and make her behave.

I said I would ask a lady colleague to see Mary if she thought that was best, but we could not take over Mrs. Bell's job, nor could we be used to punish Mary. Mary would have to trust her probation officer, and that would mean that she would have to be sure that she could tell her how she felt in confidence. Mrs. Bell asked, "You mean you would not tell me what she told her officer?"

I said that we could not promise to tell her all that Mary said, and that Mary would have to know this, just as she would have to know that we wouldn't permit her to tell us of plans that would be dangerous to her, such as running away, without letting Mrs. Bell know. Mrs. Bell seemed reassured by this and I said we would of course have to let Mary tell us about how she felt about her grandmother if we were to be of any help. Just as she had told us about Mary. Mrs. Bell sat in silence for a while and then quietly she said "That was a real hiding that I gave her". I said we might have to go further and discuss with Mary her feelings about her mother.

Mrs. Bell said "I think she is seeing her mother — that's what I'm afraid of really". I queried "Are you afraid of Mary going to her mother and staying there?" In an angry voice she faced me and said "You think I ought to let her see Mary, don't you?" I replied that I had no way of knowing the rights and wrongs of that, but I could see that Mrs. Bell was not sure herself, and from what she had told me she was unsure of her ability to meet all Mary's needs. In fact, it seemed that Mary herself would not let her, neither would her husband, and perhaps in coming to see me, Mrs. Bell was really looking for someone to take over part or all of the responsibility for the girl. After a fairly long pause, Mrs. Bell nodded and then said "He thinks I'm too hard on her. I think he has been seeing her too." I said it must seem to her as though everyone was against her. Mrs. Bell said rather gently, "If only she'd come to me. I'm her mother after all." She thought for a minute or two and then said softly, but with quite a new expression on her face and in her voice, "I'm not hard-hearted, really I'm not", then after a pause, "Only hard-headed."

3. PERCEIVING AND RECALLING

The social worker requires skills to help his client remember information and other skills in order to make inferences about things the client will not be able to recall. The defence mechanisms are processes by which motives and goals that cannot be dealt with consciously are repressed. The processes of memorizing and recalling are affected in analogous ways, i.e. in memory there is a tendency to modify and distort past situations to make them fit more comfortably with other experience and with the self-image.

Memorising is not a simple process by which present events recede into the past in a uniform progression. Although this kind of forgetting does occur it is modified by such factors as what significance was attached to earlier experience, the degree to which it was "learned", and the nature of intervening experiences. The way in which things are remembered depends on their congruence with a person's other experience and his image of himself. These factors help to determine whether or not a person remembers at all and in what ways his recollections differ from events as they actually occurred. There is a tendency for people to more effectively recall positive, satisfying things than negative, unpleasant things. It may be easier to wake early on a holiday than on a day that may be unpleasant at work. The advantages to a person in being blind to unpleasantness may be related to its effectiveness as a defensive device. Many people are able to ignore some background noise when they are working. This helps them to concentrate on what they are doing. It can be demonstrated that words with unpleasant connotations tend to be recognised more slowly when exposed for very short intervals than words with pleasant connotations. The person has to see that the word is unpleasant in order to recognise that it is unpleasant. It has, almost simultaneously, to be rejected or "defended against". This defends the individual against the entry of preselected things mildly disturbing to his equilibrium. If an animal lacks the ability to ward off minor threats it might be unable to cope with them all at the same time. Once a person has learned to perceive many threats and dangers in his environment he requires to have a system of defence against them. Of course there are wide variations in what people regard as threatening or dangerous. If someone has a great deal of frustration in his experience then more of his world or environment and new things in it especially will be seen as potentially dangerous. They have to be warded off but, paradoxically, they must first be recognised. To protect himself from more insecurity the insecure person must first see the things that will produce feelings of insecurity and then deny to himself that he has seen them.

A person's strongest needs and the goals in which he invests heavily are to do with the maintenance of self-esteem. Because of the fundamental need for self-esteem and because it underlies many of a person's goals, frustration of the need will produce extreme tensions. Efforts to resolve these tensions may take various forms, some apparently constructive and others destructive in their results. Attempts to resolve unbearable tensions may result in doing things which give relief but which do not actually resolve the objective problem. Because the defence mechanisms have been discussed quite fully elsewhere I shall concentrate on providing illustrations of their effects on communication and interpersonal perception rather than extended discussion of the topic.

When information is presented to a person he is selective both in the information he observes and in recalling data he associates with it from his past experience. Some of the factors which influence selection are easily modified. Those which are difficult to modify are deep-seated personal ones. In the case of the X-ray pictures of the hands the statement "hand A is younger than hand B because it is smaller" was influenced by the pictures' context. The two pictures were on the same piece of paper and there was no obvious line dividing them. It was easy to assume that the pictures had been taken of hands lying side by side and they were therefore on the same scale. The distinction is more easily made if the paper is cut between the two pictures. But deeper or personal attitudes could not be so easily modified, for example, if a person held the attitude that a sensible teacher would not expect to compare pictures of different scale, or if a person's attitude was suspicious so that he usually looked for catches in everything. The receipt of visual information is affected by context: this is also true of the receipt of information verbally. The meaning of an object, situation or event, to an individual, depends on how it has stimulated him in the past, on the previous and present context and his reaction to it. Before a child is old enough to eat an apple he may have seen one and possibly learned its name. He may see an apple as something to roll along the floor and to play with. He may see balls in the same way; apples and balls may be regarded as equivalent. Gradually the child comes to have ideas about the shapes, sizes, weights and colours of apples, and later their taste and smell. The apple becomes something to eat as well as something to play with. As development proceeds many other associations are linked with apples, apple trees, apple pies, cider, and so on. An apple can thus come to elicit a range of responses in terms of all the experiences previously associated with it.

The growth of meaning is related to the tendency to interpret the new in terms of the old. This is well illustrated by the way objects have different meanings for different individuals (for example, finding the hidden figure in the picture puzzle, trying to understand what a film is about when we go in half-way through it). This is also illustrated by projection tests (for example, when subjects are required to interpret ink blots): "We see what we want to see." Different expectations lead different people to perceive the same object as different; a "grey rat" or "a piece of rag" or "an old woollen sock" instead of a piece of paper. One person may see a drawing as dumb-bells: another may see it as a pair of glasses, as a result of being told roughly what to expect. Past experience also influences the perception of whole objects or symbols in terms of parts of them. If people had to examine every object or situation minutely before perceiving it they would be handicapped in reacting to the environment. In reading, for example, the meaning of words is grasped by reacting to their most obvious letters; familiar objects are recognised in terms of their parts. Some aspect of previous experience helps to "fill out" present experience. Until about the age of 2 a child tends to perceive situations as a whole. He may fail to recognise a familiar person who appears in an unfamiliar place or in new clothes. At the age of 1 Piaget's daughter saw him in the garden and smiled at him. When her mother asked where father was the child looked towards Piaget's study window where she was used to seeing him. When she was 1½ she played happily with her sister downstairs but on going upstairs was surprised that the sister was not there. Her sister had just been ill and had been in bed for a week.

Psychologists have devised a number of experiments to study memory span, factors influencing recall and so on. For example, children or adults are told or read stories which later they try to remember. When a story is read or heard repeatedly and recall is required after each repetition this is a typical memory experiment where increased retention occurs as a function of repetition. In another version of the experiment recall may be required after different periods of time following a single presentation of the story. Another variation of these experiments is to have one person read or hear the story, who then tells it to another, who in his turn tells it to another. In this way changes occur in the story as it passes from one person to another as when rumours circulate. The story which follows has been used in these kinds of experiments. I have adapted the experiment to introduce ideas about perception and their influence on communication, and have used it several times. On this occasion I read the story to one student who repeated it to another until it reached the eighth person. An interval of ten minutes was left until he was asked to repeat his version. I now give the original American version and then the story as it was given by the last student to hear it. (The original story is to be found in Munn, N. (1961) *Psychology,* Harrap, p. 458, where some other reproductions will also be found.)

Original story

The Son Who Tried to Outwit His Father

A son said to his father one day "I will hide and you will not be able to find me." The father replied "Hide wherever you like" and he went into his house to rest. The son saw a three-kernel peanut and changed himself into one of the kernels. A fowl, coming along picked up the peanut and swallowed it; and a wild bush cat caught and ate the fowl. A dog met and caught and ate the bush cat. After a little time the dog was swallowed by a python that, having eaten its meal went to the river and was snared in a fish trap. The father searched for his son, and not seeing him, went to look at the fish trap. On pulling it to the riverside he found a large python in it. He opened it and saw a dog inside, in which he found a bush cat, and on opening that he discovered a fowl, from which he took the peanut, and breaking the shell, he then revealed his son. The son was so dumbfounded that he never again tried to outwit his father.

Reproduction of the story

A young boy was in trouble with his father and tried to hide from him. His father was asleep and the boy left the house and went into the woods where he found a peanut. Opening the nut he removed the kernel and got inside, saying "Now he will not be able to find me." A wild cat came along and saw the nut. Because she felt hungry she ate it. A short time later a dog came along and ate the cat and then the dog met a snake who ate it. The father woke up and decided to go out to look for his son. He went down to the river and saw the snake caught on the bank. He killed it, cut it open and found the dog. Inside the dog he found the cat and then he found the nut. He was very surprised to see his son and the boy was so astonished to see his father he promised never to misbehave again. After this the original story can be told again or the group can read it for themselves in order to contrast the two versions.

When the story is retold or rewritten the theme is usually well retained and the sequence of events follows the original version. But a number of changes in detail are noticed. Some words or parts of the story may be missed out entirely: some words may be replaced by synonyms. A number of changes will be seen in this reproduction. The "three-kernel peanut" becomes a "peanut" and this changes to "nut" as the story proceeds. The boy (previously son) removes the kernel. In the original narrative the son had not misbehaved; he was simply intending to outwit his father. The "bush cat" is changed to "wild cat" and python becomes a snake. The fish trap is omitted and the fowl is lost from the story. On other occasions the fowl has changed into a hen or a chicken. Words or ideas may be added which were not in the original. These may increase with successive repetitions and increasing distortion of details is noticed. The distortion of details is particularly marked when one person hears the story, then tells it to another, and that person passes it on to another, and so on. In the version reproduced here, for example, the "wild" cat was hungry and because she felt hungry she ate the peanut. A further elaboration occurs when "a short time later a dog came along . . ." The father was surprised to see his son: this is an addition to the original story.

Bartlett (1932) described a number of experiments on remembering. Some verbal material, such as a short story, was told to one person who then repeated it to another. He repeated it to a third person and so on. Bartlett believed that a person's past was made up of schemas or active, developing patterns of past experiences and reactions to them. Recalling an event involved an imaginative reconstruction which was affected by all kinds of past experiences (Schemata). The more an event or story fits in with an existing schema the more accurately it will be remembered. It would therefore be expected that stories from another culture with different patterns of thought would be more noticeably changed than stories originating in a person's own culture. To examine what happens to a story from another culture when it is passed along a chain by serial reproduction two groups of students all belonging to one culture (e.g. all British) are required with at least six people in each group. One group uses the Chinese story and the other the English story reproduced below. For each group the first student is told that the tester is going to read the story through twice and the student will be asked to rewrite it in his own words after a ten-minute interval. The student is then asked to write out the story from memory. This second version is given to the next person and so on. A coin is tossed to decide which group uses the Chinese and which group the English story. Bartlett analysed the changes by counting (a) the number of words in each consecutive version, (b) the number of pieces of information that are not repeated elsewhere and which correspond accurately to ones in the story and (c) the number of themes, each theme representing a separate episode or major piece of information (usually about a sentence in length). These measures indicate the degree of literal accuracy and how far the general sense of the story is retained. Discussion of the results focuses on the kinds of change which occurred during reproduction, whether the two stories changed in different ways and what items disappeared first; what themes were well retained? Special attention is given to the overall size of the stories, additions and explanations, repetitions, aspects of the Chinese story that were anglicised, and whether the point of the story is retained. Here are the two stories.

1. The Chinese Story

Ming-Y was the son of a family renowned for its learning and piety and when he was 18 he became teacher to the children of a man of rank and high station. To fulfil his duties he had to stay in this nobleman's house some miles from his father's home. Before he left his father repeated to him the words of an ancient sage: "By a beautiful face the world is filled with love; but heaven may never be deceived thereby."

After two months away Ming-Y desired to see his family again and so with his master's permission he set out on the journey, only to find when he arrived that he had lost his purse. On the return journey he was stopped by a serving maid who told him that her mistress had found his purse and wished to return it to him. So he was led into the deepest and most silent part of the forest where he saw an old and very beautiful house which he had never noticed before.

When he met the mistress of this house he thanked her for returning his silver and learning that she was a widow in mourning wanted to hurry away so as not to disturb her; but Sie (that was her name) did not want him to go quickly. So Ming-Y rejoicing secretly in his heart, for Sie seemed to him the fairest and sweetest being he had ever known, and he felt he loved her more than his father and his mother. So he stayed and they talked and sang and drank purple wine and they kissed and the night grew old and they knew it not.

By deceiving his father and his master, Ming-Y was able to visit Sie's house every evening and each night they devoted to the same pleasures which made their first acquaintance so charming. Until one day there was a chance meeting between the father of Ming-Y and his patron and the deception was discovered.

When questioned by his father the boy was very ashamed and said nothing, so his father struck him violently with his staff and he told his father everything.

Then they all went to the spot deep in the forest where Sie's house was, but when they arrived there the autumn light only revealed an ancient tomb of a great lady of the court who had died 600 years before. The name on the tomb was Sie.

2.   The English Story

Helmut and Wilhelm were on their way back to the camp at Peronne 48. They had lost their way and stopped at the Charneau farm to ask for directions. Seeing a half-finished bottle of wine on the table, Helmut asked for a drink and was gulping it down when a girl came into the room and started at the sight of the two German soldiers. Her parents were country people but this girl was a little different. Her build was tall and slight and her long dark hair and clear brown eyes gave her a certain elegance. Her expression of surprise turned to hatred as she looked at the two men.

"Isn't it enough for you to take all our food without taking our drink as well?"

Helmut was not used to being spoken to like this by any woman and especially not a French girl. Were not the Germans the conquerors and these the conquered? He lunged towards her. She struggled fiercely and succeeded in drawing four stripes of blood down his left cheek. While Wilhelm stood back rather disturbed by this turn of events and tried to restrain the frightened mother, Helmut swung a blow at the father who had tried to free his daughter which sent him crashing into the table. He dragged Elizabeth outside. Sometime later he returned for Wilhelm and they left together. During the following months Helmut returned to the farm several times. He felt slightly guilty because of what had happened and eased his conscience by bringing pieces of cheese and ham. Elizabeth would touch none of it, though after a while her parents accepted it eagerly. It pleased him to think that they were dependent upon him.

On one of his visits Elizabeth was more antagonistic than ever. It annoyed him to think that she could still feel this way despite his gifts. Pulling her sweater tightly over her abdomen she snapped: "Does this sight make you feel like an heroic conqueror?"

The knowledge that Elizabeth was pregnant shocked Helmut and he returned to his camp dazed. He could not forget that Elizabeth was carrying his child. Unexpectedly this gave him some pleasure and he could not help feeling protective towards the girl. She was still proud and loathed the Germans for what they had done to her country and countrymen. Helmut felt he could change this. He returned to the farm as soon as he could and tried to talk to Elizabeth. After the war, he told her, they would be married and he wanted to teach his son to walk and ride and shoot.

He was unable to return for several months and the next time he arrived there was turmoil at the farm. Elizabeth had started a difficult labour early that morning and her mother had discovered that both she and the baby had disappeared from the bedroom.

A few minutes later the door was flung open: Elizabeth stood there, her face was grey and her clothes and hair were wet and muddy and sticking closely to her body. "I couldn't bear it," she sobbed, "I took him to the stream and held his head under the water until . . ."

4.   INTERPRETING WRITTEN INFORMATION

Projection "tests" require a person to respond to ambiguous stimuli by giving them meaning, i.e. by structuring what he perceives. The vague or incomplete nature of the material permits the person to project himself into the situation. An example is the Rorschach test which consists of inkblots; the person is asked to locate and describe images he sees in them, rather like seeing pictures in a fire or faces in the clouds. Another example is the Thematic Apperception Test in which the person responds to rather indistinct drawings by making up a story, saying what events have led to the situation drawn, what is now happening, and what he thinks is going to happen in the future. These are among the most commonly used projective techniques. Case studies such as those presented here provide students with opportunities to project themselves into the situation, to feel what it may be like, and to think about the reactions or possible reactions of the person in the situation. They are thus like projection tests, projection being a way in which we "put ourselves into someone else's shoes". The next step is to stand back and to try to consider the person in his situation more objectively. In studying this case you may identify with one person or other in the family. The summary does not provide a vast amount of information thus leaving scope for readers to look at what is presented imaginatively. The situation is to some extent unstructured therefore. It does not involve a situation calling for a stereotyped and predictable reaction. It may elicit many different reactions depending on who reads it. People's past experiences differ and they get different meanings from the same material. The meaning which we get out of the material may tell us something about our own past experiences and perhaps the motives which have come from it; thus such study may increase self awareness.

1. Interview with Mr. Smith

Mr. Smith was referred to the probation office by the local council of Social Service. He asked first for an assurance of confidentiality. He then said that he had married in September last year, not having had children or a wife previously, and had taken on John aged 15, now grammar school and Peter aged 13 who attended a secondary modern school. He had come to see me about Peter.

He insisted on making the legal position clear and showed me a will made by the boys' father leaving the house they lived in to his wife and then to the boys. He said that his mother-in-law had convinced the boys that they owned the house and they showed no respect for the property. The older boy was not too bad as his homework and an occasional club kept him quiet. The younger boy refused to do what he was told and had stolen £8 or more from his father's pockets. He also came home from school with expensive articles like cigarette lighters which he said he had been given there. He obeyed his parents grudgingly if at all and Mr. Smith had curtailed pleasures like TV and the cinema as he thought they were a bad influence.

Peter belongs to the sea scouts but Mr. Smith thought the troop poorly run with no discipline. He wondered whether he should have moved to a new area on marriage and given them all a fresh start. He thought Peter needed "shaking up" and said that perhaps a boarding school would be best for him, or a caution from the police. He had sought advice from his friends who had advised him to restrict, but he wondered whether he was handling the boys in the right way. He described how they had been spoiled by their mother and grandparents in the past. He stressed the need for strong discipline with the boys, especially Peter, who took advantage if he slackened off even a bit.

After a second short interview with Mr. Smith, a week later, the probation officer saw Mrs. Smith at the office. She was clearly very anxious about the family situation. She talked about the disappointment his misbehaviour had been. Since the death of her first husband eleven years before she had worked to keep the home going; the boys had to be left a good deal to relatives. On marrying again she had looked forward to a normal and independent family life. She had known Mr. Smith about twenty years. He had not been married before or courted anyone else, so his experience of family life was limited. He had had a hard time in his childhood. He was anxious to compensate for what was lacking in his own life. He was very firm with the boys who were used to having their own way. This partly explained Peter's recent behaviour.

She talked about her own difficulties in this situation, especially conflicting loyalties to husband and children. She did not like the way he had sought advice from others and made family affairs rather public. She also talked of Peter's schooling, his enthusiasm for Sea Scouts and his ambition to join the navy. She thought this wish was genuine and not a passing phase. On the whole, although she saw good qualities in both husband and boys, she was finding family life rather a strain and losing sleep.

2.   Interview with Peter Smith

Peter came to the office after being invited to do so by the probation officer. On first impression he was a well spoken, intelligent boy, perhaps rather immature.

Talked of the position at home and Peter said things had not gone too well since his stepfather joined the family. The whole atmosphere had become difficult. His stepfather was working like mad on decorating and gardening. Peter's brother John had been allowed to help but he, Peter, being clumsy with paint, etc., was not allowed to do so and felt rather left out of the picture. It seemed that his father was more interested in John who had grown up interests and was a member of the army cadets. His stepfather had an army background. Peter said he had made about £8 caddying and wanted more money to make up the price of the set he wanted. He took the money from his father's pocket hoping not to be found out. After intensive questioning from his stepfather he confessed first to his brother and then his mother. He was quite frank in talking about this. He seemed to rather like his stepfather though he found his restrictions irksome. He really wanted to go to a naval school and this was not just an idea that had come to him in recent months.

"Angela Hope": Aged 15 years

27th Sept:

Received notice indicating that Angela was being charged with Unlawful Wounding. The circumstances of the offence were that she struck a 13½-year-old boy on the head with a poker, causing lacerations on the forehead, which resulted in two stitches being inserted.

It was noted that a brother is under the supervision of a probation officer after appearing before the court as beyond his mother's control.

4th Oct:

The Headmistress of Camden Road High School telephoned. She was very concerned about the case as the offence did not at all tie with her knowledge of Angela; she was also rather bothered as she would not be able to complete the School Report in quite the detail she felt would be required. It was arranged that after visiting the home and obtaining some idea of Angela and her background, I should call at the school to discuss the situation with the Headmistress.

5th Oct:

Called at No. 2 Tor Way, Monks Park, and a young girl answered my knock.

Me: Good afternoon, are you by any chance Angela Hope?
Angela: Yes.
Me: Well, I am Miss Deacon, from the Probation Department, and I've called to see both you and mother because I understand you are in a spot of trouble and will have to go to court.
Angela [half-smiling]: That's right, but Mother is out at the moment, she goes to work.
Me: I shall have to call back again to see her but perhaps I could have a word with you now?
Angela: Certainly. Won't you come in?

Angela led the way through to the kitchen and the back of the house, where our entrance disturbed a large and rather beautiful black cat. The radio was playing rather loudly in the sitting room but did not disturb our conversation. Angela had a pleasant friendly manner and did not seem at all put out by my visit. She is quite tall for her age, rather pale, with fair hair and large protruding eyes ringed with shadows. Fidgets and gives the impression of being rather nervy.

Me: I am lucky to find you in but how is it you are not at school?
   Are you not feeling too well?
Angela: Well, no.

Me: I am sorry: what is it? a cold? [*she sounded rather "snuffly".*]

Angela [*after hesitation*]: Yes.

Me: Well, now, what is all this about? I've heard nothing apart from a notice from the police to say that you have been charged and will be attending court, although I don't yet know when. I shall have to produce a report for the court on you, your home, what you do and so on, so perhaps we could start by you telling me how it all happened.

Angela: My two sisters were playing outside when two little boys started to annoy them. They would not leave them alone and so I went out and told them to go away. As I turned round to come back into the house one of them threw a piece of earth which hit me on the back of the head. I picked up a piece and threw it back and unfortunately it went through his mother's [? neighbour's] pantry window. The boy followed me to the door and stood on the step. He wouldn't go away even though I told him to wait until Mother came home. He kept on and I threatened to get the poker to him. Well, then he started daring me to do so and I lost my temper and hit him with it.

Me: Oh dear! and then I suppose his mother went to the police?

Angela: I don't know how they got to hear about it.

Me: Do you often lose your temper like that?

Angela: Not often, but when I am roused it is pretty bad, It takes quite a lot to rouse me though.

Me: But when you are roused you tend to let fly and the worst happens.

Angela [*smiling*]: Yes.

Me: How old are your sisters?

Angela: Seven, no eight now.

Me: I suppose mother was out when this happened so that you were in charge of your sisters and felt responsible for them.

Angela: Yes mother was at work and I was looking after the house.

Me: Do the boys concerned often cause trouble?

Angela: Well, the twins used to tease them and they used to throw stones, but we haven't seen much of them lately.

Me: What does mother think about it all?

Angela: Well she thinks I was very silly to lose my temper, but that really the boy asked for it. She is paying for the new window.

Me: I expect in a way she feels the whole matter could have been settled without bringing in the police?

Angela: Yes I think she does.

Me: Let me see, you go to Camden Road School, don't you? How do you like it there?

Angela: It's all right, but I'm not very keen on school, I wanted to leave next Easter, but mother says I must stay till next Christmas when I'll be sixteen.

Me: Will you have taken the Certificate exams then?

Angela: No, I don't want to take them.

Me: Why not? It seems a pity to spend all these years at school without taking it.

Angela: I'm afraid I'm not good enough to pass.

Me: I can't think that is really the case. What do you want to do when you leave school?

Angela: I would like to be a hairdresser.

Me: What would you do? — go to work at one of the local hairdressers and study for your certificates at evening classes?

Angela: I want to go to the technical school and study cookery and needlework.

Me: Would that be part-time during the day?

Angela: Oh no, at evening classes.

Me: And you would be prepared to give up your free time and things like pictures in order to study?

Angela: Oh yes — I don't go to the pictures at all anyway.

Me: Don't you like them?

Angela: No.

Me: How do you manage about getting to school, because it's quite a way in to Camden Road?

Angela: Oh we go in by bus.

Me: School bus.

Angela: No the ordinary bus.

Me: It must get very crowded.

Angela: Sometimes in winter we can't get on the bus which gets us to school in time so we have to get the next bus at twenty to nine, but because we live a long way out they don't mind if we're late. If we can't get a bus if the weather is very bad then we are too late getting to school, so we wait until the afternoon.

Me: I suppose that if you are very late you miss most of the first period?

Angela: Well, there's no one there to know we are in school then as our form mistresses have left the class. But when we go in the afternoon we can see them and explain.

Me: What do you find to do with yourself in the evenings apart from homework?

Angela: Oh I go out with my friends and we walk about. Tonight we are going square dancing at the Canteen.

Me: Would that be at the Community Centre?

Angela: Yes.

Me: Is it a good one?

Angela: It's not very good at the moment, but they are hoping to get some men together and start on the new building this winter and when that's built it should be much better.

Me: There's not much room at the moment I suppose.

Angela: It's big enough really but there's a stove right in the middle and when you're dancing round you bump into it.

Me [*laughing*]: And it's apt to be hot! Have you any classes down there?

Angela: No, well I think there will be when we have the new building. There's a youth leader to keep us out of trouble.

Me: And how necessary is that?

Angela: Well the boys do get a bit rowdy after a time.

Me: Do you find anything else to do — do you go to guides or any other clubs, or Sunday School?

Angela: It's too far for me to go to guides.

Me: Oh, haven't they a company out here?

Angela: There isn't guides or brownies, but there's what do you call it? Girls Friendly Society at the Rectory. I used to go to Sunday School but don't now. Well, for one thing Mother isn't well.

Me: Isn't she — I'm sorry to hear that.

Angela: She has asthma and quite often on a Sunday I do the work while she rests. My brother's away in Denton too.

Me: Has he been there long?

Angela: About a month.

Me: What is his trouble?

Angela: He has asthma as well.

Me: How long is he likely to be at Denton, or don't you really know?

Angela: He's supposed to be there for six months, but if he doesn't show any progress after that time they'll keep him in there until he does.

Me: I believe it's very pleasant out there.

Angela: Oh it is, sometimes I go out to see him on a Sunday, which is another reason really why I don't go to Sunday School now. And then sometimes my other brother goes out to see him.

Me: It means that one or other of you goes most weeks.

Angela: It really depends how Mother is. If she's not well then I stay at home and do the work and my brother goes.

Me: Do you like housework?

Angela: Well, I like cooking and the interesting bits, but not the hard work.

Me: I wonder how many of us there are who are like that: It's a case of liking cooking the potatoes and not peeling them.

Angela: I like it when I'm left alone to get on.

Me: You're all right if you can go steadily on, but if people come in wanting you to hurry up or do other things you get a bit impatient.

Angela: Yes, now Mother will come along and want me to do things another way. She says I'm not doing it right. Then I get annoyed. But if she's upstairs in bed then I get on all right.

Me: Everyone has their own way of doing things and it's not easy to be told differently. I expect you have learnt cooking at school?

Angela: Well, we did for one year but I'm in the middle class and we had to drop it and take extra languages.

Me: And you don't like languages?

Angela: No, I don't.

Me: What do you do — French and German?

Angela: French, German and English. I can't understand German at all. I wanted to drop it and go down to the other class where I could continue to do cookery but the mistress said I was too far in front of the other class to do that, and I would have to stay where I was.

Me: I expect she feels you would find it too easy in the other class and there would not be enough to interest you and keep you at work.

Angela: Yes, I think that's it.

Me: Well, I'll be along again sometime to see Mother, about what time does she get in from work?

Angela: At about half past five. I'm sorry she wasn't in now. As a matter of fact she'll be a bit late tonight as she's having her hair done.

Me: If you would let her know I've called and will be along one evening to see her — I'll give her time to have a cup of tea first as I expect she needs it when she gets in.

Angela: She has Ovaltine as a matter of fact — she doesn't like tea.

Me: By the way, how do you feel about going to Court, are you very worried at the thought?

Angela: Not really. The policeman said I wasn't to worry as all they would do would be to tell me off.

Me: Well, they could do a lot more than that!

Angela [smiling]: Yes.

Me: But I think you'll find everyone kindly and helpful although they'll be far from pleased to see you there! You will have every encouragement to tell your side of the story.

Angela certainly did not seem worried over the prospect of appearing in court and she did not inquire what might happen apart from a "telling off" — she probably has some idea of the alternative already.

I turned to leave the kitchen and as I did so caught sight of the cat.

Me: Isn't he a lovely cat!

Angela: We've had him three or four years now and he's a great friend. When we came there were lots of strays, he was one. Then we decided to have another but whenever we put the kitten down and left it he hissed and spat at it, so Mother said it wasn't fair on him as he was here first and we got rid of the kitten.

Me: Cats are wonderful companions, too, aren't they?

Angela: Oh yes we'd be lost without him.

Me: [at front door]: Well I'll be along again soon and try not to get into any more trouble with that temper of yours!

Angela [laughing]: No. Goodbye.

Angela waited at the front door until I was out of the gate and then smiled goodbye again.

The short history of Mr. Smith, his son Peter and the probation officer requires a discussion group to exercise their imagination and to speculate quite widely. The case of Angela Hope may have a variety of uses in teaching since it is a more detailed record. I am not adding a commentary on the two pieces of material, leaving readers to compare interpretations between themselves and others. This book contains ample scope elsewhere to compare the interpretations of writer and readers.

5. INTERPERSONAL PERCEPTION

The written accounts of interpersonal behaviour can be used to stimulate thinking about the perception of persons and how people see social situations. Some suggestions for developing these important topics now follow.

Fig. 11. Acute or obtuse angles

The drawing is usually seen as a simple two-dimensional figure of three lines meeting at the centre point. Each angle in the figure can be described as part of the whole. Angle *aoc* is usually seen as an obtuse angle. But if additional lines are added, as in the next figure *aoc* is seen as a right angle. It appears different because the whole figure of which it is a part is now seen as a cube. A person's perception cannot be understood unless the properties of the system in which the perception exists for him are known. The person's perception of a single object is determined by the relations which exist between that single item and the other items which go to make up an organised system of perceptions. To repeat: to understand what a person sees when he looks at one item it is frequently essential to know the properties of the system of which the item is a part. If this part-whole principle is valid in the perception of people it could be of great help in describing many psychological processes. It could be helpful in helping to understand bias or prejudice in judgements of groups or individuals, social classes, or institutions. The perceived similarity among parts of a whole may tend to be exaggerated: a person may over-estimate the shrewdness of a Jew or the sexual appetite of a Negro. Stereo-typed sets of personality traits may be ascribed to particular groups so that judgements of individual members of these groups may be biased. The important point to be learned from this is that this bias in perceiving people is found in everybody and is due to the nature of perceptual processes. The specific instances given above are based on the general principle that the perception of the properties of an object are largely determined by the perceived properties of the system of which it is a part. There are several instances of the part-whole principle in person perception, for example, the so-called halo effect, implicit personality theory, and in stereotyping as already indicated. The experimental evidence is of interest in suggesting possible ways of demonstrating the principle in learning experiences. I will describe these instances briefly omitting detailed descriptions of the actual experiments.

Individuals may come to exaggerate the homogeneity of the personality of another individual. If one has a generally favourable impression of another person this impression will tend to spread to one's judgement of specific traits. He may then be judged too high on desirable traits and too low on undesirable traits. If one has a generally unfavourable impression of another he may be judged too low on desirable traits and too high on undesirable traits. This tendency has been called the halo effect. The way in which an individual perceives other persons is influenced by his beliefs about how personality is organised — what traits go with what other traits. For example, some people may tend to associate aggressiveness with being energetic, or the trait of kindness with the trait of honesty. Asch (1946) had two groups of subjects and gave them a short list of personality traits which were said to describe a fictitious person. The lists were identical except that one included the term "warm" and the other the term "cold". The resulting impressions of the two groups were significantly different with respect to fifty-three other traits. Wishner (1960) in a follow-up study required a group of college students to rate their teachers in each of the fifty-three traits and on the warm—cold dimension. All the intercorrelations were then computed. The highest correlations proved to be with those traits which most sharply differentiated the warm and cold groups in Asch's study. In an experiment by Zillig (1928) two groups of children performed exercises in front of their classmates. One group was disliked by their classmates: they were trained to perform the exercises perfectly. The other group were liked and they were trained to make mistakes deliberately. At the end of the two performances it was found that the audience had "seen" the disliked group as having made the mistakes. A bad act is easily connected with a bad person. The organisation of a cause and effect system is influenced by value judgements and emotional reactions. There is a universal tendency to group objects or events on the basis of proximity or similarity. Such perceptions may change but cognitions of cause and effect tend to be organised in this way initially.

Another instance of the part-whole principle in the perception of people is the influence of stereotypes. Stereotypes are relatively simple cognitions of social groups which blind an individual to many differences among the members of any groups. One way in which stereotyping occurs is through the grouping of people into status classes and ascribing to an individual characteristics which are believed to pertain generally to his status class.

Some attributes can be judged more accurately than others. Three voluntary discussion groups, each made up of ten adults, took part in twelve meetings. After each meeting the subjects were asked to indicate those persons in each group they "liked best", those they "liked least" and to guess which persons liked them best and least. It was found that accuracy of perceiving the feelings of others exceeded chance level. The subjects perceived liking or acceptance more accurately than disliking or rejection (Taiguri, Bruner and Blake, 1958). It seems that some people are easier to judge accurately than others. Some people are "transparent" — they wear their hearts on their sleeves. The personal likes and dislikes of some people are easier to predict than those of others (Taiguri, Kogan and Brunner, 1955).

A study of primacy and recency in impression formation by Luchins (Hovland, 1957) provides an illustration of experimental material which could be useful in teaching. If this material is used it should be borne in mind that later work (Luchins, 1957) indicated ways of overcoming the primacy effect.

Luchins (1957) made some studies of the relative importance of primacy and recency on the formation of impressions of persons which can be adapted as useful exercises or used for illustration. In one study, for example, four groups of people were given different descriptions of a person, Jim. One group (Group E) was given a paragraph which described Jim as extroverted and friendly.

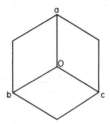

Fig. 12. The whole cube

Description E

Jim left the house to get some stationery. He walked into the sun-filled street with two of his friends, basking in the sun as he walked. Jim entered the stationery store which was full of people. Jim talked with an acquaintance while he waited for the clerk to catch his eye. On his way out, he stopped to chat with a school friend who was just coming into the store. Leaving the store, he walked towards school. On his way out he met the girl to whom he had been introduced the night before. They talked for a short while, and then Jim left for school.

Group I was given an account which described him as behaving more as an introvert.

Description I

After school Jim left the classroom alone. Leaving the school, he started on his long walk home. The street was brilliantly filled with sunshine. Jim walked down the street on the shady side. Coming down the street towards him, he saw the pretty girl whom he had met on the previous evening. Jim crossed the street and entered a candy store. The store was crowded with students, and he noticed a few familiar faces. Jim waited quietly until the counterman caught his eye and then gave his order. Taking his drink, he sat down at a side table. When he had finished his drink he went home.

A third group (group EI) was given a combined description in which the E description preceded the I description.

Description EI

Jim left the house to get some stationery. He walked out into the sun-filled street with two of his friends, basking in the sun as he walked. Jim entered the stationery store which was full of people. Jim talked with an acquaintance while he waited for the clerk to catch his eye. On his way out, he stopped to chat with a school friend who was just coming into the store. Leaving the store, he walked towards school. On his way out he met the girl to whom he had been introduced the night before. They talked for a short while, and then Jim left for school. After school Jim left the classroom alone. Leaving the school, he started on his long walk home. The street was brilliantly filled with sunshine. Jim walked down the street on the shady side. Coming down the street towards him, he saw the pretty girl whom he had met on the previous evening. Jim crossed the street and entered a candy store. The store was crowded with students, and he noticed a few familiar faces. Jim waited quietly until the counterman caught his eye and then gave his order. Taking his drink, he sat down at a side table. When he had finished his drink he went home.

The fourth group (group IE) was also given a combined description. In their case the I description preceded the E description.

Description IE

After school Jim left the classroom alone. Leaving the school, he started on his long walk home. The street was brilliantly filled with sunshine. Jim walked down the street on the shady side. Coming down the street towards him, he saw the pretty girl whom he had met on the previous evening. Jim crossed the street and entered a candy store. The store was crowded with students, and he noticed a few familiar faces. Jim waited quietly until the counterman caught his eye and then gave his order. Taking his drink, he sat down at a side table. When he had finished his drink he went home. Jim left the house to get some stationery. He walked out into the sun-filled street with two of his friends, basking in the sun as he walked. Jim entered the stationery store which was full of people. Jim talked with an acquaintance while he waited for the clerk to catch his eye. On his way out, he stopped to chat with a school friend who was just coming into the store. Leaving the store, he walked towards the school. On his way he met the girl to whom he had been introduced the night before. They talked for a short while, and then Jim left for school.

Members of the groups were then asked to write a paragraph giving their impressions of Jim and they were asked to predict how he would behave in various situations. The descriptions were coded for frequency of mention of extroverted and introverted characteristics. The order of presentation of the E and I descriptions was found to be significant in determining the subjects' impression of Jim. The EI group tended to give predominantly extroverted descriptions, though not as markedly as the E group. The IE group gave predominantly introverted descriptions but not as markedly as the I group. In Luchins' study the first block of information about Jim was more influential than the second block in determining peoples' impressions of him. The EI group saw Jim as outgoing, sociable and friendly. The IE group saw him as reserved and quiet, lonely, unfriendly and unpopular. The EI group said that he would stop and talk to acquaintances; he would accept an invitation to a party. In these kinds of situations the IE group said he would be shy or withdrawn.

An exercise based on Luchins' experiment could aim at studying the effect of different kinds of information on impressions formed about people. Four approximately equal groups could be given copies of the descriptions. After reading their description carefully each person would be asked to write a description of about 100 words giving their impression of Jim. They could then rate Jim on each of the scales in the following diagram.

5	4	3	2	1
(a) Friendly	More friendly than unfriendly	Neither	More unfriendly than friendly	Unfriendly
5	4	3	2	1
(b) Forward	Moderately forward	Neither	Moderately shy	Shy
5	4	3	2	1
(c) Social		Neither		Unsocial
5	4	3	2	1
(d) Aggressive		Neither		Passive

These scales can be scored quite easily. If the "extroverted" paragraph made more of an impression the score will be high because the left hand of the scales contain very extroverted characteristics. If the "introverted" description made a greater impact the score would be low. The 100-word accounts of Jim's characteristics may also be "scored" roughly and the relative strength of "extroverted" and "introverted" impressions can then be compared. In these ways it can be ascertained whether in the case of the EI group the E characteristics (the information first presented) made more of an impression than the I characteristics (the more recently presented introverted information). Analysis of the scores for each group will demonstrate whether primacy or recency is dominant in impression formation.

6. SUMMARY

The learning materials illustrated in this chapter are used in discussing influences on communication. Some of the important points are now briefly summarised, having been more fully discussed in the chapter commentary.

Perception is affected by the varying conditions in which individuals practise their perceiving. A perception depends not only on the sensation being received but on individual factors: (a) the past situations which the individual has perceived (i.e. learning), (b) the individual's current needs, values, desires and interests (i.e. motivation) and (c) the type of person he is (i.e. personality). These factors are fairly constant for any one individual so that his perceptions will have some degree of stability. These factors vary in different people. The perceptions of two or more people in the same situation are therefore likely to be quite different.

Perception is partly a matter of training. Primarily, differences in ways of perceiving, however, are inherent in people and cannot be eliminated by experience. Training can influence selection but it cannot correct basic differences in speed of perception and in size of the visual field. Speed of perception can be improved only in teaching people to see groupings of objects rather than individual objects. A person can speed up his reading by learning to react to groups of words rather than to single words, but even after training there are wide variations among people. Projection tests owe much of their value to perception variables. Some of the major factors in misinterpretation are therefore (a) the sense organs gather inadequate or ambiguous information, (b) attention is directed towards the wrong part of the perceptual field, (c) previous relevant experiences are of the wrong type for present sensations to be correctly and objectively interpreted, (d) a different expectation being expected by the perceiver from the one which he actually obtains, (e) possibly including a perception in an incorrect category because the perception is incorrectly completed and based on incomplete sensation, (f) a person may find a perception unacceptable because it conflicts with his existing opinions, e.g. his views about himself. Their chief characteristic is that the person gives meaning to the stimuli he is dealing with. Thus these tests elicit personal reactions and personality patterns. They indicate tendencies to behave in certain ways in real life situations. In forming an impression of another person we observe his actions, his tone of voice and expressive movements, and follow what he says and does as he responds to us. Then we use this information to make judgements about his characteristics. We make inferences about his ideas, feelings and personality traits and our actions towards him are guided by these judgements. The other person in turn makes judgements about us and thus guides his actions in relation to us. Communication is more likely to be established if the judgements of the two people are correct. The person attempts to understand and organise the complex verbal and non-verbal messages, explicit and implicit, that the behaviour of another person (or group) is conveying. Inaccurate or distorted perceptions occur when the "sending" system of the receiver is not keyed to the coding system of the sender. The person tries to convey messages either explicitly or by making use of the expectancies of the receiver. Incorrect or inadequate sending occurs when the encoder's system is inappropriate for the receiver. A person may be an effective sender and receiver or he may be effective in one role and not in another or he may be ineffective in both roles. The next chapter is concerned with applying one's understanding of communication (and I include "intuitive understanding" here) to interviewing. I have arbitrarily described aspects of learning about interviewing under the headings (1) communication with children, (2) interviews with adults, (3) roles in interviews and (4) communication and human relations training. The reader will note that the difficult problem for the learner is to apply his understanding of influences on communication. We need further work on how to facilitate this learning and how to make it more efficient and possibly faster.

CHAPTER 5

Learning About Communication in Interviewing

1. COMMUNICATION WITH CHILDREN

The key factor in establishing communication is the establishment of trust. This is a complex process. In the relationship between child and adult the way the child needs to proceed by cautiously evaluating the adult is described by Fraiberg (1952). The social worker needs to understand the child's anxieties in a strange situation and mistrust of the direct approach. He may not recognise a problem, or if he recognises one he may refuse to talk about it. He may meet the social worker at a time of crisis in his life and practical help or advice may be all that is required. Fraiberg describes some practical obstacles in the way of gaining a child's confidence, which may require unorthodox methods if it is to be achieved. The obstacles may include an inability to comprehend the function of a social agency, creating chaos in the department, talking loudly and demanding attention, being unable to sit still for very long and so on. In communicating with the younger child then, formal interview procedures are set aside. Children hate being questioned, at least until they have discovered the kind of person they are dealing with. The child's techniques for doing this are striking. Given enough time he can find out a great deal about such matters as the social worker's attitudes towards destructive or disorderly behaviour, towards children in general, towards crime and punishment. Is the social worker a lecturer, scolder or threatener? (These are useful ways to categorise adults.) If the child feels endangered by the new situation he defends himself against the danger in characteristic ways which are of great importance for the social worker to bear in mind in trying to establish a constructive relationship. The child's behaviour may be seen as ways of trying to communicate his fears, uncertainties and wishes. The social worker needs to concentrate on listening to what the child says and to be alert to his non-verbal communications. The social worker also needs to recognise that the young child's thinking is strongly affected by magic: wishes can be achieved through the magic power fantasy and thought. Like Fraiberg, Timms (1969) makes the point that communication is established by helping the child discover the kind of person the social worker is: compared to work with adults interviews with children rely more on oblique reference to problems. This involves giving attention to the variety of ways in which children may communicate, that is, to the significance in terms of communication of drawings, stories, and other vehicles carrying symbolic meaning. Various ways of communicating and sharing feelings of the unhappiness of a 10-year-old girl are illustrated in an article by Stevenson (1963).

Anne

Anne has lived with foster parents for ten years. They are very staunch churchgoers and rather rigid and among other misdemeanours Anne has caused them distress by shouting "bum" and "belly" at church meetings. The child-care officer feels that her outbursts are a reaction to the excessive rigidity and that the breakdown is due more to fundamental incompatibility than actual naughtiness on Anne's part. Anne is not very intelligent but lively and quick in her responses; she is small with "buttony brown eyes" ...

She leaned out of the car waving to Miss M as we went off and then sat down, saying nothing. I was having difficulty in negotiating heavy traffic and could not get even a look at her for a while. When I was able to I could see that tears were pouring down her face though she was very quiet about it and turning her head away from me. I drew the car to the side of the road and said that I expect she was feeling a bit sad. She nodded and did not protest when I put my arm around her and cuddled her. She began to cry more openly, saying that she was only crying because she was tired and was feeling sick. I sympathized and said I expected that it was a little bit because she was missing her

Mummy and Daddy (foster parents). She nodded to this and said that Mummy said she wasn't to cry because she was a big girl and big girls didn't cry. I said that sometimes big girls did cry if they felt very sad and this sometimes made you feel a lot better. Things often hurt people very much inside and then they cried. She said she supposed it was all right so long as I didn't mind ...

At lunch, I talked about what the children's home looked like, the names of all the people there, and the children who would be in her group. She wrapped my travelling rug around her shoulders, clutching her teddy bear and said she was going to sleep. She pretended to go to sleep, but obviously didn't and while she had her eyes shut managed to arrange herself across the seat so that her head was on my lap. She stayed there for a while then sat up, still wrapped in the rug, saying that this rug was magic and when you were wrapped in it, you could wish for anything and it came true. She asked what I wished for but when I suggested that she had first wish she said she was wishing for a nice house, ever so pretty, with a nice garden. I asked who lived in the house and she said a Mummy and Daddy and some little girls. The little girls were naughty sometimes. But their Mummy didn't mind a bit. She just said "It's all right, my dear". Nothing ever happened to them when they were naughty. I said that perhaps she thought she had been naughty and her Mummy had been cross with her. She said airily that she thought she might go to sleep now. I said I thought perhaps she felt that her Mummy had been very cross and had sent her away. That wasn't so, she had come to be near her very own brother and she was not a naughty girl; I thought she was a very nice girl and very clever too. She asked if she could have a jelly baby and took one out of the box on the car shelf. I said she didn't seem to want to think about home. Anne said she didn't know what I meant. I said I thought she was frightened to think about it because she was thinking she had been sent away. She hadn't been sent away because she was naughty, she was not a wicked girl. Anne still clutched the rug around her and said that she knew a boy who was very naughty and then he had been put down in the ground and then he went to Hell (awed sort of voice). I said I didn't believe there was a place like Hell — God didn't go around punishing people. He liked them. Anne looked doubtful about this but didn't question it.

She went on to talk about living in N, telling me about the children she knew, but carefully avoiding reference to home. I asked her one or two questions about the boys and Mr. and Mrs. H and each time she replied only in monosyllables. I asked her about the cats in the house and she began to explain that Mummy had brought one of these home, sticking at the word "Mummy" but swallowing and then going on. I talked about her going back in holiday times to see the cats and the family and she seized this avidly and asked how long till the holidays, how would she get there? I explained that it was 8 weeks and I would be taking her.

Anne finally fell asleep, and then when she woke appeared to be very depressed, saying that eight weeks was a terribly long time and I might forget. I encouraged her to talk about home and talked to her about the children's home and she finally said in quite a temper, "I don't want to be sent away from home, I don't like that place we are going to and I want to go back to N, and I want to go *now*". I said I knew it was hard and I knew she hated it and it made her feel all funny inside, but I would be there and I would see her quite often and I would help her all I could. She cried a little, saying, "Please take me back now", but became a little calmer and finally settled down in the seat as close as she could get to me with her hand on my arm. I talked about her brother and said that he was terribly excited about seeing her and Anne began to show slight interest in this. She finally began to talk about seeing him in a pleased way and continued so to the end of the journey.

Stevenson comments that in this record, one sees the worker confident in Anne's need to face grief, not allowing her to escape from it, and even more important perhaps, able to deal with the impact of the child's grief on herself and not avoid the issue. In conversation the child-care officer said, "Years ago I would have said — look at the nice sheep in that field, and tried to cheer Anne up." But here she does not let Anne take refuge in changing the subject when she says she might go to sleep now or asks for a jelly baby. She comforts the child but recognizes the need to keep the feeling open and flowing; her experience and knowledge will have shown her that if the feeling is damned up the child's pain, anger and resentment may effectively block the later adjustment, in this case to the children's home and to the foster home to which she was to return for holidays. The child-care officer's concern is not to explore deeply unconscious fantasy — but rather to recognise, as it were, the little pieces of the iceberg which show above the surface in order to help the child handle better the realities of the situation. On this long car journey, the child-care officer is deliberately bridging the gap between the past and the future by the purposive references to both. The child-care officer knows that in children who move from one place to another the images of people and places are often blurred and disturbed by the feelings — of anger, of fear, of sadness — which surrounded them, and that these are often intense. The task is therefore to try and keep the reality of the situation alive and relatively unclouded by the fantasies. In order to do this, the child-care officer must be alive to the significance of casual remarks or significant stories, such as Anne could tell when encouraged by the magic rug and the child-care officer's interest.

2.   INTERVIEWS WITH ADULTS

If a person has to communicate something to another and recognises that his aim in communicating is not just to express himself but to give information in a way that the receiver is most likely to understand he is likely to do it more effectively. He will then bear in mind the receiver's requirements and attitudes as well as his own purpose in communicating. If messages are sent with the clear aim of achieving adequate understanding between sender and receiver learning is involved. This applies whether a person is sending or receiving a message. The sender's role in a learning process is often to adapt and order the information he is communicating in such a way that it can be learned by the receiver. It follows that efficient planning and preparation is important and techniques have been developed (and can be adapted) for doing this. Similarly, in the role of receiver it is helpful to remember that the information that is being received is only of value when it is understood. If this is appreciated the application of skills in receiving processes, such as listening and reading, becomes important. The receiver has to select and sort out information he is given, according to his needs and purposes before he takes action which makes use of it. A very important part of this selection process is the forming of a general impression of the information as a whole. The rest of the selection process is concerned with fitting relevant details into the pattern of the general impression. Obstacles to this process lead to inefficient communication. The ability to select relevantly and to apply what is selected depends on listening carefully and is indispensable in effective learning. One of the commonest characteristics of two-way communication is the interchange of information which is found in asking and answering questions. The root skill in communication is the ability to ask and answer questions efficiently. Ordinary everyday conversations between two people and group discussions of all kinds involve spending a great deal of time in questioning and answering. It is also true that in one-way communication situations the ability to ask and answer questions is a vital part. In both kinds of situation information is presented in accordance with the needs of another person (or a group of other people). Sometimes the sender has to imagine the questions his receiver(s) would ask. In studying written material an important skill is the formulation of relevant questions and searching for the answers. What factors in asking and answering questions may contribute to effective communication? In the first place a question can provide a strong motivation for communication. A person may respond to the perceived dependency of another: it may be flattering to be asked for advice or information and people often make this available quite freely. A question demonstrates another person's need; in many situations it is not clear what a questioner's purpose is and he himself may be unsure what information he requires. But asking a question seems to make subsequent communication easier. In replying to questions seeking factual information a basic method is to proceed from what he does not know. In this method units of information are given in a particular order. The order of presentation can be affected by the sender's assessment of the questioner's point of view. If he is able to imagine what the other person's frame of reference is he can try to structure the information to correspond to this, for example, by going step by step through a series of actions. (The essence of questioning and answering is feedback. This involves checking whether or not another person has correctly understood the information he has been given.)

The illustration of an interview which follows links the discussion of communication and learning with consideration of the interview as communication. This detailed record, which was made by a social work student, has been used for learning. I have interpolated my comments to raise some points for thought and discussion and have added some further remarks at the end of the record.

Interview between Mrs. Read and social worker

verbatim record

S. W.: Hello, Mrs. Read.

Mrs. Read: Hello.

S. W.: May I come in?

Mrs. Read: Yes, I suppose so. It's cold in the living room, better come in the kitchen, it's in a muddle.

S. W. (to child): Hello, Mike.

Mrs. Read: Go out and play, Mike. He was going to get dressed just when you came. Can't get him to keep his trousers on.
(Wild search for trousers)

Mike: I never had any trousers yesterday; where are they?

S. W.: It's nice and warm in here — he doesn't hurt without trousers in here.

Mrs. Read: That School Welfare Officer didn't half carry on last week about the two others going to school without their coats. They won't wear them, anyway.

S. W.: If you were here when they went to school, you could see that they wore them.

Mrs. Read: I know, I know, but I'm not giving up working whatever you say. He keeps me short, spends it all on horses. I've got no more coal after this anyway until I get my Family Allowance.

(The social preliminaries are soon over in the early part of the interview and Mrs. Read and the social worker seem to "get down to business" quite quickly. They seem to know each other fairly well; there is no evidence of great defensiveness in this part. The social worker's comment that Mrs. Read could see that the children wore their coats when they went to school requires consideration. This seems to be a challenge to Mrs.

Read. It could be aimed at helping her to see what she could or should have done. The reply seems to be defensive — "I'm not giving up work whatever you say" but what the social worker says seems to count for something with Mrs. Read.)

S. W.: You're short this week?

Mrs. Read: Always am short, I'm fed up. For God's sake, Mike, stop grizzling. How am I supposed to know where your trousers are. Can't you see I'm talking. Get out. I'm sick to death of it. I nearly went last Sunday. I don't care — they can all be put away.

S. W.: You're feeling pretty bad?

Mrs. Read: I'm feeling bloody awful. I hate this house. I hate him. I hate everybody. He'll be sorry if I go. It will serve him right. I'll show him. I'll give him something to grumble about. He's always grumbling. I'll go and that will give him something to talk about. The lads won't care — they always want him and they don't want me. They can get on with it.

S. W.: I think you hate people more than they hate you. Tom was worried because you hadn't visited.

Mrs. Read: I'm not visiting him. What good would that do? You took him away from me at that Court, you can get on with it. I'm not going to see him if he doesn't want me.

S. W.: You are worried about seeing him.

Mrs. Read: Of course I'm not. All I'm worried about is that he might not want to see me.

S. W.: Oh, I see.

Mrs. Read: He doesn't think much of me. He never shows it and I get fed up. I wish he'd show it a bit more if he really does want to see me. Anyway, you took him away and you can go and visit him. Perhaps he'll make a fuss of you.

S. W.: He's awfully like you and you find it difficult to make a fuss of people even when you like them.

Mrs. Read: No, I'm not going, so don't try and make me. I'm no good to him, anyway I can't take him things.

S. W.: Giving things doesn't matter much if you go and see him.

Mrs. Read: Mike, go out and play again. He's always on about something. Always has been.

S. W.: I was saying that giving things doesn't matter much.

Mrs. Read: I know, I heard you. You don't understand how I feel. I feel awful when I go there. I know you think I'm hard, but I just can't go. I'm afraid he'll say something.

S. W.: Say something?

Mrs. Read: He's always saying that he likes his father better than me and I don't see why — I've always done all I can, but it didn't seem to make any difference. He was a terrible baby, always crying. Sometimes I couldn't stop him crying and I felt as though I'd do something dreadful.

> (The next section raises a number of points. Mrs. Read expresses her feelings of depression and frustration clearly. Her remark about her children not caring about her brings an interpretative comment from the social worker ("I think you hate people more than they hate you . . .") and a further comment about the consequences of Mrs. Read's action, i.e. Tom was worried. What effect does this appear to have? Mrs. Read continues to convey her feeling that she is no good to anyone and then, that she needs a sign that she *is* wanted. The social worker tries to reassure her but this is resisted: "don't try and make me . . ." The social worker seems to have a clear sense of direction in the interview: or Mrs. Read seems to see this. Mrs. Read seems to be able to talk quite freely to the social worker. If this is the case what factors might be influential?)

S. W.: Yes, you did have a bad time, didn't you.

Mrs. Read: Bad time? Nobody knows what I had to put up with. Nobody cared — nobody at all. Nobody cares now. I've never had anyone to help me — I never had a soft time when I was a child. My mother used me to do the housework. I used to have to get up early and do all the housework and my brother didn't do anything. I don't see why I should be expected to do everything for Tom. I bet you think I'm awful.

S. W.: You are painting an awfully black picture of yourself. You have been under a lot of pressure. It hasn't been easy for you.

Mrs. Read: I suppose I haven't got much excuse really. I used to think

I wouldn't get married because my mother and father used to row so much. Then I met him and married him. He seemed all right when I married him. I can't stand him now. He doesn't even keep himself clean and he is awful. Tom came straight away. I used to look at him sometimes and think he might die. He was ever such a little baby. He could have died. He didn't know I was thinking about him.

S. W.: Tom is very fond of you. He told me how you used to read him stories when he was little. He liked that and he remembered it.

Mrs. Read: He got better as he got older.

S. W.: You felt better towards him as he grew up.

Mrs. Read: Yes, I did, somehow he wasn't so bad. I used to wallop him sometimes — I suppose he has told you.

S. W.: No, he talks about the good times at home — those are the ones he remembers.

Mrs. Read: It's funny he remembers good things — what does he say?

S. W.: Oh, he told me about going to the woods with you in the summer and going to the pictures.

Mrs. Read: Fancy him remembering that. I take Mike to the pictures sometimes. He keeps on fidgeting. Tom always kept still. Once he got on a bit he was ever so much better.

S. W.: I've always felt you got on well with all the children.

Mrs. Read: Oh, I don't know. They don't think much of me. After all, I can't give them much.

S. W.: You are saying the same as you said before. You're frightened to admit to anything good about yourself. There is a bad side, but there is a good one too.

Mrs. Read: Nothing good about it. I'm fed up with everything. I shall go and leave the lot. Fancy Tom remembering about picnics and that.

S. W.: That was the good side.

Mrs. Read: Don't be silly. Want a cup of tea?

S. W.: Yes, please.

> [Mrs. Read *to kitchen to make tea. Returns in few minutes, without tea*]

Mrs. Read: I'm not going to see him, not if you went down on your bended knees.

S. W.: Pity, he'll be disappointed.

> (There is accumulating evidence to support the hypothesis that Mrs. Read is "testing out" her feelings about her own "goodness" and "badness" with the social worker. It may be noted that the social worker seems to respond to the feelings expressed by relating them all the time to other peoples' views including her own. She is saying that Mrs. Read seems to her to get on well with her children. She points out that Mrs. Read is frightened to think well of herself and "holds" or "structures" the interview by commenting on recurring themes. How do these communications affect her client? What is their purpose? Is the purpose achieved?)

Mrs. Read: No. I can't go, it's too difficult.
S. W.: How is it difficult?
Mrs. Read: Well, the buses don't fit in. Anyway, I can't take him anything.
S. W.: I think you are afraid of the feelings it might stir up.
Mrs. Read: What? His feelings? He doesn't care.
S. W.: No, your feelings. You probably feel mixed up in regard to your feelings about him.
Mrs. Read: You do keep on, don't you?
S. W.: Um.
Mrs. Read: Well, I'll go and get that tea. [*Fetches it*]
Mrs. Read: What was that you were saying?
S. W.: I was talking about your feelings being mixed up.

> (Now Mrs. Read is making different responses to the social worker's comments about her feelings. First of all she seems deliberately to try to avoid recognising the reference to being frightened of feelings which may be aroused, and which may be painful, if she visits Tom. But the ambivalence noted previously is still evident, as the social worker says. Mrs. Read finds this message a difficult one, and goes to fetch the tea. What does this behaviour convey to the social worker and to readers of the record? Before she goes: "You do keep on don't

you?" On one level can be seen as a defensive response. It might also mean that Mrs. Read recognises that the social worker is maintaining a clear focus in the interview.)

Mrs. Read: I think I could go one evening. What was that about my feelings — I don't know what you mean.

S. W.: I think you have a job to see yourself as anything good.

Mrs. Read: Well, I'm not much good to him. I had an awful time when he was born. They thought I would die, but I didn't. He was ever such a little baby.

S. W.: You must have been frightened. It was rather horrid for you.

Mrs. Read: Yes, they didn't understand how I felt. What do you mean about seeing anything good.

S. W.: You have told me a lot of things which you think are bad about you. Tom told me the good side, so I know there are two sides.

Mrs. Read: Yes, it was funny that he told you he had a nice time at home.

S. W.: You don't appear to the children as a bad mother.

Mrs. Read: Ah, yes, but what about other people. What about you?

S. W.: Most people are a mixture of good and bad.

Mrs. Read: I suppose I could get a bus to W ... on Saturday. I wouldn't stay long of course. Mike can come with me. I shan't stay. I don't suppose Tom will be worried. He doesn't really care whether I come or not.

S. W.: Yet he does ask when you are coming.

Mrs. Read: Oh, that's just because he wants someone to visit him. Anyone would do.

S. W.: That's not true, is it? If it were he would not be content just to see me and he isn't. It's you he wants to see.

Mrs. Read: Well, I don't know. I might go, but it all depends on the buses. Is there one?

S. W.: Yes, there is one you could catch.

Mrs. Read: I'll see anyway.

(Earlier parts of the conversation are repeated and thought about again. Mrs. Read continues to test her thoughts by seeking the social worker's reactions and she learns about other points of view and other peoples' feelings. This part of the interview illustrates again the different levels of communication. Part of the time Mrs. Read is discussing the practical problems of going to see Tom. Mingled with this is discussion of her mixed feelings and the influence that her previous experience has had on how she feels now. Throughout the interview the social worker has listened attentively and it is remarkable that she remains consistently open and responsive to the emotional content of what is said. This is well shown in this section. Focus on how Mrs. Read feels is maintained: when the social worker is asked her view of Mrs. Read as a mother she comments again on people being "mixtures". Further study of the record could be related to alternative responses such as more reassuring remarks about "good" qualities, and whether the reply quoted was itself sufficiently reassuring. The social worker makes it clear that Tom asks about his mother coming, and that not "anyone" would do. As she moves towards her decision Mrs. Read communicates the extent of her dependence on the social worker. She seems to do this in making her request for information about a bus at a suitable time. This could lead to thinking further about the client-social worker relationship in terms of transference and counter transference.)

S. W. I have been thinking about the complaints the School Welfare Officer made.

Mrs. Read: Now don't you start: he was bad enough. Just went on and on. [*Screams out of the window*]: Mike, what are you doing, come in at once.

S. W. Do you think you will be able to do anything about the boys going to school with coats?

Mrs. Read: Don't start nagging. Once you start about a thing you don't let it drop, do you?

S. W.: You sometimes don't want to face things that make you uncomfortable.

Mrs. Read: I don't do anything if I'm bullied. Mike, where are your shoes? I'm sick of looking for your things. I might give up working after Easter and then I shall be at home when they go to school. Satisfied?

S. W.: Well, we'll see.

Mrs. Read: I shall go on Saturday to see him. If he wants to see me, of course.

S. W.: Yes, he does.

Mrs. Read: I'll ring up to say I'm coming.

> (There is more evidence of what seem to be attempts at effective structuring of the interview in this section. The social worker again raises something which seemed to have worried the client at the beginning of the interview. She asks about the School Welfare Officer again, not by an explicit probe, but by telling the client she had been thinking about this. It is probably worth thinking about possible reasons for raising this again now and whether the statement about effective structuring above can be supported. Mrs. Read again responds to the social worker as a nagging, organising parent. This response can be noted throughout the interview and it raises questions about non-verbal messages conveyed by the social worker. There is no information in the record and there is thus room for speculation. This point may well arise in discussion earlier and perhaps it needs to be dealt with early if discussion of the usefulness of the interview to Mrs. Read is to be considered. Was it a well-focused interview? Was it successful, and in what ways?)

The interview between Mrs. Read and the social worker (in fact a professional course student) raises some clear points for discussion. First, it would be helpful for a group to try to clarify the purpose(s) of the interview as seen by the participants. Second, questions may be asked about their relationship and the effectiveness of communication between them. What do they think of themselves and of each other? Mrs. Read several times tells the social worker she is nagging or suggests she does not like being pushed around. But at some points she seems to be asking for this to happen. There seems to be evidence in the record to suggest that there is really a relationship of trust and mutual acceptance between the two people. Third, the material invites discussion of defensive responses in interviews and how they effect communication. How does the social worker facilitate discussion of uncomfortable subjects? Does the social worker inhibit such discussion at any time? What might be the reasons and what results seem to follow from these actions? A fourth point may be linked to the previous ones. What role does the boy, Mike, play? There are brief exchanges between Mike and mother recorded by the social worker. Fifth, a number of people are mentioned during conversation, a special person apparently being Tom. The record gives a little information about him and also about the School Welfare Officer. Questions about their roles should be considered. No doubt other questions about communication between Mrs. Read and the social worker will occur to readers. I have interrupted the account six times to raise some more questions. These comments are in brackets. One further focus for discussion and learning can be suggested, that is, to compare and contrast this interview with the communication problems of Mrs. Mead and her social worker described in my previous book (Day, 1972).

3. ROLES IN INTERVIEWS

Understanding of the process of interaction between two people in an interview may be furthered by some understanding of a series of stimulus-response episodes. It will be increased more if the goals, motives and attitudes of the participants are also subjects of study. The record of the interview between Mrs. Read and the social worker may be used to illustrate this and to serve as a basis for the discussion of interviewing as a process of communication which follows. The aim of this discussion is to indicate some important teaching points about the application of communication concepts, and some of them will be developed in later sections. Individuals develop methods or habits of interaction that are intended not to facilitate communication. They are designed to help individuals protect themselves against revealing information which they feel might make them look inadequate in some way. Communications from other people may be attempts to influence an individual to do things he does not wish to do. Defences are thus erected against this: their function is to mar communication with omissions and inaccuracies. Individuals have learned what is likely to be said in some kinds of situations. As a result of anticipating what is going to be said they may not pay full attention but respond instead to their own ideas of what they expect to hear. A person recognises that people communicate with him for various reasons and these reasons may forward or frustrate his purposes. He is likely to give more attention to topics which engage his interests or feelings in positive ways. Both respondent and interviewer bring to an interview habits of behaviour based on similar experiences of communication. Both are likely to have developed the same tendency towards evaluative reactions. Like the interviewee the interviewer may be under pressure to express or conceal his opinions, to convey a certain impression of himself, and he too will listen selectively.

If the respondent sees the interviewer as approving an attitude he has expressed it is likely that the respondent will be motivated to repeat or over-emphasize that attitude and to avoid expressing feelings that might be in conflict with it. If the respondent sees the interviewer negatively defensive reactions are likely. They may be simply a refusal to continue the interview or a tendency to modify or withold some kinds of information so as to avoid risk of disapproval.

A person recognises that people have varied reasons for communicating with him and that these may further or frustrate his own aims. He is likely to give some attention to evaluating messages he receives (whether questions or answers) in terms of the sender's possible motives, the possibility of adapting messages to his own needs. The tendency to make evaluations is heightened in situations where feelings are deeply involved. An effective interview will be one where the forces to distort or withold communication are reduced as much as possible. Usually, the interviewer plays an important role in bringing this about. People have an image of themselves which they need to project. This is done through a variety of non-verbal actions. It is also done through words. It is important for the interviewer to think about what feeling the interviewee invests in what he is saying. This involves "listening and responding" to feeling, and, in particular, to what the person feels about himself. What is his subjective assessment of his situation and of his role in it? The interviewer is interested in what the other person is saying in words as one medium of communication. He is also interested and alert to what is communicated by other media. What is the other person conveying by his silences or hesitations, his gestures and his tone of voice? Interpreting words literally can be misleading. Sometimes they may be used deliberately to protect the speaker from saying what he feels. An interviewer has to interpret and react to the difference between what is said and the way it is said.

When a person expresses anger it is often appropriate for an interviewer to attend and respond to the manifest or literal content of the communication. Sometimes it is understandable that an interviewer does this but it is not always appropriate if the aim is to help the angry person. If the interviewer defends himself or some other object of attack by becoming angry himself this may serve only to contribute to difficulty in communication. It is the angry person's feeling which requires attention rather than the literal meaning of what he says. Interviews deal with information that is factual, objective and readily verbalised. They also involve attempts to clarify attitudes and private feelings, i.e. material that is not frequently verbalised. The interviewer may contribute, through the relationship he establishes with him, to the interviewee's ability to formulate his attitudes and organise his ideas about particular topics.

Partly at least, the relationship between interviewee and interviewer affects what things will be seen as threatening. When an interviewer finds that the other person is beginning to "block" or give evasive answers to personal questions it is very likely that the respondent feels threatened. If an interviewer asked "how are you getting on with your wife?" a defensive interviewee might respond "I do not discuss my private life with other people". The interviewee is indicating that his relationship with the interviewer is not one in which this kind of topic can be discussed (at least at this point in time). The interviewee might ask what the question has to do with the subject of the interview. If he sees the question as irrelevant and /or impertinent he is likely to decline to answer. If this happens the interviewer may abandon (at least temporarily) an attempt to pursue the topic or he might try to overcome the other person's resistance by trying to show that the question was relevant. Alternatively he might wait for an opportunity to return to the question at a later stage. By then the relationship with the interviewee might be better established and sufficiently strong to permit discussion of this subject. Even in situations where an interviewee is highly motivated and well disposed towards the interviewer there may be psychological barriers which hinder him in giving information. He may have forgotten it, or he may recall only part of the information. Emotional factors influence the way the memory alters or distorts information; remembering and forgetting are selective. These obstructions to communication are not due to a wish to withold or distort information but simply in the psychological inability to give it.

There are times when adults as well as children express anger because they require help with their hostile feelings as well as with the situation that provoked them. It may not be helpful for the interviewer to become angry too. If the interviewer interprets the hostility as arising from some other source than that which is expressed ("You are not really feeling angry about A, but about B because . . ."). This may be seen or responded to as an attempt to disarm the interviewee. It might be seen as suggesting that the feeling of anger is unfounded. This can smack of condescension and make the angry person angrier. He might also feel angrier because it evades discussion of what he is expressing anger about, or because it seems to be an evasive manoeuvre on the part of the interviewer (Keith-Lucas, 1957). The detailed recording of an interview which follows was also made by a student in professional training. Following the discussion of expression of feelings of imitation or anger (above), it will be seen that this interview provided an opportunity to express annoyance. The interviewer's comments indicate that this appeared to be a helpful conversation in which a positive foundation seemed to be laid for further work.

Interview with Mr. Kent

      Agency: Probation service
      Family: Wife: Mrs. Kent — divorced.
               Children: Ann 15
                          Susan 12 In local authority
                          Peter 9   children's homes.
                          Roy 7

Mr. Kent is a tall, quietly spoken, friendly and unassuming man of 36, who was made subject of a probation order three months previously as the result of an offence of theft (£1.50) from an electricity meter. He had been known to the probation officer for less than two months, as he had recently moved from the south of England, where he had lived for fifteen years. He settled quickly into employment as a crane driver, and lodged with his sister and her family, an arrangement which he did not find wholly satisfactory.

His recent past was a disturbed one. His marriage deteriorated as his wife became increasingly in need of psychiatric help, and eventually in divorce in 1970, since when he has not seen Mrs. Kent, who spends extended periods in hospital. Mr. Kent has custody of the four children of the marriage, all of whom are slightly subnormal (I,Q.'s of 60) and in care in the south. Although he had spoken little of the circumstances of their leaving him, it appears that the younger two were compulsorily removed because of his ill-treating of them, and the elder two Mr. Kent placed voluntarily in care owing to his inability to provide adequately for them on his own. His continuing affection for them was quite clear.

In addition to this, both of his parents died last year.

Circumstances of interview

During the previous weeks Mr. Kent had shown every readiness to report to the probation officer, who had expressed a wish to use their meetings in any way which Mr. Kent would find useful in meeting his problems. As Mr. Kent confessed to an incapacity to manage his financial obligations (of which he has several) this was used as a focus for the early meetings, but as his confidence grew, he began to put forward more of his past, and his feelings concerning the present. The weekend immediately prior to this interview, Mr. Kent had spent visiting his children, for the first time in over two months. The interview was conducted without lighting owing to restrictions upon its use in the office.

Monday 1.30 pm.

Mr. Kent telephoned me requesting me to contact the Social Services

Department and to explain that he was unable to pay his weekly contribution of £5 towards his children's care. I suggested that he may prefer to speak to the officer concerned himself, as he had met the man previously, but he said that he did not feel able to and repeated his request that I should telephone for him, which I subsequently did.

4.15 pm.

Mr. Kent reported. He was more smartly dressed and well groomed than usual and without his by now familiar duffle-bag containing his working gear, which made it fairly clear that he had not come from work. The meetings were by now sufficiently routine for him to sit down opposite me without waiting to be asked, but he had time only to say that he had not in fact been to work today before he was interrupted by my having to answer the telephone. I apologised for this short interruption and urged him to start again by repeating what he had told me about being off work.

Mr. Kent explained that he had been excessively tired by his weekend journey to see his children, but immediately went on to say in a tone of virtual confession and grave import, "Tell you the truth, I've been a bit annoyed". He related in great detail, much of which was repeated, an incident in the children's home in which he felt that his son, Peter, was unfairly treated by the housemother, who had immediately taken another boy's side against him following a quarrel and had punished him without questioning. Several times during his telling me of this incident, I tried to participate by adding comments, but was so firmly talked down that I could not fail to see his quiet determination to say everything he had to say and his firm intention not to be interrupted in his flow. I felt it best not to become embroiled in a situation I could not judge, but after a quarter of an hour, I was able successfully to inquire if his feelings about the inadequacy of Peter's care applied to Ann and Susan also, but he thought that they were better able to fend for themselves, and he quickly returned to Peter. He acknowledged that Peter was "slow", but felt that the houseparents, because they are so concerned with order in the home, were suppressing his emotions and making him withdraw into himself. Mr. Kent added in a tone of importance, "In fact I've written to ask for him to see a child psychiatrist".

Mr. Kent is slow in his speech, and appears constantly very tired (although he has refused to see a doctor concerning his sleeplessness). Consequently, his directiveness and the relative urgency of his tone today approximated most nearly to a show of emotion that I have seen from him. I said that he appeared to have been upset by this incident, to which he replied with a half-laugh and a look at me which flickered from anxiety to confident indifference, "Well, I lost my temper with her" (the housemother). He justified this, saying that "she shouldn't ought to treat him like that" and "if she did that when he (Mr. Kent) was there, what would she do when he was gone?" "People should be like they are all the time." I asked if he had had cause to suspect wrong treatment of his children before; he had not, but Peter told him after he had again transgressed that "Aunty won't do anything till you've gone". I conjectured that Peter might be saying this as a means of getting his father to stay longer, which Mr. Kent acknowledged was possible, but he then proceeded to counterbalance this by referring back to his own childhood in care, a subject which had rarely been mentioned before.

Mr. Kent described first of all the staff of the home, who were male nurses, and focused on one particular man, whom he described as a "sadistic bastard", and to whom he referred again three or four times during the remainder of the interview. His focus during this description was very firmly on the way in which authority was exercised. "The staff", he said, "thought they were there for their own benefit, not the kids." He recalled seeing a boy on the floor being kicked and beaten by staff, but remembered with some feeling that they were "as nice as pie" on visiting days.

I commented that he must have felt very lost and frightened in such a situation. He agreed that he did, but remembered the "night nurses" who put them to bed — "I suppose we looked at them as substitute mothers". This prompted me to ask where his own mother and family were at this time. He told me of his father ("he gave us a pretty rough time") who went away to fight with the army during the Second World War, and after the war "went his own sweet way". Consequently, Mr. Kent and his sister, then aged 6 and 5 respectively, lived with their mother and aunt. One day whilst out playing they found a tea chest full of toys ("I always remember the fireman's axe and a dartboard") which they dragged home with them. A neighbour had told them to take it back to where they had found it, but their aunt had hidden the articles, which were later found by the police. The aunt was imprisoned and the children placed in care. He continued in the same rather expressionless tone, saying that if his aunt had not hidden the articles, the police would never have been involved. As his mother was not involved in this, I suggested that the commital of the children to care "must have said something about the conditions at home" with which he merely agreed whilst staring thoughtfully at the wall.

After a few moments, pensive silence on both sides, I remarked that there seemed to be very little consideration of emotion in the homes where he lived. In a very matter of fact tone, which created the impression that he put this behind him in a "ca ne fait rien" manner, he agreed that this was so, and then returned directly to Peter's situation and the lack of emotion he displays. This clearly concerned Mr. Kent very greatly, and for the first time he compared Roy with Peter. Roy was far more expressive and affectionate, as were the girls, perhaps this was why he focused the conversation on them so little. When I inquired how the home and his visit affected them, he replied "Oh, they're all right; they keep asking when they can come to live with me, and that, but they understand now". I felt that Mr. Kent perhaps took their reactions a little lightly and so commented on the difference between understanding and feeling. He at once acknowledged that they must have had feelings about it, and spoke rather bitterly and pensively of how being in care was not good for children, because, he said with slight hesitation "I know, what kids want is love". This stimulated a rather unhelpful regression to the inadequacies of the houseparents' care and attitudes.

It was only at this point, however, that he described how during his visit Peter had walked away from him after speaking to him for only a few minutes, and went over to the other side of the large room to play with his fort. I asked if Mr. Kent was annoyed with him for this, but he responded that "it was only natural, I suppose. He probably enjoyed playing with his fort and thought he could play and talk at the same time" (though this had not been possible). I said that even so Mr. Kent must have found it rather hurtful to travel 150 miles to see his son for the first time in three months, only to find that he did not show much interest in him. He clearly did not want to express annoyance and anxiety, saying mildly "Well, I was a bit". Seeing him reticent on this I decided to pursue the matter a little and queried if it was not so that Mr. Kent was concerned at Peter withdrawing into himself and away from him also, but he was fairly swift to deny that he thought Peter was growing away from him. The denial was followed by another pause, broken by myself, saying that his position was a difficult one, in which he would, I supposed, feel rather helpless, as he had had to entrust the upbringing of his children to other people, and perhaps he did not approve of the way they were being "moulded". His reply that "he did not care about that", was quickly altered to "I mean I don't mind about the moulding of their characters. The main thing is that they're getting fed, clothed, a roof over their heads and schooling, but I just think that the way he's going (Peter) his schoolings going to be spoilt." Mr. Kent felt that Peter's repressed emotions and his inhibited nature would lead him into "delinquency" and "trouble". "I know I was always getting into trouble myself when I was about 16." After a few more moments of conversation, concerning Peter's needs, I felt that we could not properly discuss his feelings, or importantly, their meaning for him, in this interview. We had been talking for an hour and a quarter, and the room was in almost total darkness. I, therefore, lit a long-overdue candle and drew the interview to a close by returning to Mr. Kent's financial problems, and telling him the result of my conversation with the Social Services Department, obtaining his ready agreement to their suggestion that he should make up the payment he has missed by small increases in his next few contributions.

When he left, I remarked that we had talked for quite some time, and hoped that he had found it helpful. He replied that he did want to talk about his problems, but did not like to burden his sister with them, saying 'she's got enough of her own". I said that it must be a real burden to carry his problems all by himself, to which he remarked quietly and rather selfconsciously that it did "get him down" at times.

He said that he would report again next week.

Comment

As the field of his difficulties was so broad, it appeared wisest for each to familiarize himself with the other and for the probation officer to appraise the scope of Mr. Kent's problems before arriving at a focus for long-term treatment goals. They were therefore working with a very open-ended brief, with the initial aim set in the broadest possible terms of "helping with rehabilitation".

Before this time, Mr. Kent had shown little eagerness to discuss his feelings about his situation, and in this respect, this interview represented a considerable step forward. It seems likely that his inhibitions regarding feeling were overcome because of the emotional stimulus the meeting with his children had created; though Mr. Kent was still reluctant to discuss some significant feelings, as was shown by his consistent concentration on the externalised aspects of his children's care.

I felt that it would be too great a step founded on inadequate thought and evidence to draw Mr. Kent's attention during this interview to the emotional links between past and present (e.g. (1) transference of feelings of anger against those who undertook his care on to those into whose hands he has had to entrust his own children in a similar situation, (2) the use of this anger as a defence from current realities, (3) possible guilt and inadequacy in precipitating the family break-up by theft, and his shared responsibility for his inability to provide a family home at present.)

This interview made it possible to identify several areas where attention could profitably be focused. His past life was composed of many conflicting elements which, once discussed and brought individually to the surface, could be drawn together within the realm of present conscious experience, enabling him to overcome his hesitancy at acknowledging realities of feeling central to his problems, and hence removing a major obstacle to his overcoming of them.

4. COMMUNICATION AND HUMAN RELATIONS TRAINING

As the interviewer said on his comment on the interview with Mr. Kent the meeting was an opportunity for two people to get to know each other. It is likely that Mr. Kent responded to the interviewer's empathic response and respect. Trainee interviewers can be provided with guidelines to the facilitation of communication and work on this perspective on interpersonal learning and helping is now surveyed. To break the monotonous use of the terms client and counsellor I will sometimes refer to "helpers" and "helpees". These names may be more felicitous. They will also indicate that references are to Carkhuff's work on counselling. Carkhuff (1969) describes the helping process not as something dominated by technique and as apart from other human relationships. He regards it clearly as having the characteristics of all good human relationships. The relationship is not one in which the helper remains aloof, wearing a mask and maintaining a sterile neutral atmosphere. To Carkhuff the helper cares deeply and cannot be unconditional in his responses. "If I care for you what you are and what you do make a difference to me and I must react accordingly, sometimes approving but sometimes disapproving, sometimes with pleasure, sometimes with disappointment — yet always caring." Counselling and psychotherapy are aspects of interpersonal learning and relearning processes. Significant human encounters may have constructive or deteriorative consequences. Counselling or therapy may be "for better or worse". Clients of counsellors who offer high levels of the facilitative conditions of empathy, respect and concreteness as well as more active conditions of genuineness and self-disclosure, confrontation and immediacy improve. Clients of counsellors offering low levels of these conditions deteriorate. A great part of a counsellor's effectiveness can be accounted for independently of his orientation.

Some simple guidelines may serve the helper-trainee in his role playing and also in his helping experiences. The helping process may be thought of as having two principal phases: (1) the phase in which a relationship is established and the helpee explores his areas of concern and (2) the phase in which an attempt is made to define and implement courses of action. (Later, in Chapter 8, an approach to the analysis of interviews will be discussed, which is broadly similar to this one.) Empathy is the most critical of the helping process variables and the other ingredients of the process flow from it. Several guidelines are helpful in formulating empathic responses. The purpose of these sensitive interpretations is to communicate to the client a degree of understanding of him and his situation in such a way that he can clarify his own understanding of himself and other people. The purpose of the empathic response is to communicate to the person seeking help a degree of understanding of him and his situation, in such a way that he can clarify and extend his understanding of himself and of other people. Some guidelines are helpful in the formulation of these responses.

The interviewer tries to avoid making premature judgements about the interviewee by concentrating on his verbal and non-verbal expressions which provide cues for understanding his frame of reference. He also tries to respond in ways that refer to no one person specifically but which might refer to himself. He does this in an open but cautious way. This is important because it helps the interviewer to become attuned to the interviewee's emotional state and the meaning of what he says. He may also try to encourage the interviewee to express feelings he was not able to express before. In the early stages of the helping relationship a high level of verbal responsiveness on the part of the interviewer provides an active model for the interviewee. This also serves to increase the probability of accuracy in communication. This does not imply that periods of inactivity or silence are not appropriate. But the more frequent or prompt the interviewer's responses are the more likely the interviewee is to take an active part in the process of helping.

Active encouragement of expression and absence of negative regard towards a person seeking help is perhaps the most effective way of communicating respect. By being open to his client the social worker can indicate that he will listen to his views before he makes critical judgements. Warmth is one aspect of communicating respect but it is sometimes inappropriate, depending on the background and circumstances of the client. Initially, however, it may be effective for the social worker to communicate potential warmth. The most direct communication of respect is through paying careful attention to the client and through showing that he cares about what he communicates. The helper tries to be genuine and spontaneous in his relationship with the client. The communication of respect in these ways is aimed at establishing a relationship based on trust and at enhancing the client's feelings of self-esteem.

Guidelines for the communication of genuineness and self-disclosure are not easily summarised. However, the helper will be most effective in communicating genuineness when he tries to minimise the effects of his role, i.e. to minimise the role façade and role expectations. This maximises the possibility of involvement on the part of both the helper and the helpee. The helper avoids inauthentic responses and communicates on openness to authentic ones. Increasingly he tries to be as open and free within the helping relationship as possible. He will be most effective in communicating genuiness when he can share experiences with the helpee as fully as possiblé. There is a case for not permitting questioning and probing to be the predominant style of communication in helping interviews. But in the early stages specific and concrete information is required by the helper who may need to frame questions about the other person's situation and experiences. Questions may be economised if they are effective in opening up areas for further discussion. The interviewer controls the helping process to the extent that he maintains a focus on information relevant to the client's problem, i.e. he ascertains as accurately as possible the specific nature of the problem. When the client's communications are vague or confused the helper tries to respond with greater specificity and concreteness. In framing communications in this way the helper reduces the possibility of being remote from the client's feelings and experiences. He encourages the person seeking help, in his turn, to be concrete and specific, and may thus assist him in sharpening his awareness. Concreteness and specificity of expression serve complementary functions to empathy enabling the helpee to deal specifically with areas of concern to him.

To enable the helpee to confront himself and others effectively when it is appropriate the helper must confront the helpee for discrepancies in his behaviour, for example discrepancies between the helpee's verbal expression of his awareness of himself and his observed behaviour. The helper therefore concentrates on the helpee's verbal and non-verbal expressions and raises questions about specific discrepant communications from the helpee. The helper focuses on the implications of the discrepancies that occur. In questioning discrepant communications from the helpee it is as if the helper says (or he may actually say), "On the one hand you say this, while on the other hand you say that." The fact that, in a social work relationship, the client is seeking help because of environmental or personal limitations, means that the social worker should reach out towards the client. This reaching out means placing emphasis on how the client feels and on other aspects of his communications. The social worker's interpretations or responses will be cautious and tentative, however. Following on from this the social worker (and other counsellors) try to concentrate on what is not being expressed by the client verbally as well as on his literal messages. In other words, it will frequently be helpful to fill in what is missing as well as simply dealing with what is present. After the person seeking help has explored the problem or situation the helping process may concentrate on sensitive understanding before constructive action or action may be emphasised as a way of learning. These phases are not mutually exclusive. Action and understanding are complementary components of helping interaction. Each can aid or facilitate the other. The person may have problems in interaction with others. The problems may also be because the person cannot communicate with himself in certain areas. It is the verbal and behavioural expressions in problem areas that lead a person into difficulty. If this is a correct assumption the goal of the helping process becomes the helpee's reconstruction of the communication process both with himself and others. The key ingredient in the reconstruction of the communication process is helpee self-understanding. When he understands himself effectively he will be able to understand others and then communicate his understanding.

An approach to learning about the way you carry out a task, such as interviewing someone and about what it is like to be in the roles of client or of social worker is to act them in front of other people. This is not an alternative to practising the real thing. It is a substitute for it which enables you to anticipate the interview. Rehearsing your part is a way of learning it. Role playing involves trainees in lifelike experiences; they have opportunities to interact with others in effective ways. It enables them to experience being in need of help as well as helping. The role playing experience offers continuous feedback: the people engaged in role playing develop understanding of their own behaviour and the observers are also able to contribute their assessments. Role playing has been described as the key means for developing effective communication in helping (Carkhuff, 1969).

One way of role playing in interview training is for one trainee to play the part of the interviewee, perhaps identifying himself with someone he knows, and who responds to the interviewer in terms of this role. Another member of the group plays the interviewer. The other members of the group watch what goes on and when the role-playing session ends there is a general discussion of the techniques used by the interviewer, the strengths and weaknesses which he showed and the problems posed by the interviewee. In preparing for a role-playing session the student acting as interviewer thinks about the purpose of the interview and may discuss this with other students. The person who is going to play the role of the interviewee needs to have a general idea of the kind of interviewing situation that is going to be played. He has to think about his role in more detail. If he is to play it effectively it needs to be a role with which he can identify easily. In preparing for the session the rest of the group are asked to note the interviewing methods that are used and to evaluate them. The actual role playing session need only be brief (fifteen minutes is probably enough). When it is over the interviewee tells the group how he felt about the way he was interviewed, and about such things as when he was prepared to give information to the interviewer, when he was unwilling, and his reasons. The interviewer explains why he acted as he did, where he felt he was unsuccessful in the interview, and at what points he felt the interview had gone well. The role of the tutor as observer and monitor of the playing session will be apparent. It is important that he should pick up points the group may have missed, that he should underline the principles of effective interviewing and relate these to the exercise, and encourage the students in discussion.

The interviewee is well placed to observe where an interviewer failed to obtain information that was potentially available and when things the interviewer said or did were irritating. Looking at his own reactions to being interviewed helps a student to become more sensitive to the kinds of reactions people might have. Similarly, the other members of the group can see how the interview has gone. They see the performance in a more detached way and can feel "safer" than the two role players. They can benefit by relating what they observe to their own interviewing practices. Often in role playing a person makes the same mistakes that he makes when actually interviewing. After role playing he may well be more able to see these errors himself quite quickly. He thus becomes more self-aware and this, of course, is partly because he learns of the effect his behaviour as the interviewer has had on the other members of the group and on the person who played the interviewee. Role playing provides a chance to practice techniques which may be used in a real interview situation without some of the constraints which the real situation imposes. Some of these points are taken up in a different way in the next chapter on simulation. One condition that can greatly reduce the forgetting of knowledge is the opportunity to put it to practical use. Knowledge that is quickly put to use, for example in writing projects, or in group discussion or in interviewing (or other social work activity) is reinforced. In order to act confidently it is helpful to rehearse beforehand. Before carrying out "real-life" interviews and learning from them, some preliminary learning through rehearsal, with a sympathetic and constructively critical audience, may help in reducing some of the learners' anxieties and in increasing his confidence. In the next chapter simulation exercises will be described.

CHAPTER 6

Simulation Exercises

1. GAMES

A wide range of methods is used in "sensitivity" or "human relations" training either singly or in combination. They are based on experiences in groups of varying degrees of intensity. The methods range from simulation exercises (case studies, games and role playing) to unstructured group sessions. The use of unstructured group sessions and combined methods of training will be discussed in the next chapter. Illustrations of course content will be dealt with as well at that stage. Games are useful in examining changing situations which it may be too risky or at some stages in learning too remote to study at first hand. Even if first-hand study is possible simulations may be helpful in reducing unnecessary complexity and by eliminating trivial detail permit more concentrated attention. Games involve decision-making. They can reproduce simulated consequences of decisions that have been taken. Students do not have to be the person involved in the decision but they are enabled to study the kinds of situations that are relevant to decisions and action. Decisions are often required about directions and methods of communication in groups and organisations. For example, if a group cannot meet face to face at all times it is important to consider the consequences of the communications network for group functioning. A person's feeling of participation is related to his position in a communications network and group leadership may well emerge from the more central positions. Centralised communications are very effective in carrying out a specific task but relatively inflexible in developing new solutions to fresh problems. Information is lost and distorted as it travels through a number of separate communication links (Leavitt, 1951).

Directions and methods of communication depend on existing patterns of organisation. If methods of communication are used which are not in keeping with the existing pattern of organisation they are more likely to have to change than the organisation. An authoritarian organisation or group will not change simply because a member says that it should or because an instruction is issued. Established patterns of relationships are slow to change and they help to determine the relationship which exists between people involved in a communication situation. The way groups operate and the way in which their members communicate with each other affect the decisions that are taken. These points are illustrated in the following games.

In groups information is transmitted through a number of people, i.e. from A to C via B quite often, and not just directly from A to C. The structure of the net that a group uses affects the speed and accuracy of communication between members. Another aspect of the process is that one person (A) may talk to another (B) without return talk from B to A. Or a communication may be in the form of a conversation in which B can talk back to A. The two methods can be tested experimentally. A is supposed to tell some other people a short anecdote, give them a piece of information, or some instructions about a pattern. They are required to write down what he says or to follow his instructions and produce the drawing. Two forms of the experiment are used. In the first one A is told to turn his back on the group and to tell them to write or draw exactly what he says. He is to give them their instructions as quickly as possible and they are not allowed to question him nor give him any indications of how they have received his message. In the second form of the game A is required to communicate the information or instructions and the group are again required to perform the stated task. But this time A is allowed to face the group and they are allowed to interrupt him and to ask any questions they wish. The results of the games are first that it is found that one-way communication is considerably faster. Under two-way conditions more people in the group perform the stated task correctly, i.e. under these conditions communication is more accurate. The group members usually feel more confident in monitoring their own performances. The person sending the message to the group, however, feels more vulnerable psychologically in two-way communication. Group members identify his mistakes and make him aware that they have detected them. They may express hostility towards him thus provoking a similar reaction from him. In the two-way method interruptions and irrelevancies are common and the group appears not to work as smoothly or efficiently as in the one-way system. In these games when the sender is told that he is to send one way it usually happens that he requires or uses more time to get ready. He has to think about how to communicate with the group in order to try to ensure that they will receive and understand the instructions he is to give them. It is different in the two-way situation. The tendency here is to use less time in preparation in the knowledge that feedback is possible and that it will give him the chance to correct mistakes. Although the sender feels he does not have to plan so much he has to be prepared to listen and to be sensitive to feedback if he is to achieve his aim. Although group members are told that they are permitted to talk to and ask questions of the sender it nearly always happens that some of them know their answers are wrong but they do not use the opportunity to ask questions in order to correct them. It is illuminating to ask why they did not. Usually the answers are quite varied. Some people do not ask questions because of boredom and lack of interest in the game. Sometimes they feel annoyed by the sender because of the way he presents the material for example. They just do not want to imply that they are curious and therefore interested: they do not want to give the sender the satisfaction of asking him a question. Sometimes they feel too fearful to ask a question. They may fear a curt or hostile reply (especially if someone else has already been given one). People may say they did want to say something, but they could not find the opportunity because so many others were talking. Thus many barriers to two-way communication exist even when attempts are made to facilitate the exchange of views and ideas. This game demonstrates the advantages and disadvantages of one-way and two-way communication and it may also be useful in learning about the problems of group discussion and leadership (as well as of other roles in groups). It shows, for example, that one-way communication is faster and more orderly. From the sender's point of view, it is the preferred method if he prefers to avoid hearing criticisms of his mistakes, and if he wishes to protect his power over the group. In studying communication it is important to recognise that controlling information is a method of exerting power. The implications for the management of resources may not be as obvious as this statement might seem to imply. But one-way communication may well be a way to simplify the task for the leader. It does this by structuring the situation in such a way that the leader only has to make decisions about the content of the problem he is communicating. With two-way communication he also has to think about the people involved in the discussion. The differences between approaches to communication in organisations or groups may be shown. The ordering, systematising approach to one-way communication may be contrasted with the apparently trial-and-error nature of the two-way method. There seems to be a conflict between the short-term efficiency of two-way communication and the need in the longer term to maintain power and authority at various levels of an hierarchial organisation. Two-way communication results not only in more accurate transmission of facts but also in the opportunity to revise perceptions of relationships.

The next simulation exercise may be used as a script for role playing, but I am including it here because it could also be used as a "game" involving decision-making. (Unfortunately I do not know the origin of this script.)

Application for a child to be placed for Adoption

Case presented to adoption case sub-committee for a decision

This baby is expected in three months time. The child will be legitimate. Mr. and Mrs. Snow were married 10 years ago. They both hold posts of responsibility in administrative local government and enjoy their jobs. They are also champion ballroom dancers, both in England and abroad, and have cups they have won lining their sitting room. They seem to spend the whole of their lives completely together. Their house is fairly large, and very comfortable; it is meticulously clean and tidy and they are very proud of it. There are pictures and statues of cats all over the house. Mr. Snow is a tall slim man with a moustache; he has a very smooth manner, but seems genuinely concerned about this problem and concerned for the baby. The wife is small, neat, blonde and very attractive: she is thin and very tense. When the Snows were married, they were determined not to have children. Mrs. Snow says she literally loathes children, and as their married friends have had children, they have deliberately lost touch with them. A child has never entered their present house, which they have had for five years. No one knows about the present child. Because of this loathing, the Snows have done everything they can think of to dispose of the child. I rather suspected they might have attempted an abortion. Mrs. Snow has said she will leave her husband if he insists she keeps the child. She has also said she refuses to see it once it is born. Mr. Snow said he was not particularly fond of children though he did not feel as strongly as his wife: if there was a choice between wife and child, he had of course no hesitation in choosing his wife. He indicated he was prepared to go to any length not to keep the child — to publicise a child for adoption through the local newspapers, or to place the child with the first possible people who presented themselves, if the Adoption Agency did not accept the application. They wish to know now. I felt they were both in a brittle and nervous state. A further complication is that they are Catholic. They wish to stipulate the child should be brought up as a Catholic in spite of the fact that Catholic adopters are few and far between. They are not, however, prepared to put this problem to their priest, fearing what he will advise them to do. They are prepared to tell him once the whole adoption is legalised.

Task for the committee

1. To appoint a Chairman.
2. To decide whether in principle this child should be placed for adoption.

    In this decision one should take into account:

    (a) The mental health of husband and wife, i.e. possible reasons for their feeling.

    (b) The future for a baby within this family. Are they likely to change significantly.

(c) Whether one should tell this couple of a nursing home where the nurses would be prepared for her not to see the child.

(d) The religious question.

(e) Their possible actions if the Committee refuse to accept this application, and the likely effect of this, i.e. the responsibility of the Committee.

(f) Possible work recommended to the adoption officer with this family.

Committee

1. A woman doctor with some psychiatric interest.
2. A Catholic mother who was once a teacher.
3. A staunch Labour woman with six children and very strong maternal instincts.
4. A Conservative maiden lady.
5. An ex-probation officer.

2. CASE STUDIES

The use of case studies in interviewer training has been discussed. Records of group processes are useful tools for learning and, like interview records, they may be drawn from students' field experience or specially prepared or adapted from a group workers' record. Thus the situation presented for project or discussion work may be real or imaginary. As in interview records students are asked to discuss certain aspects of a situation and what courses of action might be taken by the people involved. This can be a useful and effective method of initiating discussions. As in the case of games, to be referred to later, such records permit students to "stand back" from situations. This carries certain risks, one well-known one being that members of a group may spend more time in negative criticism of the record, for example the typing errors, the poor grammar of the group worker, and so on. This can mean that more important aspects of the content are not discussed at all: the group avoids the learning task. The group leader or tutor has the current responsibility of maintaining orientation to the work in hand; this is not always a congenial task for a tutor nor is it for other group workers, and it is not an easy one to attempt, since we are ignorant of the techniques involved. Groups tend to blame their leaders. This tendency may arouse a leader's anxiety, make him doubt himself, and act impulsively, defensively or stupidly. If he cannot view the hostility objectively he may "punish" the group by acting in an authoritarian way. This leads the group to further acts of sabotage. Alternatively he may try to place the members because he accepts that the problem is really his fault. He may try to win the group over, to ingratiate himself with them. In this way he communicates his over-anxiety and this in turn renders him incapable of focusing on the task effectively. An attempt to navigate between these two hazards will go some way towards helping group members to maintain focus on the material. I now provide some studies of group situation which have been found useful in studying communication and roles in groups.

The record which follows has been widely used in discussions on group process. It was made by a student of the University of Pennsylvania. Traveller's Aid societies in America have desks in railway, bus and air terminals and as their name indicates they are to serve travellers in need.

Group interview with three runaways

21.11.62. Mike, Tom, and Jim were brought to the Traveller's Aid desk in Pennsylvania Station by a railroad detective, who asked that I help the boys go to Trenton, New Jersey, where they were supposed to be going for Thanksgiving. The boys had been turned over to the detective by a train conductor who found them on the train between Wilmington and Baltimore. They had no money or tickets and claimed that they had not known where to get off the train and had stayed on through Trenton, Philadelphia and Wilmington. The boys had convinced the detective they belonged in Trenton, and then had given false names and addresses for themselves and the person they were supposed to be visiting in Trenton. After I asked the boys a few questions, it seemed obvious they were runaways. They did not even know what state Trenton was in.

Mike was 14 years old. He was a tall, stronglybuilt boy. His clothing was neat and clean but of inexpensive quality. Mike had a pimply face of which he seemed self-conscious.

Tom was 13 years old. He was average size, very well dressed. Tom was a fine-looking boy with dark curly hair, large black eyes and clear olive skin.

Jim was 12 years old and small for his age. He badly needed a haircut, and his clothing was patched and shabby. His shoes were so worn and torn that he could hardly keep them on his feet.

Mike, Tom and Jim seemed to come from entirely different backgrounds. They were different in many respects other than their physical appearance. Mike acted aggressively. Tom was very mannerly and seemed worried. Jim had an "I don't care about anything" attitude. The boys were interviewed together because of the worker's apprehension that if they were interviewed separately, the two not being interviewed would have run away. As soon as the detective left, Mike said to the other two, "Okay, let's go". I told them they were not going any place but behind my desk, and I opened the door and all three meekly filed in and found themselves places to sit. After several attempts to obtain the boys' names and addresses, all of which were unproductive, I told them I would have to let them sit until they decided to tell me the truth and let me help them. I continued with other business since many people were coming to the T.A.S. desk and I was the only person on duty. While I spoke with other people, the boys held quick, whispered conferences. After about fifteen minutes, Jim the youngest boy, asked, "What happens if we don't talk?" I directed my answer to all three. "At a quarter to nine I'll have to call the police and turn you over to them" — glum expressions followed. A little later came the question from Jim, "How's the detention home here?" I was sorry, but there wasn't one, and runaway boys were held at a police station until they were identified and their parents came for them. More time passed, and there were more whispered conferences. A few times, Tom wanted to say something but his companions told him that if he "squealed" they would get even. Occasionally, uncommitted-type questions were asked. "Where are we?" "Are you a cop?" "Can we go if we promise not to get on any more trains?" The revelation that I was a social worker evoked a response. Jim fell off the high stool he was sitting on — but carefully arranged to fall on a duffle bag. Tom passed out cold on top of Jim, and Mike assisted in the tragedy by slapping his friends in the face with a rolled newspaper to help them recover from the shock. I was unimpressed, and when the boys recovered they went back to their original places. The tension of the situation seemed broken, but I waited for a few minutes and asked, "What are social workers like?" I got an answer from each boy. Mike said, "They rat on you to your parents when you hook school". Tom said, "They're worse than cops". Jim said, "They come snooping around the house butting their nose in everybody's business". It was decided that I wasn't like "social workers", and the boys thought they might be able to talk with me.

I asked the boys why they had run away, but they protested they hadn't run away. I begged their pardon and asked if they could think of any reason why boys would want to run away from their homes. This was different. All three gave many reasons why *boys* would want to run away — their families might not care about them, maybe they had been caught stealing, school might be too hard, and they might be afraid to go home because they had been hooking school and got caught. We found out that *boys* would want to run away for many reasons, and then we found out how difficult things were for *boys* who ran away from home. They had to hide from the police, go hungry, and not know what to do, etc. My comment was that running away wasn't like what most boys think it will be. Tom cracked first. "I don't care what you guys do, but I'm going to tell him." Mike said he knew Tom "Would chicken out". Jim agreed with Mike until I asked him how much longer he could have held out, and then he admitted that he was ready to crack but didn't want to be the first one. Tom and Jim then taunted Mike that he was more afraid than they were but wouldn't admit it to me. Mike insisted that I wrote on my paper that Tom cracked first I wrote, "Tom cracked first, Jim second, Mike third." Then, I showed the paper and asked if I could throw it away. There being no objection, it went into the waste basket. Everyone was ready to give me the information I needed. Names, addresses, schools, ages were all given. The boys told me about their decision to run away from their homes in Connecticut, what they had been doing for the past two days since they ran away and how they got to Baltimore. Also they let me know they ran away after they were caught stealing from a car while being truant from school. They were afraid to go home. "Now what happens?" one boy asked, but all three wanted to answer. All three were quick to say they wanted to go home. I suggested that we make plans for them to go home and all agreed, but each one sympathised with the other two about how hard it would be to go home "and get our heads knocked in". I explained how I would have to get in touch with their parents through the police in their home town since none of them had telephones. Other procedures were explained and accepted. Also, when I asked if they wanted to talk with me separately before they went home, each boy said he did. The boys let me know they were starving, and they asked if I could get them supper while I was waiting for their parents. I said I would like to let them go to the station restaurant, but I asked how I would know that three runaway boys would return when they were supposed to return. "Now cut the boys stuff out", said Mike, "we're leaving our coats and cigarettes here so you'll know we'll be back." This record has been used to stimulate discussion about the relationship between the three boys as this is revealed in their conversation and behaviour. It indicates that the Traveller's Aid worker influences their decision about what to do. Careful attention is given in the record to the kinds of boys they are who form this small transient group of runaways. They soon united in confronting authority and their whispered conferences were clearly vital to their cohesion. These communications helped them to reopen conversation with the T.A.S. worker. Gradually resistance is decreased as the T.A.S. worker becomes better acquainted with them and helps the boys to relax, partly, it seems, by conveying a non-social-work image. The boys seem to identify positively with the worker ("I wasn't like 'social workers' and they thought they might be able to talk to me") and they are then able to move on from the initial testing out. The worker demonstrates verbally acceptance of the boys and ability to help them. Another discussion topic is to say what was the turning-point in this group interview. This came when the T.A.S. worker having discussed impersonally why boys might run away from home, said that "running away was not like most boys think it will be". This comment seems to describe very well how the boys were feeling and led Tom to say he was ready to give information about himself. This illustration leads on to some further points about group work processes. These processes (i.e. the development of relationships in the group and [later in this case] between the group and the wider environment) develop from the content of group meetings. In the single-group session described above, as well as in longer-lived groups, there is emphasis on what members have in common; what concerns have led them to come to an agency in the first place and what has been their experience since. In groups who live together in residential establishments the problems of living together, and doing things together provide a range of content for group discussion and action.

The next record, while not of a residential group, illustrates this point about wide-ranging content of communications. It concerns people at a markedly different stage in life experience from the three runaways and facing different crises: disability and death. The record shows how group members who are accessible to each other become vital factors in the helping process in the group. It also shows that in a group, situation and member-worker relationship need not be as intense as in individual casework or counselling. Some of the older people in the group were defensive and tended to deny dependency. In a one-to-one relationship their defensiveness and isolation might have become more pronounced. In the group, participation with people with similar problems enabled them to engage more readily and more comfortably in reality testing. The record shows how communication within the group provided opportunities for members to derive certain personal satisfactions from their membership. It also shows how the work was focused on specific objectives, stated at the beginning, and how the group developed as a unit in working towards them.

A group of older people

This group of elder clients, whose average is 74, was started in January 1963. The eleven members were chosen mainly on account of their social isolation and loneliness; all were living on pensions or marginal incomes. Some were physically handicapped, some quite withdrawn. I saw this Group as a mutual helping group around problems of old age; a way of helping lonely, isolated older persons to form some relationship with others, and eventually, perhaps, to move out to larger community groups: a way of stimulating them intellectually by use of their reflective judgement in discussion, and to bring them back to "living". I felt that in a group of this average age changes in individual attitudes and behaviour would be a limited expectation, and have been impressed to see the occurrence of changes through interaction within the group. Some of the members have never risen much above the marginal income level, others have had a more varied and rewarding life experience and higher educational status, e.g. Mrs. G. was trained as a professional singer and piano accompanist, married a wealthy businessman, now many years a widow. Miss M. has held responsible positions as manageress of large restaurants, and in hotels, and has travelled. Mr. B., of European origin, has been a composer of music, conductor of orchestras, and is still writing on music for European periodicals. I have been interested to note that this difference in status has created no difficulty in the interaction between members; there has been a friendly sharing of interest and knowledge on many subjects. Several members have commented, "We always learn something here, don't we?" Cultural differences abound, their native lands being England, Germany, Austria, Scotland, Russia and Canada. On joining this Group all members were shy of entering larger groups as Golden Age clubs; they were not too interested in recreational activities. Men predominate in the Group, there being only three women members. Five had moved out to more active community groups, three of whom still attend this Group; three members had died during the year, leaving a sadness and sense of loss amongst the others. The vacancies have been filled by new members. Group meetings are held weekly, coffee is served; the only break is during the month's vacation, at which time members are firm in expressing their feelings of loss in missing the meetings, and their pleasure at being together when we reassemble. Attendance has been very regular, absences being due to illness or occasionally to extreme winter weather. In working with this Group, I have been impressed by the warm emotional climate which has evolved amongst members, and appears to act as an enabling process, both in assisting the casework to reach the rigid, reserved and defensive client, and also in helping the individual members to become less withdrawn, self-engrossed and more "other-centred". Both these processes are clearly illustrated in the case of Mr. B. (mentioned above), physically handicapped and socially isolated, who proved so rigid, proud and defensive in individual interviews that I failed to reach him. His response to any suggestion of further appointments was, "I'll come if you need me". Since his entry into the Group a year ago, he has never missed a meeting. When asked, after the first two months, how he felt the Group was helping him, he remarked, "It is bringing me back into society". Shortly after entering the Group, Mr. B. picked up a comment by Mr. W. and said "I'd like to comment on your statement about our [i.e. pensioners and old people] being regarded as second-class citizens". He then loudly ventilated his feelings about government authorities and wealthy members of Parliament, who deny pensions to older people whose needs are real. (Mr. B. is ineligible for a pension on account of his wife's earnings, i.e. $40 a week, and is without income for himself.) While expressing his angry feelings and firmly controlling any member who interrupted, I purposely avoided intervention. Finally Mrs. G. said, "They'll hear you outside". Mr. B. shouted, "I hope they do, and I hope they do, and I hope they'll hear me in Ottawa and Quebec". Following this angry outburst, Mr. B. was given sympathy by other members, and recognition that his situation was hard to bear. After which he lowered his voice and responded with the others to a joke by Mr. W. which caused general laughter. Expression of negative feeling persisted, in Mr. B.'s case, for some weeks. It was necessary, at times, for me to control his expressions of anger when they were threatening to other members, and to intervene in such a way as to cause Mr. B. to face facts, rather than distort and project, "But this is not really the case, Mr. B. The facts are . . . etc., etc." Other members, particularly Mr. W. and Mr. R., would then interact with Mr. B. to bring him back to reality — gradually his anger would subside — he would end up with a smile. At other times I have given support to Mr. B. in his attempts to involve himself with other members in a helping role, and to offer suggestions of positive action around community problems, recognising his deep need to establish himself as a worthwhile person with some purpose in life. After five months Mr. B. began to show real concern for other members and to encourage them in handling difficult problems. On a later occasion he asked me if he might visit Mr. L. who is physically handicapped and mostly housebound and has no friends. He did so, took Mr. L. over to his small apartment, played records for him, as Mr. L. has little conversation. Mrs. B. invited Mr. L. to their evening meal. Mr. B. has continued to show interest in Mr. L. and to help him in this way. I feel this has given Mr. B. a feeling of usefulness and purpose. He has also made contact with a local French "Centre for the Aged" discussed in the group, to discover that this is a small racket for collecting fees from older people on the promise of helping them secure employment, and should be looked into. Mr. B. was prepared to report on his feelings to the Director of the City of Montreal Social Welfare Department; resulting in a careful watch being kept on this Centre and its activities. At our last meeting, Mr. B. suggested that it might be helpful if we, as a group, could draft a letter to be sent to our local Members of Parliament, pointing out the housing problems met with by many older persons in Montreal, especially since so many of the central rooming houses are now being demolished. I have been particularly interested to note Mr. B.'s changed attitude of completely negative feeling towards all municipal and government authority, to a more positive feeling that perhaps something can be done — that our Group should examine these problems. I believe that this has occurred as a result of recognition of his own problem by the Group; a penetration of his defences of denial and projection, a feeling of usefulness to others, and a development of some sense of mastery, and his knowledge and wisdom has been appreciated. Interesting in this connection is the following extract from a Group session. A comment on Princess Irene's marriage in Rome at which she wept, prompted Mr. B. to say, "Women crying doesn't mean anything." Mr. W. — "Don't you think all girls who marry are happy? At least they are happy for a time, even if it doesn't last, because they've got what they want." Mr. B. — "Some people are only happy when they are unhappy — they want to be always the victim." There was nodding and agreement about this. Mrs. G. commented again that Irene was missing her mother, when she cried at her wedding, and Mr. K. said he thought her tears were really around her change of religion. I picked up Mr. B.'s remark that woman who is crying doesn't really mean anything, and asked him if he would like to explain this remark — what did he really mean? Mr. B. — "Often crying is good for a woman, it relieves something, and afterwards they feel better." There was some discussion here about releasing of feelings. Mr. K. explained that after he'd had an accident and was very upset, the doctor had told him to go into a room himself and really release his feelings about it, that he would feel better for this. He had done so, but he said he could not cry, though he recognised this would have made him feel relieved. There were comments that men don't usually cry — only women do this, and Mr. B. said this was no longer true nowadays, that many men do cry and it does relieve them. After some further discussion I said, "What you're really saying is that release of your feelings does relieve you, but you have to be able to control this." Mr. K. said yes, this was what he meant. I said, I thought the same thing applied to anger, that it was sometimes helpful to express your anger, it relieves you and you get over it more quickly, but you had to be able to control this. Mr. B. commented that there are people who fly up in an angry temper and may break china, etc., but this relieves their anger and is quickly over. I said I thought sometimes this was better than keeping all the anger inside. Mr. B. said, "yes, because then the person tends to blame everyone else for what is making them angry". I said I thought this was very true. Mr. K. and Mr. W. agreed. Mr. W. made some amusing remarks about breaking cups and saucers. Mr. B. said, "It might be better to break a cup and saucer than brook over your anger for days, and upset a whole lot of other people by doing so." One or two individual interviews with Mr. B. after several sessions in the Group, proved most revealing. Mr. B., feeling freer to discuss his family history, expressed deep feelings of hostility towards his mother, who had been an over-protective, rigid woman, and controlling in a subtle manner, which he had only recognised in later life. He expressed guilt around his having forbidden her to enter his home. She tried to interfere in his marriage, and was able to accept clarification of his present feelings. His "return to society" in Group meetings, restoration of confidence in himself, as he became accepted by other members, and increase of self-esteem enabled Mr. B. to reveal himself more comfortably to me in individual interviews and to recognise his deeper needs. Recognition of past and recent achievements has proved a powerful factor in enabling members to gain more confidence and self-esteem, and to accept their present situation and losses more comfortably. Most members have, at one time or another, told of their past activities and upbringing, and been listened to with interest and lively recognition. Mr. C., for instance, a solitary bachelor, who retired from the "Y" as handyman at 76 years, too shy to participate in discussions for some weeks, was an interested observer, and laughed readily at Mr. W.'s jokes and witticisms. At one meeting he announced to me that it was his birthday, and on my repeating this, the Group offered warm congratulations and sang "Happy Birthday to Mr. C." Mr. W. asked, "Can you remember being born?" and Mr. C. looked pleased, but embarrassed. I asked him whether he'd like to tell us about the first thing he did remember. Mr. C. said, "Yes, hanging on to the back of a haycart on my way to school, and being whipped for it by my father". He continued on to tell of his hatred of his father, his loss of both parents at an early age, his upbringing by a cold and unsympathetic aunt, who blamed him for everything. (There has been much working through of negative and hostile feelings towards parents and authority figures in early life, which I have encouraged, where appropriate, and observed as healthy outlets for the members concerned.) Mr. C. then launched into a long story of his experiences in the R.A.F. and World War 1, his efforts to stand up for his rights, even if it meant defiance of authority. The Group were silent during the recital, and showed interest, at times amusement, and finally several members commented on Mr. C.'s ability to look after his own interests. Two members said they had enjoyed his story. He has now shown more readiness to participate in discussions, and is obviously more comfortable with other members. Mr. C.'s dependency needs have never been adequately met, and he has built up a strong defence of independency; since joining the Group he is beginning to recognise his needs — to consult me, as his caseworker, when various problems arise and he needs help. It seems clear to me that this kind of recognition from peers, not only helps each member to accept their present situation, but enables them to move towards facing their future and eventual death. In the early stages of our meetings there were many negative comments, particularly from Mr. W. which I felt expressed their mutual feeling, such as "We're no use now — we're old". "What do I care what happens to me when I'm dead — the City can bury me." I have taken up the feeling in such remarks, tried to help members face reality; encouraged discussion of anxiety-provoking subjects, including death, when it seemed appropriate and where I could see ways for myself and other members to interact towards relieving this anxiety; at times questioning "Is there something we could perhaps do about this situation?" Such negative comments are less frequent now, and if occasionally expressed, are mostly thrown out in a joking manner. Some positive steps have been taken towards community action to improve difficult situations for older people, e.g. in hospital clinics. This, I believe, has given the members a feeling of some mastery over their future; a feeling of movement forward in a further stage of their lives as opposed to stagnation and "waiting to die". When one member presents a problem in their present situation, others are quick to interact with advice, suggestion and real concern. For instance, Mrs. G. was concerned, having made preparation for her burial, as to what would happen if she died outside Canada, possibly on a visit to friends in U.S.A. Mr. B., who finds Mrs. G. tiresome, aggressive, and repetitive in stories about herself and tries to control her, appropriately recognised her real anxiety here, bent over to her, and explained courteously and tactfully how she might prepare for such an eventuality. The crisis situation around Mr. S.'s death in March provoked interesting interaction amongst members, and aroused discussions around death and burial plans, which reoccurred for several weeks. Mr. S. was a smiling, gentle old Englishman, with a calm, philosophical and uncomplaining attitude to life, much liked by other members. Mr. W. had visited him from time to time, and when his admission to hospital revealed cancer of the lung and bowel, Mr. W., Mr. T. and Mr. McG. all visited him. These visits meant much to Mr. S. who had no relatives and few friends left in Montreal. Mr. S. — "A man is worthwhile who has friends." Mr. W., on learning of Mr. S.'s death, called me, sounding upset and asking "Who will see about his burial and look after his things?" On being told that I would do this, Mr. W. was reassured, and relayed his news to other members at the next meeting. "Mrs. Schwarzmann looked after everything for Mr. S. — the funeral and everything." I noticed a sigh of relief from several members, and explained carefully how Mr. S. had consulted me, even before he became ill, as to plans for his burial, had made his Will, and having no one to act for him, I had assured him that F.S.A. would see that his wishes were carried out. There was general expression of feeling that if plans were made in advance, you didn't have to feel so worried about dying alone. During the following weeks several members asked to see me, or their own caseworker, to discuss burial plans, and Mr. W. told me privately that he had drawn up a Will and made his plans, with the help of an old friend; of course he "wasn't wanting to be buried by the City". I have noted in this Group that fear of chronic incapacity and illness would seem to be even more acute with some members than fear of death. Interaction between members around specific health problems relieves some of this anxiety, and the concern shown by others, advice given, even if not always too appropriate, seems of real meaning to the anxious client beset with health problems, who is led to feel less "alone" with his difficulties. Mr. H. is a frail old man, with quite serious physical incapacity, and a wife who is stone deaf and also handicapped. Despite this he has a lively sense of humour, good educational status and employment record, and a capacity to "give" to others. Several times Mr. H. has called me before the meeting to say, "I don't think I'll come, I've had a terrible week — so many troubles — they don't want to listen to my troubles." I have encouraged Mr. H. to come, and at the meeting to tell us of his weekly problems — having his wallet stolen on a bus, being nearly knocked down by a car due to failing eyesight, falling down and injuring his knee, etc. Mr. H. will start this recital with, "I don't want to bore you with all my troubles". A brief reminder from me as to why we are meeting together will enable Mr. H. to proceed, and others will listen attentively and with interest to him. Eventually, we discuss the reality of Mr. H.'s health problems — recognition, concern, suggestions all help to increase Mr. H.'s confidence, and he leaves, saying, "I felt terrible when I came today, but it's good to share your worries. I feel much better now." The transference situation in a Group can be complex, and the therapist should be aware of this. These members, when asked to define their feelings about the Group as a whole, were quick to reply, "We feel like a family now — we're so used to each other." This recreation of "family" reactivates sibling rivalries, rejections, etc., in many different ways. I have found it necessary to intervene in an attack on a member, where he or she was obviously threatened. Several times a member has come to me privately to comment that a certain other member was irritating him with constant interruptions, inappropriate jokes, or was boring with repetitive reminiscences. These private comments contained much repressed anger, and were also attention-seeking from me, as the authority figure. Each time I have encouraged the member to bring this feeling out directly in the Group, and in most cases this has been done — members learning to express anger appropriately, to control each other, and to accept controls without hostility. "Most persons find an attack by a peer less threatening than one from an authority figure." The truth of this statement has also been borne out in this Group. The therapist must be well aware of his own counter-transference reactions in these situations, of his own feelings towards older persons and parental figures. The handling of resistance to emotionally charged and painful material also poses a difficult task for the Group therapist, who must be aware when to remain passive and accept the Group's defences, and when to support them in facing the painful subject, and thereby relieving some intense anxiety around it. Members learn to accept support, but also challenges from others, to develop sensitivity to the needs of others. Through identification members may absorb new standards and new values in life. There has been fascinating discussion within this group around human values, that money is not the be-all and end-all of existence, although you do need to have enough to manage on — the rewards gained by giving to others, the interest derived from learning. Mr. H. is a firm supporter of "giving" being an active hospital visitor, frail though he is, to several friends more severely handicapped than himself. He is emphatic in stating the satisfaction it gives him to be able to "give" something to these friends — if only "a bit of sympathy and comfort". He was supported by Mr. R., Miss M. and Mr. W. Mrs. G., a self-centred, lonely and aggressive woman, following this discussion, decided to visit Miss I. regularly, now in hospital with a severe heart ailment. Among the development tasks, which the older person must face and solve successfully, are

1.   Redefinition of social identity through development of "new social roles".
2.   Redefinition of value systems.
3.   Development of a new self-image.

Other tasks are adjustment to physical and mental changes, linkage of past and present to future, and development of a "sense of integrity". A geriatric group would seem to offer the most hopeful emotional climate in which the older person can be helped towards facing such tasks. Concerning prevention of mental illness, Mr. R. who has been acutely lonely since he lost his wife, and made an apt comment when asked how he felt about the Group, after his first three sessions. "If you stop walking, you lose the use of your legs, and if you stop talking and discussing things with older people, you lose the use of your mind; so I want to go on coming." These descriptions of work with groups and analyses of the content of communication in the groups can be used to stimulate discussion of further problems in social work and education practice. These are problems of (a) assumptions about communication in therapeutic groups and (b) assumptions about skills required in communicating with groups. It is a basic assumption that guided group interaction is a helping tool in social work. Relationships among human beings — their feelings and their thoughts — are expressed in many different ways. One of the major ways of expression is words. As in individual interviews the group worker uses this form of communication purposefully and skilfully. Encouragement of interaction in discussion groups is a significant quality of social group work. The group worker always tries to increase the interaction and mutual help among the members. The primary group is important because it is the social instrument through which the individual acquires his attitudes and it is the most potent influence in regulating his behaviour. In groups where members feel a sense of belongingness individuals participating in group discussion are enabled to identify with new information. They are able to sift evidence, examine their criticisms and suspicions, and by examining new ideas, to learn and acquire new information. In a group the behaviour of each person affects, and is affected by, the behaviour of the others. For members to facilitate each other's efforts they must share some of the same ideas and feelings about the aims of the group and the methods to be used in working for them. For active co-operation to occur there needs to be some basic agreement about the nature of the task. Earlier we noted the importance of the primary group as the social instrument through which the individual acquires his attitudes and which is the most potent influence in regulating his behaviour. The relationship between a person's values and attitudes is not a simple one but group norms prescribe what actions are "right" and what attitudes are acceptable. One of the most successful ways of promoting attitude change is the creation of a group in which members feel they belong. In these circumstances the individual accepts some new information or some new values. Participating in group discussion enables members to identify with new information; they are able to voice their criticisms, to express hostility or suspicion of new ideas and are thus enabled to acquire new information or ideas for themselves. Change can be produced in a group by allowing or encouraging members of the group to participate in communication and decision-making. Where individuals can participate in the communication process they are likely to feel committed to the message. This may be because group participation is another way by which individuals learn social reality. It is obviously assumed that the worker with groups has to establish a relationship between the group members and himself. Also he has to try to help each person to find satisfaction in his relationships with the other group members. Such general goals apply in work with families and other community groups of course. Part of the group worker's skill consists in helping a person experience in a group that one can relate to other people in constructive ways. This can involve learning that it is possible to feel angry and to say so and still work through the conflict and that it is possible to make decisions with other people while still expressing and holding to one's own opinion. The group worker has to enable members to help each other in this. Social workers and social work students usually pass through a stage where they have felt annoyed or inhibited because of the presence of other family members during interviews. They come to not only accept their presence but learn to involve them in working together. In working with groups the worker has to develop skill in enhancing interaction between group members. The group worker has to be able to provide focus and continuity in a discussion. From the several strands of content put into the group discussion by group members the worker has to select which are central. He has to make deliberate use of the various contributions, valuing them and connecting them with what has been said before or using them for further consideration of particular points. It also involves responding to non-verbal communications like facial expressions, and to remarks in such a way that others are stimulated to respond thus being actively part of the community. The leader thus provides focus and continuity in a way that has meaning to the whole group and each of its members because they too are enabled to help in maintaining continuity. The skill of a good discussion leader lies in helping others to participate. This involves trying to create an atmosphere in which people feel free enough to contribute and where they can experience the satisfaction of having accomplished something. It involves feeling when it is appropriate to enter the discussion to try to push it forward or to summarise what has been said; this means judging when and when not to encourage specific individual's contributions. The group worker has to be able to let group members work things out with each other without his verbal participation and to know when this is appropriate. This means not responding verbally to everything that is said. Sometimes a leader does this by directing a member's comment, by a gesture or glance to others in the group for a response. Group workers work through activities as well as through verbal communication. People have a wide variety of ways of expressing feelings and thoughts. The deliberate use of an appropriate programme of activities involves assessment of individuals and their group norms and of situations, if it is to be useful. Choosing the wrong games or activities with the group of young aggressive delinquents can serve to increase their hostility or deepen their resentment of the imposition of other standards. It can lead to distrust and to disaster. So-called therapeutic activities based on preconceived ideas like "water play helps to get out hostility" or "painting is helping because it helps self-expression" can seem ridiculous to some groups. One group worker met a group of teenage boys who said they wanted somewhere to play football. Some of the boys seemed solemn and defiant, others were boisterous. The group appeared not to be particularly united — there were two sub-groups — except in the wish to play football. One of the sub-groups was dominant and it seemed that the boys related to each other only on an authority basis and were suspicious of adults. Through sensitive assessment of the situation the group worker felt that he had to help the boys with their football but that he might also use the informal situation to help them with conflicts about feelings of dependence and independence and with their relationships with each other. This kind of skill of using informal situations contributes to work with delinquents and to work with people who suffer from psychotic illness.

The next record of a group session is from a paper by Hallowitz (1965). In this he says that many different group approaches are used which can be classed under four headings. In Family Life Education groups the people who go are not seeking help from social agencies although they may have quite serious problems. The emphasis in these groups is on assisting members to develop new perspectives about their role in their own family situations. The worker uses the group experience to enable members to analyse particular situations and to become more sensitive to the needs of family members. The use of group methods with clients is described by a wide variety of terms such as group work, group therapy or group counselling. Some of this work might be indistinguishable from Family Life Education. Hallowitz suggests that

   (a) people are selected for different types of groups on the basis that "this is the treatment of choice for this particular client";
   (b) the placement of clients in a particular group is based on ideas about their potential contributions to the group, i.e. a balanced group is looked for;
   (c) additional forms of help can be used by the agency with the client or other members of his family.

These distinctions should not be lost sight of. An important feature of group therapy is that it is mainly directed to increasing self-understanding. This is the principal means by which changes in behaviour feelings and attitudes occur. This means heavy reliance on an atmosphere in which it is safe for the client to reveal his anxieties, fears and frustrations both about current and past experiences, including his relationships with significant members of his original family. Destructive attitudes and feelings that lead to self-defeating activities are identified and worked through. This involves linking consciously remembered past experiences and current reality so as to decrease the use of pathological defences. Transferences and resistances of members and the group as a whole have to be identified and explored. According to Hallowitz, "how the member uses himself within the group, how he relates to others, and how he characteristically responds to group tension comes under scrutiny". He then gives the following account of a group session.

In the twelfth session of a mothers' group Mrs. Johnson was describing the fight she had with her 13-year-old son the night before, about whether city employees have a right to strike. She prefaced her account with the statement that "children think they know everything today". Then she went on to give a blow-by-blow account of how she "tore his thinking to pieces". The gloating and the air of superiority were apparent to all. The argument ended when the son slammed out of the room yelling, "You never listen to a thing I say!" and her countering with, "Of course not, when you talk nonsense!" She paused momentarily in self-satisfaction and then went on to tell the group that when her husband came home she asked him very innocently whether he thought city employees had the right to strike. He took the same point of view as his son and again she described with evident satisfaction how she "wiped the floor with him". When the group started to argue with Mrs. Johnson about her point of view on the issue, the therapist intervened asking what the group thought was going on. It was obvious to the therapist that the group members were reacting more to Mrs. Johnson's manner than they were to the issue. One woman said, "You know, I agree with Mrs. Johnson's point of view, but I found myself wanting to argue with her. As she was talking, I felt myself getting mad all over." Other group members were nodding. Another group member said, "That's no way to treat a 13-year-old boy, making him feel like a dummy". Another woman said, "If that's the way she talks to her husband, no wonder he rarely has anything to say to her". A few similar comments from other members and Mrs. Johnson's face was filled with consternation. "What did you expect me to do, let them get away with silly statements?" she blurted. Another member said softly, "Now look, Mrs. Johnson, you may not like what I am going to say, but don't get mad. You always act as though if someone doesn't agree with you that they are stupid, or if they are right, then you must be stupid." Another member also in kindly voice, quickly joined in, "Everytime we have a discussion here, to you it's not a discussion to exchange points of view. For you, it's a battle as to who's right." Another member said, "You have a habit of saying things in a way that implies if anyone doesn't agree she must be a dummy." And another member, "either people get angry with you and fight back or they ignore you". At this point, in an attempt to cushion the confrontation and make it more palatable, the therapist said, "Mrs. Johnson, what the group is trying to do is to help you to see that there is something about the way you present ideas to people that rubs them the wrong way. They are doing this because they believe you would want to know the effect you sometimes have on people." Grudgingly, Mrs. Johnson admits, "people have said I am opinionated". Another woman, Mrs. Wilson, said, "I am just the opposite. I never know what to think. At times I find myself envying Mrs. Johnson. I wish I could be as sure of myself as she is." Another member: "is that why you don't talk much in the group? Here, I've been sitting all the time thinking you're quiet because you're sitting in judgement over us, and I took your silence to mean superiority." Mrs. Wilson responded with, "I guess I find it safe to keep quiet. I'm never sure how what I have to say will be received." When asked by another member why she felt that way, Mrs. Wilson replied that she didn't know why except that maybe it goes back to how she was raised. She had an older brother who was the favourite and her parents constantly compared her to him. She remembers when she was a little girl her parents always saying to her "why don't you talk more?" The thing they never seemed to be aware of was that whenever she did express an opinion, they always found something wrong with it. Turning now to Mrs. Johnson, Mrs. Wilson said, "when you were telling the incident with your son, my heart bled for him". She quickly continued with, "I know you didn't want to hurt your boy. This is the way you are. But what made you this way?" Mrs. Johnson was obviously touched by the compassion in Mrs. Wilson's voice, not only for her son, but for her as well. She shook her head, looking down at her hands, she said, "while you were talking I was thinking maybe we're not so different after all. I am really not sure of myself. When *you* are not sure of yourself, you keep quiet. When I'm not sure of myself, I talk as though I know what I'm talking about and if someone argues with me, I sometimes feel panicky and I hear myself saying things in a most outlandish tone of voice." She was silent for a few moments and still not looking at the group continued, "I had two younger brothers. No matter what they did, it was perfect as far as my parents were concerned. No matter what I did, I was always wrong.

Whenever I could, I would show them up to my parents." Shaking her
head she continued, "but it never did any good". At this point, she
picked her head up, looked at the therapist and said, "and that hurt
even more". (Note the symbolic acting out of husband and son as the
younger brothers, the group as the mother and therapist, the father.) At
this point, other members came into the discussion to reveal similar
hurts and disappointments at the hands of father, mother or both
parents. The revelations of Mrs. Wilson and Mrs. Johnson had
triggered similar associations in the other group members and they
used the opportunity to unburden themselves as well. It is interesting
that Mrs. Johnson, increasingly during the discussion was able to look
at people, nod her head, and occasionally make comments elaborating
her own experiences. The theme was clear: parental preferences for
siblings, lack of support and consideration for them as individuals in
their own right. The therapist towards the end of the session intervened
again, giving recognition to how painful it can be for children when
parents show marked preference for another youngster; also how
painful it was when siblings got into conflict, even when it was the
preferred sibling who started it, the parents somehow always made it
clear that it was their fault. Then turning to Mrs. Johnson, he said,
"how painful it must have been today for you. You had come in today
to report how way off base were your husband and your son and how
you attempted to straighten them out and instead of getting recognition
for this, it was you whom we held accountable." Mrs. Johnson smiled a
bit and said that yes, she had been feeling hurt and angry at the whole
group and particularly at the leader. She really had been expecting
praise, but as painful as it was she thinks she learned something today.
If she had gotten praise today, it wouldn't have helped her. She paused
thoughtfully and then went on to say, "I think I have been for many
years sore as a boil. Today that boil was lanced and some of the poison
drained off and while I feel better that boil still hurts." At this point,
one of the women stood up and said, "Mrs. Johnson, you have guts. I'd
like to shake your hand!"

It will be seen that in this group the mothers are able to discuss their
family problems and their individual difficulties. They also discuss
what is going on in the group in terms of looking at each other's
behaviour and feelings. Thus what may seem to be "irrelevant" noise or

disorderliness in the group may represent members' attempts to express and to satisfy their personal needs. If they are not allowed such expression the emotional forces may be concealed (or repressed) but continue to affect the group's operation. There may be too little noise in a group: relevant information in the possession of a member may not be made available because of jealousy or status differences. Ways then have to be found to promote rather than limit communication. This involves accepting and dealing with information about personal feelings as well as information about the group's task, make their recognition possible. Two people may reach a point where they can tell one another about things they dislike. They may then be able to understand each other's points of view more easily and, as a result, be able to talk to each other more freely about other things. Some of these points, of course, do not apply to groups which meet only for a short time. They are more important in the case of continuing ones. Such groups need to develop ways of dealing with problems of relationships and to pay attention to their own processes. They have to look ahead and to generalise, perhaps by framing guidelines, about their ways of working. In this group it seems evident that the group members feel free to argue with each other openly and to say that they can feel angry, e.g. with Mrs. Johnson. The group worker or therapist has an important role, it seems, in communicating about the effect Mrs. Johnson might have on other people.

One outcome of discussion of this material may be to question what it is that blocks the communication of relevant information in groups, because, this helps to focus attention on non-verbal aspects of communication. A group member may say that he has understood a piece of information but it later emerges that he misinterpreted what he was told. Probably the more significant barriers relate to feelings about status, interpersonal hostility, and resistance to control or leadership. Thus a person may be inhibited because of existing feelings of inferiority or because of fear of appearing to be inferior. Such fears of disapproval may be verbalised as "if I say that the others will think that I am stupid or incompetent" or "if I ask that question or make that comment he will disapprove or criticise me". Hostility may lead to the wish not to share ideas with the person who is disliked and may inhibit the offering of encouragement or support to a colleague. In many ways resistance to authority is very similar. It may be shown in ways such as those just quoted or simply by refusing to make a contribution. Withholding information which could be useful to a group is a means of wanting power and undermining the work of the group.

3. ROLE PLAYING

If a person acts in a play he pretends to be someone else and is given directions about how to do it. He has to identify strongly with the character he is portraying: he has literally to speak the lines supplied for the character by the writer. Role playing is different. The role player is given information about the person whose name he is to adopt but he may not be given as much information as the actor. In a sense he is encouraged to retain more of his own independent personality. In the interaction between the role players their own personalities are represented, supplemented or changed by the instructions in the script. They are influenced, of course, by the way the role playing situation develops, and by the feelings engendered by it. It is possible that some students may find that this provokes anxiety. If it becomes too lifelike it could be quite alarming for some people. Clearly a great deal depends on the nature of the material that is used and the way an exercise is presented. The fact that the focus is on learning is an important aid to feeling comfortable about an exercise. This should indicate that it is acceptable to express feelings because they have value as data for discussion. It is also helpful to recognise that students are not playing their own roles. They are playing other people's and in doing this they communicate and interact with each other. They will be studying this behaviour and trying to generalise about their observations. The student is given the bare bones of a situation and has to elaborate on them. The challenge lies in making this interpretation and then in making deductions and links with theory in thinking about what has happened afterwards. This important step in learning cannot be stressed too much and it will be referred to again later. The exercise which follows is used to illustrate a method of learning about the concept of role. The commentary indicates some of the areas of special interest which are usually illustrated. The exercise has been used during the second year of a social-work course when students were at quite an advanced stage in sociology, and in social work were looking more critically and deeply at the roles of "helper" and "client".*

AN EXERCISE

"Jane's Day"

A day in the life of a shop assistant in a departmental store.

Characters. Scene I. *The Shop* Department

(1) A young shop assistant, Jane, who is the chief character, and is called upon to play many roles.
(2) A colleague of similar age, who is a "larky" type.
(3) An older colleague who flaps.
(4) A departmental manager — supervisor to above.
(5) The Boss.
(6) A customer — of similar class and age as (1). She is late for work.
(7) An older customer who can't make up her mind.
(8) A customer of higher class who expects immediate attention.
(9) An older customer of lower class.

Scene II. *On the way home in the tube*

(1) Jane and
(10) An acquaintance

Scene III. *At home — teatime*

(1) Jane
(11) Father
(12) Mother
(13) Kid brother.

Scene IV. *The Youth Club — an "activity" club*

(1) Jane who is a part-time leader.
(14) A girl friend who helps.
(15)
     Young people at the Club.
(16)

Scene V. *An exclusive and expensive restaurant "The Cheltenham"*

(1) Jane.
(17) Her boy friend.
(18) The waiter.
(8) The upper class customer with some friends.

Scene VI.   *On the way home*

(1)   Jane.
(17)   Her boy friend.
(19)   A poor thing in need of assistance.
(20)   A policeman.

Finis

Role 1 will be taken by the same person throughout.

This is the plot

Scene I. 15 minutes

It is early in the afternoon. (1) and (2) are larking about while (3) is trying to check them — just then the departmental manager (4) comes in and wants to know why the department is so untidy. He demands that the floor be swept, the till checked and the window display completed immediately. Then the four customers (6), (7), (8) and (9) enter more or less together and (1), (2) and (3) try to cope with all the demands made on them. Of course the Boss chooses just this time to make his daily tour of inspection. He flatters (8) whom he knows socially. When she goes he comments on the chaos — reprimands (4), who later passes this on to (1), and (2).

Scene II. 5 minutes

On the way home Jane meets an acquaintance. She has to straphang all the way.

Scene III. 10 minutes

At home — teatime with Mother (12), Father (11) and kid brother (13) — he teases her — she flies off the deep end, (11) gets "stroppy" and (12) tries to keep the peace.

Scene IV. 10 minutes

Then she goes off to the Youth Club where she is a part-time leader with her girl friend (14) who helps there. She tries to involve (15) and (16) in table tennis which doesn't interest them and they become difficult. Can she cope?

Scene V. 15 minutes

Later she meets her boy friend (17) and persuades him, very much against his will, to take her to the very exclusive and expensive new restaurant, "The Cheltenham", where they encounter a supercilious waiter (18). Sitting at a nearby table is the upper-class customer (8) with some friends. The bill is huge.

Scene VI. 10 minutes

On the way home things are a little strained between them. As they are beginning to make it up they come across a poor old thing in need of assistance (19). What shall they do? A passing policeman (2) may supply the answer.

Finis

*The Script was written by Mrs. Ruth Fanner and she monitored the action and took a leading part in discussion. The exercise was conducted jointly by Ruth Fanner and Peter Day. The latter sometimes took certain roles, e.g. the Departmental Manager and the Policeman. The commentary refers to his performance as the Policeman.

Commentary

In the shop situation one can see the case with which people very often change their behaviour according to the status of the people with whom they are communicating. In the ordinary day at work Jane assumes a number of time-limited and transient roles. She acts in one way towards the departmental manager and although she varies her approach to different customers, probably there are some recognisable common features of her behaviour towards them. These short-term rather superficial roles depend on the firm base of recognising another person's status and therefore one's own position. Frequently we are largely unaware of the process. As the script says, Jane, the chief character, is called on to play many parts in the course of her day. It is evident that she has to respond to the varied expectations which the other actors have of her. She has to deal with conflicts between her own ideas about how she wants to behave and to play her part, and her ideas about how the other people she meets expect her to behave. Her ideas about their expectations may not, of course, coincide with their versions of these expectations. Jane, then, has a complicated life; complicated because she has to play several different parts. In Scene I Jane is perhaps expected to lark about with the other girl. The other girl might want to play around by "trying on" items of clothing for sale in the shop, wanting Jane to join her in wearing various smart or showy hats; carrying this further could involve playing a game of pretending to be someone else like a customer who is well known for affectations of dress and manner, or someone else like a member of the staff. If, basically, Jane is a serious, shy or conscientious girl who thinks the other is behaving stupidly she might find it hard to join in the games. On the other hand, the girls are about the same age, and they may understand each other and get on well together: they could well both enter into playing around wholeheartedly: other people might expect that "girls of their age" or "girls like them" would do this: "it's a way of letting off steam". There could be other expectations. For example, it is very likely that many people would expect girls who are shop assistants to "behave properly and not mess around with the stock". There are many possibilities in this early situation; much depends, of course, on the kinds of people who play the parts of Jane and the other girl. If they are given the choice it is very likely that people will choose parts which they "feel they can play". Perhaps a "larky type" will choose to play the "larky" girl in the exercise. How does Jane react to the older person who tends to panic about things? This colleague often finds the "youngsters" boisterousness irritating and worrying and perhaps she tries to get them to stop playing around and get the department tidied up. Jane's behaviour to these two colleagues and to the other actors in the first scene (how she talks to them, whether she obeys or disobeys them for example) will illustrate Banton's (1965) identification of basic roles. "In almost all societies distinctions of sex and age are identified with basic roles. In many societies a similar part is played by distinctions of race and sometimes of rank and these differences may affect people's rights and obligations in many circumstances. Basic roles are those which predetermine most of the positions open to an individual and which have implications for the way the parties behave towards one another in a correspondingly large proportion of social situations" (1) (Banton, 1965). Basic roles are usually ascribed to people by fixed criteria and they are exhaustive in that they can be applied to everyone. They are mutually exclusive too. Everyone belongs in one or the other: juvenile or adult, male or female. With the appearance of the departmental manager on the scene we have someone whose status is different to that of the three actors who we have observed before. He is a supervisor or "middle manager". He carries a high degree of responsibility for the work of Jane and her two colleagues. He is responsible for the smooth running of his department to the store manager or boss. Probably most adults have some general ideas about supervisor's roles, and what their status is. In other words they have some general ideas where "a supervisor" is usually located on a map of statuses, i.e. where he stands in his organisation's hierarchy — in this case, the packing order of the shop. A person's position simply describes his rights and obligations and how these regulate his interaction (and this includes his ways of communicating of course) with people of other statuses. The departmental manager in this sketch has different rights and obligations in his relations with each of his subordinates, his customers and his boss. His relations with these different people or group of people may be complicated by the varied range of expectations each may have of the others. This has already been evident earlier in the sketch in the cases of Jane and her colleagues; ideas about status, of course, apply equally to them. As with the others the department manager enacts his role: he puts his rights and duties into effect. One thing he may feel he has to do is to stop the junior staff "larking about" (if they were when he came in) and to get everything tidied up and organised ready for the afternoon's work. He may feel he has to be "very particular" (from his point of view) or "far too fussy" (from Jane's angle) in getting the display of goods looking as attractive as possible. This could involve rearranging the shop window to incorporate some new products as well as the floor and counter displays inside. By issuing a succession of orders the supervisor could quite soon have his three subordinates "falling over each other" in trying to obey him and to cope with a multiplicity of jobs. Jane, for example, might find herself trying to cope with checking the till (even though this is usually the older colleague's job), sweeping the floor and trying still to resist the "larky" type. She might feel that she "does not know whether she is coming or going", and "there's just no pleasing him". If Jane, or any of the others, at this point, "do not know whether they are coming or going" they are confused and uncertain about what is expected of them. They may try to adapt in trial and error fashion. They may feel that what they are being asked to do conflicts with what they want to do, or feel they ought to do, or what they are accustomed to do. They may interpret the supervisor's and each other's expectations inaccurately; confusion results. All of these points are quite clearly illustrated in this part of the script if the supervisor plays his part in the way indicated. This is quite a useful way to observe the repercussions of role conflict. The arrival of someone of even higher status underlines this for observers. It is also reinforced by the different behaviour of the four customers and the different ways they are treated by the staff. In the general confusion the young customer becomes even later in getting to work, unless he or she "pushes" very hard because that is the kind of person he is. The older customer who cannot make up her mind may be left on one side to look through some samples but receive little in the way of advice or suggestion because the staff are too preoccupied. What happens to the higher-class customer who expects immediate attention is interesting because, again, conflicts are involved. The boss treats this customer with considerable respect when she comes in and gives her special attention or tells the departmental manager to give special attention. Or, because they are acquainted, the boss may spend more time in talking with this customer leaving the department manager to cope with the increasing pressures or competing demands. The older, lower-class customer may try to attract attention in the matter of activity. But he (or she) may be portrayed as inassertive or "humble" and is pushed or retreats into the background. The boss may act as if he feels rather ashamed of the apparent inefficiency of the department and this (the feeling of "being shown up" in front of someone he would have liked to impress) may help to make his reprimand stronger or more bitter: the department manager in his turn feels ashamed at being "shown up" in front of his staff or is fearful as a result of the boss's hints about the insecure nature of his job. He may well threaten his juniors with dismissal if things do not improve. But he is dependent, at least to some extent, on the goodwill of his staff if things are to improve; he may not express his anger directly towards all of the staff: perhaps he will make the younger ones take much of the blame. This provides Jane with a major topic of conversation during her journey home. At one session Jane's friend in the train said that she knew the department manager: he was sometimes very awkward with his family. "I don't know how his wife puts up with him. He's always been like it you know." Jane seems to feel relieved at being able to tell her friend about her troubles at work. The friend is an older person who tends to "mother" Jane who finishes the journey feeling less humiliated. When she reaches home we see Jane as daughter and sister. She is provoked by her brother and mother tries to act as mediator. The role structure of a family is to do with the way tasks are allocated to the members: how are the jobs to be done and who is expected to do them? The reasons for the answers to such questions in the case of particular families, such as Jane's, are to be found partly in the family's place in the social system. What is the social-class background of the members for example? What do the relatives (the extended family) expect of the nuclear family? What stereotypes do people have about how Jane, her parents and her brother see and play their roles in the family? The "answers" to these kinds of questions emerge in role playing and help people to learn what stereotypes they have about family roles. They may learn too how stereotypes are necessary in social life. Life would be intolerable if we could not take for granted many assumptions we make about social and family life. Within family groups three sub-systems can usually be discerned, the marital relationship, parent-child relationships and sibling relationships. These relationships affect relationships in the various sub-systems and in the family as a whole. Thus a mother's protective attitude towards her son affects the marital relationship, other parent-child relationships and relations between the children as indicated above. In this piece it sometimes happens that this kind of relationship is acted, presumably because "mother" feels she should protect "kid brother" from father. The stereotype of the family that is quite often acted is one where father is seen clearly as the bread-winner. It is expected that father will go to work every day and earn enough money to keep the home going: when he comes home mother does not expect him to do a great deal in the house and father tends to leave the discipline of the children to her. This does not mean that father opts out completely of course. In one session he emerged from behind his newspaper to castigate "kid brother" for his laziness, long hair and general sloppiness. He soon retired behind the paper again when mother and Jane united in trying to pacify the two male actors, saying "you can't get any peace even at tea time now". The parents' roles are usually played as being complementary and satisfactory to each partner. It is as if the family rows and grumblings are apparently quite superficial. The play seems to show well, in practice, that conflict is commonplace in families although the way it is expressed varies a great deal. The way Jane's family deals with conflict and resolves problems seems often to indicate a basic stability and strength. In other words, it illustrates that although definite tensions are noticeable the roles of family members with each other seem to fit in smoothly and in orderly or patterned ways. It also illustrates, of course, that complementarity breaks down: mother is not too pleased when father involves himself in her jobs. This scene then underlines what Perlman has said about social expectations: ". . . like most social rules by which we live, they have become second nature to most of us, unrecognised as socially imposed most of the time because we take them so much for granted and also because they have become role-rules for good reason: they oil the wheels of daily living and free us from what would otherwise be innumerable and exhausting small decisions and choices" (Perlman,

1968). At the club Jane has to respond to another range of expectations. Having been in subordinate positions for most of the day she is now supposed to be a leader. But she finds it difficult to exercise authority or to persuade the club members to play table tennis. Perhaps it is because she is close to them in age. The "being awkward" roles appear to present actors with little difficulty: they are able to discover several ways of defying the leaders or more passive resistance, e.g. by saying or showing that they are quite simply not interested in table tennis and just want to sit and talk (or just sit). There may be very little that Jane and her friend can do: sometimes they play table tennis themselves but the two members show no inclination at all to join in. She appears to be more successful in using her powers of persuasion with her boy friend but his grudging reluctance seems more understandable when the upper-class customer and her friends clearly disapprove of their behaviour and when he finds he has insufficient money to pay the bill. In one session the boy friend questioned the size of the bill. This gave the head waiter a further opportunity to express his scarcely veiled distaste by indicating that he is not accustomed to customers of this kind. Most people, of course, have a general stereotype of the head waiter role but, of course, different actors have very varied styles in performing it. As in the case of the policeman in the next scene or of the boss in Scene I deviations from the norm or individual idiosyncrasies in playing these roles are quickly noticed by observers. On one occasion a man who had been a policeman was, of course, very quick to observe the ignorance of police procedure of one actor and was critical of his performance which was too much like that of a social worker and not sufficiently close to the role the policeman would usually play with a very difficult old lady who seemed to be confused, intoxicated and not to know who or where she was or where she was going. The real-life policeman pointed out that the "problem" could be dealt with by a simple threat of "making a charge" if the "poor old thing" was still there after an hour. Offers of cups of tea at the station, he thought, were pointless. The old lady had ignored these blandishments! Jane and the other people involved in this sketch occupy a number of positions within the various social systems to which they belong. We see in the case of Jane, the basic role she plays as a young, single woman. Because it is basic it determines a great deal of her way of life. Also,

Jane has an occupation: she has a general role of shop assistant: she is a member of the staff of her department store, she has a place in its organisation and hierarchy. Members of the store's staff, including Jane, carry these general roles in various social groups. The boss, for example, was a friend of one of the store's customers. These general roles influence behaviour in a variety of settings. This dynamic aspect of role is well illustrated in the play: we saw Jane talking about her job on the way home: we saw her talking about it at home. The influence of her general role on her behaviour can in fact be seen throughout the day. She was also a voluntary club leader. Here is an independent role: it does not seem to have tremendous influence on some other aspects of Jane's behaviour. But what Jane "puts in" to this part is affected by the kind of girl she is, her basic role and her occupation. It should be possible to show this point out in the play. To take one obvious aspect of this: in the shop we have seen Jane in a subordinate position, trying to meet the expectations of customers and bosses. At the club she has to switch to become a leader, that is, to change from being a subordinate. This is not necessarily an easy change to make: even in a role-playing exercise it can be difficult. It is probably unnecessary to labour this point further: most people are aware of the nature of this general kind of adaptation, from their own observation and experience. This can lead to reconsideration of the question of role conflict. Jane is close in age to the club members. They may seem to see her, or they may choose to see her, as "one of themselves" — "just a club member" — rather than someone who is "different" or, as a leader, more distant or authoritative. A person has a number of "social selves": he has as many as there are distinct groups of people whose opinions he cares about. It is quite easy to identify several groups Jane cared about in the sketch. Goffman (1959) put it this way. It is a basic assumption of role analysis that each individual will be involved in more than one system or pattern in society. He will therefore perform more than one role: he will have several selves. How are these selves related? It was said above that what Jane put into the different roles she played was affected by the kind of girl she was. This raises the difficult question of the relationship between "role" and "self". Ruddock (1969) does not attempt to explore all the ramifications of the questions which arise but he makes a number of useful suggestions. The idea of personality includes structures of needs, wishes and fears derived from past adjustments to experience. These very complex structures in the personality will determine the range of roles a person will be able to play whatever environment he is in at a given time. The term role tree is introduced by Ruddock in discussing how a person integrates different roles into his living from moment to moment. At first sight the personality and the role tree appear to be the same. The role tree is a way of describing a person's total capacity for relationships of various kinds and this is near to a definition of personality. But the role tree can be seen as growing out of personality and as its means of expression; it is therefore open to interpretation in terms of personality. What does a role tree consist of? Ruddock uses the following example. The trunk corresponds to the basic role, say, a middle-aged man. The main branches would be his general roles: husband, father, worker. The secondary branches would correspond to special roles belonging within the general roles. A tree's leaves are the organs by which it interacts with its environment. The leaves represent transient roles, meaning those positions people occupy in conversational exchanges. They change from minute to minute as in conversation a person seeks information, reassures another or seeks reassurances, tells someone to do something, and so on. What happens in this, as in any other piece of role playing, of course is that the actors put into their parts a great deal of their experience in other roles and of themselves. The kind of person who plays Jane can be clearly seen "through" the way she plays Jane's various roles in the script. The same goes for the other characters, of course. I have also tried to show, in this commentary, that this particular exercise is a useful way of illustrating role conflict and forms a sound basis for usually timely discussions. It also raises useful questions about occupational roles and stereotypes. Role conflict is very clearly seen in the youth-club situation. Jane's leader role seems to be incongruent with her occupational role of being helpful to and trying to please the customers. As a daughter Jane tries to play a similar part, in trying to help things run smoothly at home. This is another illustration of the way a basic role may affect behaviour at work. Jane also experiences conflict in the final scene. She is torn between wanting to help the old lady and wishing to go home with her boy friend. He makes it plain that he is reluctant to spend too much time with the old lady and is only too ready to seek the policeman's help. We have little evidence about how effective role playing and simulation exercises are as aids to learning. Role playing seems to enable people to obtain new perspectives on other behaviour. It is an important part of learning to develop the ability to try to see how things might seem to other people or how they might appear to you in a given situation. Hopefully one might go further. If role playing is to develop the kind of sensitivity to other people described here this will only be effective if the general points are teased out of the action and they are analysed and underlined. Discussion of the action would seem to be essential. We have found it useful to students to have breaks for discussion after one or two scenes. Alternatively, discussion could be left to the end but it might be difficult to remember all the important events in Jane's day and the observations to be made about them. But it is the discussion itself which is important if students are to develop social skills and to enlarge their awareness of social interaction as a result of role playing.

The next sketch for role playing was devised by some social-work students to introduce a discussion about the use of authority in social work and its possible abuse. The sketch may well have other uses. Commenting on the material the students said they had tried to show how a family under stress reacted in childish and irrational ways. This raised the question in what way the social worker might use authority in trying to help the family. What would you do if you were the social worker?

Referral   Authoritiski family: 9 Wakefield Avenue, Heathfield Estate

Father: Edward John (43 years). Employed as a lorry driver till last year — now slaughterman.
Mother: Edna Doris (40 years).
Son: Peter (17 years). Unemployed.
Daughter: Mary (16 years). Works as a machinist in clothing factory. Baby due 3.9.73.
Son: James Arthur (12 years). St. Andrew's School. On voluntary supervision to Mr. Smith (social worker).
Son: George (8 years). St. Andrew's Junior School. Continually absent from school.
Baby: Garth (6 months).

Home is a three-bedroomed council house on the Heathfield Estate.

Mother refers herself to social services department because of father's attitude towards daughter who is pregnant.

Presenting Many Problems

Scene 1. *The living room of the Authoritski's home.* Mother *and* Daughter *present*

Daughter: Mam. I can't go on much longer like this — it's only another month before the baby's due and look at me. What am I going to do, I can't stand Dad ranting on any more.

Mother: Well, it's no use asking me to speak to him — I can't talk to him about the baby — he just seems that he won't listen and I'm frightened he'll hit me as well as you, like he did last week when he'd had a bit too much to drink.

Daughter: Oh, it's no bloody good, I shall just have to leave home and try and find a flat or somewhere to live — one of the girls from work might put me up for a bit until I have to go into hospital, but he's not going to hit me like he did when I was a kid. He's not perfect anyway — always messing around with that woman down at the pub — I don't see why he thinks he can lay the law down. You should try and stand up to him more, Mam, he's always going on about his weak heart but if you ask me it's just a lot of cods wallop — he's quite capable of walking down to the pub and propping the bar up there every night.

Mother: I think I've just about had enough what with you going to have this baby and Jim in trouble with the police [*sigh*] then there's George not wanting to go to school and the bloody school attendance officer snooping around — I'm worried to death [*pause and sigh*] and our Peter losing his job at the supermarket — what he brought home was going to be thrown away so I don't know why the manager made such a fuss about it — he's a good boy really and he only wanted to help out a bit knowing how short I am of money. I don't know how I am meant to manage on your Dad's money — to feed you lot and buy things for the baby, let alone help you out. I feel so fed up and if you go then there won't be anyone I can turn to.

Daughter: Why can't he work at a decent job and bring his money home proper like anyone else does.

Mother: I think the best way out will be for me to put my head in the gas oven.

Daughter: Don't be silly, Mam, it's no good giving way — he's not worth getting upset about. Perhaps Mr. Smith who comes to see our Jim might be able to help, or at least talk some sense into our Dad.

Mother: How can he help — he's just another snooping bloody social worker — they're all alike up at the Welfare — want to know all your business and then turn round and say "get him to give you some money every week, Mrs. Authoritiski" — they want to try living with him and see how they'd get some money. There's no money anyway and no-one I can ask — and if Jim has touched that gas meter again he's for the chop! I think everyone in this street is fed up with us borrowing and never returning. I hardly feel I can lift my head up again in this street — Mrs. Harris passed me in the street yesterday and never even looked.

Daughter: Well, Mr. Smith did help a girl at work and he always listens to you, so he might be able to do something. When you go down town tomorrow go and see if he is in — tell him what a right b   our Dad is. Mind you, Mr. Smith hasn't done much for our Jim and George does as he likes about going to school. God knows what he can do for me . . . !

Scene 2. *Reception desk — enter* Mrs. Authoritiski

Receptionist: Good afternoon, can I help you?

Mother: Is Mr. Smith in?

Receptionist: Just a moment, I'll see, would you take a seat, please. [*Picks up 'phone and when* Mr. Smith *answers says*]: Mr. Smith, there's a Mrs. Authoritiski to see you — yes, from off the estate — I think the family is well known to the department [*voice loaded with meaning*].

Mother [In a flat voice]: Just tell him I want a word with him — about our Jim.

Receptionist: Well, you will have to sit down and wait Mrs. Authoritski. Mr. Smith is very busy, but he will come when he can — just excuse me . . .
Waiting time . . .

Mr. Smith: Hullo Mrs. Authoritiski, how nice to see you — would you like to come into the office.

Mother: I don't suppose you can help really, but it is getting worse especially with our Dad and now our Mary is expecting — and he's a married man! Our Dad is going to throw her out of the house if she isn't gone by tonight. I'm just about at the end of my tether — and WHAT ARE YOU GOING TO DO ABOUT IT! [*bangs on table*].

Mr. Smith: Tell me a bit more Mrs. Authoritiski — what has Mr. Authoritiski actually said?

Mother: He talks a lot and does nothing. He always says he will do things but never does. Always telling people what they should do, but never does anything himself, but I think he will really hit our Mary and I don't seem to be able to do anything about it . . . He won't have another baby in the house and that's flat — I daren't even talk to him about it. I think I shall leave home or do something silly with myself [*sobs*].

Mr. Smith: Don't you think it would help if I came round and saw you all and had a word with Mary at the same time? What time would be best to come?

Mother: I don't know what you can do Mr. Smith, and it's no use coming before he's had his dinner — he's like a bear with a sore head until he's had something to eat. I don't know what you can do, I'm sure . . .

Scene 3. *Living room*. Mother, Mary *and* Mr. Smith *present*. Door to kitchen opens and Dad comes in

Father: What the 'ell are you still doing here, I thought I told you to get out! [*addressing daughter*]. [*Then turning to* Mr. Smith]: And who asked you to come?

Daughter [*Defiantly*]: He's come to help me.

Father: Help you do what, get rid of your kid?

Mother: You can't treat her like that, she needs help.

Daughter: I don't need his bleeding help — he's not even my proper father!

Father: What do you mean by that — I brought you up didn't I — so I'm your father, and if you don't like it you can get out of it right quick!! No daughter of mine would get herself into trouble [*speaking to* Mr. Smith] are you going to take her away — you're welcome to her, the silly bitch.

Daughter: I'd have left here a long time ago if it hadn't been for Mam.

Mother: Oh shut up the lot of you — you're waking the baby. I'm sick to death with the lot of you.

Father: How do you expect him to help — he can't even make George go to school and
    what good has he done for Peter for God's sake!!

Mr. Smith: Well, you do seem to have a lot to worry you at the moment, let's see if we can
    start to sort things out . . .

    [*Everyone talks together — their voices getting louder and louder.*]

4. CONCLUSION

Simulation used one or more of three basic methods of presentation,
case study, role play and games. They are not new aids in teaching but
it is only recently that they have been used widely. Business methods
have developed management simulations, training in the armed forces
has employed strategy games while in school children run "shops" thus
learning about weights and measures and the use of money. Examples
of simulation exercises potentially useful in studying interaction and
communication in groups have been given. These are sometimes
helpful in studying topics or situations which it may not be possible to
study at first hand and in bringing theoretical material "to life", or
perhaps more accurately, looking at the relevance or irrelevance of
theory in practice. To illustrate this we may recall the games concerned
with the direction(s) of communication in groups or organisations.

It is often presumed that two-way communication is necessarily
preferable to one-way communication. Two-way systems of
communication are becoming more common in industry, for example,
with worker participation in various ways, for example, in joint
consultation committees. In education also, greater emphasis is placed
on teaching methods, such as small tutorial groups, which, depend on
co-operative enterprise involving teacher and student in a different way
to the formal classroom situation. But to assume that two-way
communication is always preferable could be a mistake, because a firm
choice between the two methods may not be called for. Most situations
of any complexity involve both one-way and two-way methods. The real
problem is to decide how both may be used for what purposes each is
better suited. For example, if a large group is to be given a certain
amount of factual material it saves time to give it to them on the one-
way basis. The large group might later be divided into smaller sections
if the material was to be further analysed and discussed and if problems
arising from it were to be worked on. Thus, problems of

communication have to be considered in relation to the purpose of communication. In deciding choice of method the problem is not either one or the other: it is to decide how to use each method in particular circumstances. We may learn that two-way communication in groups or organisations does not come naturally and it does not come merely in response to the information that it is encouraged or an instruction that it should occur. The group leader or sender who wishes to ensure that two-way communication will in fact occur needs to be self-aware. This means being aware of the extent to which his own behaviour might deter people from making a contribution. He will also need to develop insight into relationships between group members. Sometimes people do not contribute because of the attitudes they have towards others and because of the attitudes they assume other people have towards them. He will be concerned about the structure of the discussion. Effective control of the discussion will be aimed at ensuring that the person who wishes to speak but who has difficulty in getting a hearing will be helped to do this.

If the misuse, or indiscriminate use, of simulations is to be avoided a teacher needs to consider a number of points:

1. Is a game really needed at a particular point in a course? Is it going to teach about a process or represent a decision-making situation more effectively than other methods?
2. Is the game that is adopted or chosen a reasonable representation of reality?
3. Does the teacher know enough about the game to run it properly? Can it be managed effectively? Does the teacher have a sufficiently clear understanding of the basic intentions of the game?

A major factor in how effective groups are in performing tasks and supporting their members is the sensitivity of members and leaders to group problems. Many kinds of problems are chronic in most groups even though members may be unaware of them and therefore unable to deal with them. For example, members may fail to pay attention to one another. They may communicate (intentionally or inadvertently) a lack of respect for one another. Preoccupation with their own emotional needs for status, security, attention, influence and comfort may lead members to fail to listen to others. If leaders fail to observe such problems and try to pressurise the group, and if they are insensitive to status differentials in the group which, if they are not resolved, block communication, they may exacerbate tensions rather than cool them. I will now review other training methods using direct experience in groups in unstructured situations and how "openness" in communication between group members may develop. The use of combined methods using two differently run courses as examples can then be considered and learning in the field will also be mentioned.

Notes and Acknowledgements

1. The script of the first role-playing exercise was written by Mrs. Ruth Fanner. When we used it she introduced the exercise and took a leading part in discussion. The exercise was conducted jointly by Ruth Fanner and Peter Day. The latter sometimes took certain roles such as the Departmental Manager and the Policeman. The commentary refers to his performance as the Policeman. The second role-playing script was by John de Roussier and his colleagues. They took the different roles, conducted the exercise and led the discussion afterwards.
2. An experiment in the use of closed-circuit television and role playing aimed at enhancing the skills of social-work students is described in an article which has appeared very recently. It is: Howard, J. and Gooderham, P. (1975) Closed-circuit television in social work training. *Social Work Today*, Vol. 6, No. 7, pp. 194-197.

CHAPTER 7

Group Experience and Learning

1. UNSTRUCTURED SITUATIONS

In unstructured situations group processes are analysed as they occur. A traditional training (or T) group is usually composed of ten to fifteen people who have no other agenda than to use their own experiences in trying to operate as a group and to use them for their own learning. The permutations of groups and group exercises starting from this kind of base line are almost endless. Usually a leader or trainer is assigned to a group and helps them to analyse group processes and interpersonal behaviour. He may also provide a model for other participants, demonstrating his own approach in supportive relationships. It may be misleading to regard this as a single method but this approach to developing communication skills and helping people to become more effective in groups is sometimes referred to as laboratory method, as well as sensitivity or T-group training, while the term encounter groups has also come into use. Before describing the process of training it may be helpful to summarise briefly some misgivings which have been expressed about these developments which became fashionable during the 1960s. All kinds of people and organisations jumped on the bandwagon some of them more incompetent than others. Rapid changes in fads made it difficult to evaluate what such groups could be expected to accomplish. But certain serious drawbacks to sensitivity training, especially in the hands of the less competent or more sadistic leaders have been recognised, and this may help to put this often effective method of behaviour modification into perspective. Perhaps the most serious risk is the emotional upset or nervous breakdown of a participant. Often a breakdown will be recognised and psychiatric help will be sought.

232

There is also the less noticeable withdrawn behaviour or increased defensiveness that may not appear until the experience and may go on for months. Little follow-up is carried out. Some trainers put on a great deal of pressure to produce a "deep" emotional experience but appear to have a casual off-hand concern for possible personal problems which emerge. The potential of T-groups for developing self-insight can lead to freer and more open communication. Changes in individual values and life styles may also result. These may lead to changes in occupations, divorces and marriages, and changes in priorities at home and at work. Some people find that they are less task oriented as their interest in other people increases. This may affect their status at work, recognition and income. For some this may work out well. For others it may not be so fortunate. It is sometimes suggested that these drawbacks can be reduced by screening out unsuitable applicants. Rigid people, and people with emotional problems, could be eliminated, it is suggested. But in practice there appear to be no clear criteria for differentiating good and poor risks. A second problem is evaluating the changes which take place in participants. However, there seems to be some recognition that very disturbed people should not participate. If applicants are well informed about the procedures and possible outcomes and are encouraged to decide for themselves whether they want to go this might be an effective selection method. Some groups refuse to accept people who are *sent* by their organisations to take part. Lawrence (1972) reviewed the "vast array" of group-training activities and referred in more detail to historical developments. He did not deal with the possible risks to individuals mentioned above: he thought that an holistic approach to persons would rescue group training from some of its trivial perspectives. It seems to be important therefore to be clear about what happens in group training. Some people seem to find certain groups artificially divorced from reality: others have found that their groups seemed to facilitate more open communication and greater effectiveness in work teams.

2. TYPICAL DEVELOPMENTS

Typically there are two early developments which may be observed in lab. groups. A group may find that it is having difficulty in obtaining agreement about a topic to discuss or about a decision on what to do. Second, it is also usual to find that members of the group seem to pay little attention to each other or actually do not listen or fail to hear each other. As the group develops some further trends are discernible. Each person tries to listen to others even though he may feel impatient; this listening may be described in two parts. It involves understanding other people's ideas or points of view and examining them objectively or logically. But this is not a primary objective. It is rather to understand the subjective meaning of events or ideas to the other person. If empathy of this kind and at this deep level is communicated to and received by the other person this may have quite a profound emotional impact. It may enable the other person to gain insight in a vivid and sudden way. It may be that participants come to feel more free in their communication in the group. Although this development, becoming less guarded or less defensive, cannot be forced, being honest and realistic may develop progressively. In lab. groups searching and sharing communication and relationships often occurs more quickly than in many other situations. Participants express their judgements and perceptions of each other but these become modified as communication proceeds. Participants gradually do not seek to sit in judgement on each other, but of course they do provide each other with personal feedback. Feedback consists of direct messages from another person about qualities and characteristics that he sees in a subject, that relate to the subjects' awareness of his own potentialities or aspects of his personality that he would like to change. This kind of communication seems to reflect the fact that members are very attentive to one another in the group and that they see each other acting on a variety of levels. The pictures which they form of each other are based on substantial evidence and mutual communication about these pictures may significantly advance self-knowledge. When questions for joint decision arise in a group every member has the opportunity to say what he thinks or feels but he may not be pressed to do so. Remaining silent might be taken to mean that he felt he had nothing to add to the discussion. On the other hand, some people find it difficult to tolerate another's silence and may try to provoke him to break it. Sometimes it may be better to postpone making a decision if one or two people are uncertain, or because, as in the instance just cited, other personal or relational developments become the focus of attention or concern. Another reason for postponement may be a need for further information. The group leader usually takes it upon himself to a greater degree than other members, to observe and attend to all the participants and to try to make sure that no member's contribution becomes overlooked. As the group develops the leader becomes assimilated into group membership as a partner in learning. In the earlier stages the leader is usually recognised as being experienced in such situations. Members are accustomed to people in a leadership position providing a model for their behaviour. They therefore tend to take their cues from him in what is for them a new and ambiguous situation. But this influence of the leader as a model gradually diminishes as indicated above (Schein and Bennis, 1965).

3. OPENNESS IN COMMUNICATION: SOME IMPLICATIONS

Certain assumptions about learning and communication are basic to the laboratory method of training in group relations. It is assumed that people can learn effectively from analysis of their current psychological experience. The facts from which such learning proceeds are the feelings, reactions and observations of other people and understanding how people withhold them from one another. The forces responsible for such inhibitions of communication are essentially attitudes which have been learned. These attitudes are related to conventions about social behaviour. It is assumed that in a training group these forces against communicating attitudes and feelings about other people can be overcome. This enables participants to obtain personal insight into their own and other people's reactions and feelings about events in the group. Quite early in its history members of a training group often find they are having difficulty in agreeing on a topic to be discussed or a task to be performed. They often find that members do not pay much attention to each other and fail to hear what they say to each other. These discoveries may lead to the interpretation that the difficulty of making a decision is due to the inability of group members to have much concern for others or for total group performance because they are preoccupied with their own personal needs.

Training groups foster open and honest communication and a kind of scientific openness to new learning. It might be thought that by helping people to be more open and honest they are helped to be more democratic and to question the uses or abuses of formal authority. In many situations where formal authority has been assumed to be necessary it has been found not only unnecessary but also inefficient by creating a variety of human problems which undermine task performance. Formal systems of authority tend to foster hostile anti-organisation informal groups (Likert, 1961). The effective exercise of formal authority implies a limiting of communication to task relevant information and the exclusion of feelings in the interests of efficiency. It has been found that people whose work is very individual and independent preferred a more task oriented, authoritarian approach which maximized efficiency of communication. People whose work involves more dependence on others preferred employee centred supervision. The nature of the task thus seems to influence workers' preference for style of leadership. Workers' personalities also seem to affect preferences for different types of supervision. Dependent authoritarian men seem to respond well to that kind of leader. Highly independent men seem to be more productive when allowed to participate in decisions by employee-centred supervisors (Vroom, 1960; Vroom and Mann, 1960). An insight which may come out of a training group is that a group should be run autocratically in order to achieve its goals. Weighing the advantages and disadvantages of autocratic and democratic leadership styles is difficult. The issue is whether this kind of human relations training, in teaching democratic leadership methods, undermines traditional forms of authority and thus many organisational settings where authority is highly centralised. For individuals resolving this issue depends on developing awareness of when it is and when it is not appropriate to be open and honest.

It will help to illustrate these developments and one person's reaction to a T-group experience by quoting an account written by a student (Central Training Council in Child Care, 1970).

> The group was made up of 11 female students and a male consultant. We were told that we would look at the group in the "here and now" situation. I found we looked at interaction in the group as it happened. We were expected to, and made to, look at ourself and each other in order to see what we were feeling and doing to one another. What we found we were supposed to express at the time, rather than admit it later or swallow the feelings altogether. When it came to negative feelings I, and I

think others, found this very difficult to do. The consultant was ruthless in squashing attempts at "escapism" from the present situation.

My first reactions to the group were mainly confusion and mild apprehension. I did not grasp the purpose of the group or the role of the consultant. By the end of 3 days I was still not clear about the group's purpose but felt I had gone through a long, painful and very emotional experience.

Fairly early on I began to feel very angry towards the consultant because of the way I felt he was treating the group. I could not bring myself to express this, however. Several times I wanted to get up and slam out in protest but again I did nothing. By the second day I was still getting angry, at members of the group occasionally as well as at the consultant, but I no longer wanted to leave. I felt compelled to stay and see through whatever it was we were "doing". There was a need to deal with the situations which developed, round them off and bring them to some sort of finished, positive end.

I began to feel that "the group" had an existence of its own quite separate from either any one member or the total number. It was some kind of being.

There continued to be times when I was explosively angry wanting to jump up or shout out loud. Usually this anger was directed still against the consultant, sometimes other members. At other times I felt shocked at the way I thought the consultant dealt with members. Sometimes tension in the group became almost unbearable. Once or twice it seemed we must take sides when a conflict developed between 2 members.

It became clearer how little we really knew of one another and how necessary honesty was to reach this knowledge but also how difficult it sometimes was to be that honest.

Pressure and tension became so great at one point that most of group wept at the end of the session. This was something I and several others admitted we found difficult to do. In fact I could bear to have only one other group member with me as I cried. This experience did not help to keep further tension down in the group for again in a following session I felt I would cry helplessly, but without understanding why.

By the end of the final session nothing had been neatly rounded off and finished.

We returned to our placements the following day and for the remaining 3 days of the week I felt completely unable to cope with anything especially clients. I felt paralysed. By the next week this had begun to wear off but there was still a terrible need to talk incessantly about "the group". I spoke mostly to other students on the placement who were also group members. But social work and secretarial staff also received a good deal of the flood. I felt I was trying to carry out the tidying-up process that had been denied at the end of the group. Until about 2 weeks later I felt very emotionally battered and raw. I also felt as if I had grown a new dimension and because of my own emotional upset, I was able to pick up or sense much more quickly other people's feelings and emotional conflicts. This applied in personal life as well as professionally with clients.

Another result was that I seemed often to see situations that had occurred in the group occurring in groups in which I was involved on the placement. I belonged to 2 groups. One was of about a dozen workers from various agencies who met weekly to discuss cases and ideas in general. The second group was 3 or 4 mothers talking to a psychologist about their children, homes, problems, etc. In both groups I felt at times as if my own group experiences were being repeated and I was able to pick up the feelings and undercurrents much more quickly, examine them and see why they were occurring. To some extent the same thing happened on a social level also.

Much of these intense feelings have now gone but I did, and still do, feel expanded as a person. I can see why all feelings, negative and positive have to be dealt with and to some extent I think I try to do this more now than I did. The 11 in the group had ostensibly been friends or at least friendly for almost a year. We all were intelligent enough and spoke enough of the same kind of language to understand one another. Yet we found it hard to really speak, reveal feelings and express honest opinions of and to one another. I know often I was so worried about myself in a situation I was unable to see the need of the person next to me for reassurance about their position, for help, for backing.

My ultra-sensitivity after the group made me aware of all these things, it seemed. I also began to see how difficult it must be for a client who is as articulate as I am, does not feel on my "level" and who may not know me very well, to be able to speak to me about feelings he had about this situation and my part in it.

At the time I found the experience painful and disturbing. Looking back I still feel that but I also feel it was something I am glad I had as it has shown me how I can function better as a person and as a social worker. I feel almost as if I have been privileged to see something few other people have and as a result have had something added to myself.

Smith (1969) has made it very clear that research into behaviour modification should evade the problem of values, and that theoretical work which has implications for practise (for example, on social skills) probably cannot evade this. Those connected with T-groups training argue that the personal and immediate nature of what is talked about make it more likely to enhance social skill than other methods rooted in abstraction or detached intellectual insight. In enhancing interpersonal skills sensitivity training is seen as correcting the effect of contemporary education. How effective is sensitivity training? It seems, from work so far, that it has a long lasting effect on approximately 60% of people who undertake it. As far as their subsequent behaviour is concerned people who work with them find them more perceptive and co-operative, and not as defensive as before (Cooper and Mangham, 1971). They appear less authoritarian and less concerned with control behaviour, and more with affection behaviour (Nadler and Fink, 1970; Smith, 1964). T-groups appear to produce changes in behaviour. However, it is not clear whether the new kinds of behaviour lead people to be more effective in all kinds of social situations. It seems, though, that they will increase effectiveness in developing co-operation between people, in improving communication with others, while they will decrease the effectiveness of a person for whom it is necessary to keep secrets and to use bluff with others (Campbell and Dunnette, 1968). Further evidence assembled by Cooper (1974) seems to support the findings quoted above. This study assessed the disturbing effects of sensitivity training using questionnaires completed by participants and their families and friends. Participants showed increases in neuroticism as a result of training but this was not confirmed by the family and friends two weeks after the T-group. A large number of trainees saw themselves, and were seen by their family, friends and children, as slightly better able to cope with personal and family problems, more happy, better able to get on with their children and better able to communicate. It was pointed out that participants seem to have a halo effect as a result of the course. Second, a sizeable group of participants and close family and friends recorded "no difference" or "the same", that is, that no change was perceived. However, the study indicated that fears about T-groups are misplaced and for a large number of trainees they seemed to be beneficial.

4. COMBINED METHODS: FIRST ILLUSTRATION

I now review and summarise training schemes which employ combinations of methods. There is evidence of the strong influence of the laboratory methods described earlier but the contrasts noted are of interest. It will be seen that the courses described were not primarily for social workers. The search for illustrative material for this chapter was greatly hindered by monopolistic capitalism and a pseudo-religious orientation towards T-groups. I was told by one facilitator or leader first of all that he had ethical objections to releasing information. Later I was told frankly that the assembly of material had been a time-consuming business and the material had a monetary value. In some other cases it was said that the sending of written material would be of no use to me (even though I explained that I had had group experience). Personal explanations by trainers and actual participation in *their* groups were the *only* ways of developing understanding. My inquiries have had to be comprehensive. The prevalence of the attitudes illustrated unfortunately lends some credence to the criticisms summarised earlier. To balance the account (and possibly to counter the bias introduced by the writer's experiences) the reader would be well advised to look at the literature that is available on the subject (e.g. Smith, 1969; Cooper and Mangham, 1971). It will be seen that the courses which are now described are very ready to communicate their ideas and experiences: both John Heron and Lawrence Nevard took great trouble in facilitating my use of the material they have developed. The reader is thus enabled to make his own assessment of these approaches.

The Human Potential Research Project of the University of Surrey has run a series of courses described as training for change. These two courses have been for members of staff of hospitals for the mentally handicapped (and a third course was for voluntary help organisers in the Health Service). Among the objectives of these courses have been the development of skills in communication and exploring attitudes to personal and organisational change. Both courses were experimental and designed to discover methods of training suitable for reorientating staff toward modern concepts of residential care. The report on the course contained a full description of what happened on each of the fourteen days. It included feed-back sheets from participants and their accounts of the problems involved in the care of the mentally handicapped. The excerpts which follow are selected so as to provide a picture of the learning methods employed and how the participants viewed the course (Heron *et al.*, 1972).

Staff conceived the course as a co-operative and multi-disciplinary venture combing staff resources, participants' resources and external resources. These three groups combined together to constitute a learning community. The course was titled "A Multidisciplinary Skills Laboratory". The term "laboratory" implies the creation of an experimental climate for innovation and risk-taking as a means of facilitating change of attitude and behaviour. Staff resources comprised skills in group relations training methods and relevant background theory in the behavioural sciences. The design for the course was as follows:

1.   The first two days were spent in highly participative communication exercises and role-play, in order to de-freeze participants and prepare for an imaginative and creative use of the third day.

2.   The third day called upon the resources of participants to plan

the remainder of their course in a co-operative exercise with the staff: thereafter we could all say it was *our* course, not "just another course".

3.   The remainder of the course fulfilled the programme devised on the third day, bringing in outside resources to meet participants' stated needs interests, with many periods left free for team-development exercises involving staff and participants only.

4.   The final day was devoted to planning evaluation and a course report.

A brief description of these methods follows:

Communication Exercises: in small groups of five or six.

(a)   Pattern of verbal interaction: anyone can talk but only when holding the group's single beanbag.

(b)   Non-verbal interaction: each silently explores by sight the non-verbal cues of other members of the group.

(c)   Members give each other feed-back on the non-linguistic aspects of each other's speech.

In pairs

(d)   Non-verbal interaction: silent gazing.

(e)   Image sharing: comparing how I think my partner sees me with how my partner sees me.

In groups

(f)   Tacit norms: identify redundant tacit norms in the group and adopt alternative behaviour.

(g)   Self-disclosure: each talks of hidden aspirations and unfulfilled ambitions.

Role-play: participants explore attitudes and communication processes by enacting on-the-job situations.

Confrontation and role-reversal: the clash of attitudes between two real-life protagonists is made overt; each then assumes the role of the other to explore the other's attitudes "from within".

Problem-solving: a cycle for dealing with a particular problem.
(a) Clarify the symptoms.
(b) Discriminate all possible causes.
(c) Isolate relevant causes.
(d) Generate wide range of alternative solutions without premature evaluation.
(e) Evaluate solutions and select the most viable.

Critical incident analysis: participants examine from their experience a critical incident in the human relations of an organisation — a crisis of communication, decision-making, decision implementation and so on. This can be used to identify a problem in terms of its symptoms and causes and to lead into a problem-solving cycle; or it may lead into role-play.

Action-planning: a cycle for leading to a decision about action. It assumes a goal or viable solution is to hand.
(a) Discriminate the relevant obstacles and difficulties in implementing the idea.
(b) Distinguish between alterable and unalterable constraints.
(c) Generate alternative means to implement the idea without premature evaluation.
(d) Evaluate the means in the light of the constraints and select the most viable.
(e) Decide specific action steps.

Group discussion: a discussion on specific issues and their underlying attitudes.

Group interaction with ground-rules: an exploration of personal and interpersonal attitudes by discussing a topic in accordance with the following ground-rules:
(a) Speak only in the first person.
(b) Speak directly to others in the group (i.e. address them in the second person singular).
(c) Avoid generalisations, intellectualisation, and speaking for anyone else but yourself.

Fishbowl discussion: two or three start a discussion in an inner circle; as participants enter the discussion they move from the outer circle to join the inner circle.

Monodrama: one participant has two or more chairs to represent different aspects of himself and his attitudes. He moves from chair to chair to speak for each in dialogue with the others.

Creative brainstorming: generating ideas in small groups without pausing to evaluate them.

The course had a block of three continuous days at the outset and a similar block at the end, with eight days at weekly intervals between these two blocks — a total of fourteen days. Each day was from 10 a.m. to 5 p.m. with four periods of about 1 hour and 20 minutes each — a total of fifty-six periods. Thirty-four periods were devoted to a variety of team development exercises involving staff and participants only: these occupied the whole of the first five days and all but six periods of the last five days. Twenty-two periods were spent with outside resources: they gave talks and/or engaged in discussion for sixteen periods and participated in task groups and other activities for six periods.

In the morning session of day 11, participants examined the following question in a group dynamics session, using the same ground-rules as before: What effects on your attitudes and behaviour in your job can you attribute in any way to attendance at this course?

Comments

"I appreciate different opinions and points of view."

"I understand someone else's point of view (by imaginary role reversal)."

"Gain in self-confidence: enough strength to discuss new ideas in the hospital."

"I listen a little more, realise other people's problems more."

"More aware of problems, more able to discuss them."

"More knowledge; have courage to ask to go to case conferences; starting to think about discussing problems with superiors."

"More tolerant to people who are subjected to a hierarchy."

"Increasingly aware of other people; more consideration of other points of view; less quick to make value judgements; less tendency to rule out ideas as impractical."

"More tolerant with voluntary workers."

"More conscious of other people; look at people more directly; plucking up courage to introduce negative feedback in the department."

"Have found other people with the same problems; put myself in other people's positions; still find great difficulty with difficult people; opportunity to view attitudes of other people on the course, how they react in their roles."

"I know more about other people and their ideas."

"More self-confidence; able to fight more in the hospital; less afraid of victimisation."

"Learned by listening."

Participants' evaluation of the course was effected by a self-report questionnaire containing twelve questions, which was completed in the week following the end of the course. There was also a course review discussion on day 11: see feed-back sheet for details.

Of the fifteen original participants, fourteen responded to the questionnaire (one was hospitalised for surgery immediately after the course).

Course Content and Design

Question 1 asked which of the following activities was most valuable (they are given here in rank order with the number of mentions each received): group discussions with visitors (11), creative brainstorming (8), action-planning (8), role-playing (6), talks (5), group discussions with ground rules (5), critical incidents analysis (1). Group discussions with visitors also appeared at the top of the list of responses to question 3, "What did you enjoy most?" (it was chosen by six respondents). Question 2 asked what was disliked the most: top of the list was "being talked *at*" (seven respondents).

With respect to question 1, which also asked in what way the activities named have been valuable, group discussions with visitors were valued because of their effect in giving an appreciation of the problems of others working in the field. Brainstorming and action-planning were valued because of the way they facilitate creative involvement. Role-playing was valued because it gives insight into the attitudes of others. Talks were valued for their information content. And group discussions with ground rules for their effect in sharpening group members' appreciation of each others' points of view.

The most controversial part of the course design introduced by the staff was the allocation of the first two days to experiential exercises that challenge conventional rigidities. Question 5 asked for comments on each of the first three days. With respect to day 1 on communication exercises, nine of the fourteen respondents made positive comments: six said they could see the point and purpose of it in retrospect although they found it embarrassing/difficult/pointless at the time; three commented that it "increased alertness", was "very informative", was "very interesting and valuable". Three others saw the day as "waste of time", "difficult", "painful"; one was "not impressed" and one made no comment. The whole of day 2 was spent on attitude exploration through role-play. One respondent made no comment; the other thirteen appreciated the day and found it insightful / informative / destructuring / creative / beneficial / enjoyable, but six of these also found it embarrassing / difficult / frightening / threatening. Day 3, spent on designing the rest of the course, receives a strong flood of positive comment from thirteen respondents (no Comment from one). They saw the day as interesting / efficient / revealing / beneficial / worthwhile / constructive / satisfying; and six commented on democracy in design / participants' direction of course / team spirit / group cohesion.

Proposals for Future Courses

Staff views

1. The highly participative type of course, based on the concept of a peer-group learning community, should be repeated, since it involves participants in the exercise of skills that can be directly transferred and applied to bringing about organisational change. And improved patient

care is very much a function of improved communication, co-operation, delegation within the hospital organisation, within local authority organisation and between the two.

2. But the overall effectiveness of this type of course in influencing organisational change could be greatly improved by a wider selection of participants. The most comprehensive mix would include the following:

(a) local authority staff as well as hospital staff;

(b) a diagonal slice through both the local authority organisation and the hospital organisation.

A diagonal slice means that all hierarchical levels should be represented, especially senior medical and administrative staff, and that those on adjacent levels should be from different departments/hospitals. Such a diagonal slice relieves participants of the immediate constraining tensions of a direct chain of command. It is particularly important that representatives of top levels should be present on a course of this kind.

3. It is also important that judgements about training needs should be related to the fullest possible consultation with prospective participants, including a pre-course briefing in the hospitals by university staff and previous participants.

4. A similar initial design could usefully be followed, with two days of destructuring exercises, devised and designed to bring out fully their relevance to on-the-job performance, followed by a day spent on course design in which staff and participants co-operate by sharing their resources. It is possible that a greater incidence of experiential forms of learning should be included in the subsequent part of the course.

Participants' Views

Question 10 on the post-course questionnaire asked participants what changes in design they would suggest if the course were to be run again for a different group of people working in the field of mental handicap. The experiential forms of learning receive the greatest amount of comment. Four respondents recommended more of it, especially role-playing; four suggested a reduction of experiential exercises in the first two days; one wanted the first three days eliminated and replaced by hospital visits; one suggested having the course design session on the first day; one suggested less role-play and more talks and discussions; one found the design adequate, one suggested two days a week rather than one; one suggested that medical staff should attend. On balance, the consensus, explicitly or tacitly, is in favour of retaining experiential exercises.

A second course was held and reported in 1973. The selected excerpts which follow indicate the way in which the first experience was used in the further development of the training (Brown, 1973).

The project staff used the notion of a self-directed learning community of peers. This model suggests a framework in which staff resources, participants' resources and external resources are made available, and in which distinctions between trained and trainee dissolve. In addition, the model included the use of highly participative exercises. These functioned as community building techniques, and as training devices for self-directed and experiential learning. The participants were a Group Liaison Officer, a Voluntary Services Organiser, two senior nursing officers, a ward sister, a student nurse, a teacher, a speech therapist, member of the League of Friends, two charge nurses, a Training Project Officer, a Mental Handicap Project Officer, a member of the Hospital Management Committee. They represented a diagonal slice through a hospital organisation. The course was voluntary, and the initial membership included a second ward sister, a principal psychologist, and a Research Assistant in Management Training, who dropped out after the three-day introductory block. Project staff thought it necessary and desirable that a course using the model of a self-directed learning community should be planned co-operatively by course members. Consequently, the extent of the design which was presented to participants on the first day was:

1. An introductory three-day block.
2. Eight days, once a week.
3. A closing three-day block.

The introductory block was further structured into a two-day meeting and defreezing period, to make way for a creative use of the third day, spent designing the rest of the course.

The model of a self-directed learning community has a restricted and general use, which are not mutually incompatible. The restricted use is as a training device pure and simple; that is, it forms part of an hypothesis about learning processes in groups, which predicts that working together in the context of shared leadership improves the uptake and retention of knowledge. The general use suggests in addition that an individual is best seen as having a capacity for self-directed agency, and that a learning community of this sort will reveal his human potential more readily than other contexts. Implications of the wider use of the model are that members of the community will engage in close interaction, will take risks in disclosing and sharing their views, will be aware of and take steps to avoid patterns of dominance and self-effacement, will be aware of and respect the needs of other members. I would suggest that the success of the restricted use of the model will depend largely on the extent of the incorporation of these elements of the general use. The construction of such a community presupposes abandoning the traditional roles of lecturer and audience, trainer and trainee. The actions of staff in this context are facilitative or enabling, rather than directive; that is to say, staff suggest techniques and exercises designed to create an atmosphere of trust and support, to disclose the self-directed potential of the participants, and to ensure that creative use is made of community resources. These exercises will necessarily be highly participative; they are also open ended, inasmuch as one function of a self-directed community can be to adapt and invent techniques for its own use. Exercises which were used in this course, during the defreezing period and elsewhere, included:

(A)   Open Meeting, Here and Now Focusing, Self-actualisation Exercises

A person explores the patterns of verbal and non-verbal interaction within the group by:
  (i) Silently meeting and holding the other's gaze.
 (ii) Describing as fully as possible the immediate experience of sitting with a partner.
(iii) Disclosing to a partner hidden aspirations and unfulfilled ambitions.

(iv) Openly appreciating another person.

(v) Openly describing and appreciating oneself.

(vi) Attentively and without interruption listening to a partner describe the tensions during the day.

(vii) Using the space of the room to mill around and introduce oneself to others.

(viii) Using simple games to overcome and discharge embarrassment by laughing.

(ix) Using the ground rules of speak only in the first person, speak directly to others in the group (i.e. address them in the second person singular), avoid generalisations, intellectualisation and speaking for anyone else but yourself.

(B) Exercises for Understanding and Resolving Job Conflicts

Role play: participants enact a situation, playing the characters who took part.

Alter egoing: the "audience" assume the different aspects of the characters and speak for them as they think appropriate.

Confrontation and role reversal: the clash of attitudes between two real-life protagonists is made clear; each then assumes the role of the other to explore the other's attitude from within.

Surplus reality: participants explore the range of possible alternatives to a situation by enacting them.

Critical incident analysis: participants examine from their experience a critical incident in the human relations of an organisation — a crisis of communication, decision-making, decision implementation, and so on. This can be used to identify a problem and its symptoms and causes (to lead into a problem-solving cycle) or it may lead into role play.

(C)   Producing an Open Dynamic within the Community

Group confrontation: participants form groups in which all members hold similar attitudes, and jointly challenge or confront another group.

Image sharing: members of a group compare how they see themselves with how the members of another group see them.

Identifying and abandoning redundant norms: participants identify the patterns of behaviour which the community has covertly adopted and explicitly abandon those it does not require.

(D)   Co-operative Approach to Tasks

The community uses voting and consensus procedures to engage in task oriented exercises.

Action planning: a cycle for leading to a decision about action. It assumes a goal or viable solution is to hand.
  (i) Discriminate the relevant obstacles and difficulties in implementing the idea.
  (ii) Distinguish between alterable and unalterable constraints.
  (iii) Generate alternative means to implement the idea without premature evaluation.
  (iv) Evaluate the means in the light of the constraints and select the most viable.
  (v) Decide specific action steps.

Creative brainstorming: generating ideas in small groups without pausing to evaluate them.

This is a summary of what happened on particular days.

Days 1 and 2.   Destructuring period; individual and group experiential exercises.

Day 3.   Course planning; small and large group tasks.

Day 4.   Work and involvement; discussion with ground rules; counselling.

Day 5.   Leadership styles; decision-making exercises.
Day 6.   Personal attitude exploration.
Day 7.   Organisational change (outside speaker).
Day 8.   Identification of job conflicts; hospital communication.
Day 9.   Parents (outside speakers); strategies for parental involvement.
Day 10.   Hospital friction.
Day 11.   (Regional Board Member); communication issues (Outside speaker); therapy and assessment.
Day 12.   Euthanasia; personal fantasy and disclosure; nursing teamwork.
Day 13.   A clinical psychologist on multi-disciplinary teamwork; identification of on-course change job attitudes.
Day 14.   Evaluation and questionnaire design.

Outside speakers were asked to interact with the community with respect to one or more of the following issues: organisational change; sharing job descriptions, clarification of role; leadership styles and the use of power; use of resources; constraints within organisation; areas of conflict; hospital morale; staff-patient attitudes; acceptance of community role; relevance of various professions to mental handicap; needs of patients; objectives and policies of a hospital group.

Community sessions. The purpose of these sessions was seen to be to develop the following skills: interpersonal skills (awareness of self and others, communication skills, decision-making, interviewing); creative thinking; action-planning skills; team-building skills, appreciation of each others' job descriptions. Possible methods to be adopted by the community were listed as follows: group discussion; group discussion with ground rules; structured exercises; role play; psychodrama; monodrama; brainstorming; communication exercises; problem-solving cycle; action-planning cycle; critical incident analysis; case study; seminars; theory inputs; co-counselling; CCTV; films; play and games; feedback sheets. It was agreed that an appropriate strategy for these sessions would be to plan them as a function of the unfolding dynamic of the group. An overall strategy adopted by the community was that it would use the course as an agency of organisational change and development.

Day 14

We spent the morning discussing follow-up strategies to maintain a community nucleus. The afternoon was spent designing the questionaire. The final form was:

1. What value has the course been to you?
2. How has the course helped you in your present work?
3. How do you see the course helping you in the future?
4. Would you have preferred fourteen *consecutive* days?
5. How do you *now* evaluate the first three days?
6. What has been the effect on the course of the absence of medical staff?
7. Have you been usefully occupied while on the course?
8. How will the patients benefit from your attending the course?
9 How would you improve this course?
10. Would you have preferred a more traditional course?
11. How has the course affected your perception of Hospital Management?
12. Has the course affected how you see your role in the Hospital Team?
13. Was the day at Royal Earlswood beneficial to you? If so, how?
14. What did you enjoy the most?
15. How well do course members represent hospital staff?
16. Would you have liked to have had more hospital groups represented?
17. Would you have preferred a smaller or larger number of course members?
18. Please comment on the balance of outside speakers, Royal Earlswood visitors and community sessions.
19 Has the course had any negative effects on you?
20. Was community effectiveness diminished by the periodic absence of John Heron?
21. What is your opinion of John Heron's facilitative style?
22. What did you find the most embarrassing?
23. What made the most impact on you? In what way?

Questionnaire

During the final day community members produced a questionnaire based on a consensus of the questions they wished to ask and to answer about the course. The response rate was 11 out of 12, and the responses themselves were encouraging, perceptive and implied a high degree of commitment to the training methods used. A full analysis of the answers is given below, but a summary of the results suggests that:

1. The acquisition of skills gained in community interaction are relevant and applicable to on the job situation.
2. Post-course reactions to the hospital structure are typically ones on increased understanding.
3. The use of a defreezing period was vindicated, though participants found this one of the most difficult aspects of the course.
4. The questionnaire alone is a rough indication of the effect of the course on participants; there are six questions which concern positive responses, four questions which concern community composition.

Analysis

The questionnaire consisted of twenty-three questions (see feedback sheet for final day). They appear to be grouped in the following way:

(A) Questions 1,2,3,8,14,23 ask about the positive personal and professional effects of the course; (B) Questions 11,12 ask about attitude changes which have been taken place during the course; (C) Question 4 asks about the course structure; (D) Questions 6,15,16,17 ask about the composition of the community; (E) Questions 9,10,13,18 ask about the course design; (F) Question 5, and the majority response to question 22, ask about the effect of the defreezing and planning block; (G) Question 19 asks for negative effects; (H) Questions 20 and 21 ask for participants' reactions to the facilitator.

Responses to group (A) indicate that the most valuable gains were increased understanding of and liking for on-course and off-course colleagues and patients. This reply occurred nine times to question 1, four times to question 2, five times to question 3, four times to question 8, five times to question 14 and five times to question 23. Six responses concerned an increase in the skills and confidence of handling people, four referred specifically to the application skills in hospital teamwork. Five responses to question 14 and five to question 23 expressed gains from particular sessions with outside resources. One response to question 14 mentioned the value of the "small day" (see feedback sheet). One response was that the course was an exercise in changing other's attitudes; one response was that the course had affected attitudes to organisational change. Nine responses to this group could not identify or doubted gains.

In group (B), five participants found that they understood Hospital Management better after the course, three found that the course confirmed their previous view and three were unable to answer. Six participants said that the course had not affected their view of their hospital team, four thought it had promoted closer teamwork, and one said there was no team. Five participants were satisfied with the structure of the course, five considered fourteen consecutive days more suitable; one participant was undecided.

In group (D), responses to questions 15, 16 and 17 indicated that the size of the community was satisfactory and that the members were a fairly good representation of hospital staff. This was tempered by the replies to question 6, where seven participants would have liked medical staff to be represented. The issue of drawing a larger cross-section from hospitals was also expressed in three responses.

In group (E), six responses suggested a larger cross-section of hospital staff for a similar course; seven responses regretted the allocation of so many sessions to community resources. Further improvements included a suggestion that a future course be residential, that more small group exercises be introduced, that Project staff invite outside speakers and hospital seniors for protocol reasons. Nine participants preferred the model of a self-directed course, two would have preferred a more traditional one. Six participants did not find the day at Earlswood helpful, of these one found his work intruded into the community, and two said they were sufficiently familiar with the hospital. Two participants found they could not relate more to community issues by being on the spot and four welcomed the feedback from strangers to the hospital. The reply to question 5 indicated the value of the introductory block. All participants found the use of experiential exercises useful as defreezing techniques, two particularly enjoyed the planning on day 3. However, there were qualifications that the defreezing period had been too long, and additionally, eight participants listed this part of the course as the most embarrassing.

Retrospect

A distinctive feature of the course was the frank exchange of views and experiences between community members. The gains from this kind of interaction are typically the enjoyment of the concomitant atmosphere of trust, a sensitivity to others' views and needs, a willingness to use the support of the community to take risks as part of a process of innovation, Staff would suggest that the growth of this openness amongst community members was due in large measure to the radical methods used on days 1 and 2. The correlation between the views expressed via the questionnaires, that these days were necessary to get the course off the ground, and that they caused the most embarrassment, is consistent with the thesis that was used as an introduction to the defreezing period. The construction of a self-directed community of peers requires the dropping of role defences by participants; it is precisely this action which causes embarrassment and uncertainty. As the course progressed it became apparent that the consensus orientation was towards process rather than task. This can be unsettling, inasmuch as it represents a break from the traditional view of training programmes, which are geared to visible work outputs. However, what were essentially staff fears that participants would feel that they were not getting anything out of the course were discounted by the continuing enthusiasm of participants. The responses to questions 2 and 3 of the questionnaire indicate the recognition of participants of the application of process skills in their work situation. Proposals for future courses of this type are:

1. That staff assume responsibility for approaching outside speakers and inviting them in to participate in selected sessions.
2. That the cross-section of the hospital organisation which participants represent be extended vertically and horizontally to include group secretary, consultants, and other members of the professional executive.

3. That the use of "block" periods be increased, so that a structure might be 3 days + 2 single days + 4 days + 2 single days + 3 days. These blocks might be residential.

The use of outside resources was organised with only modest success. This was partly due to an apparent reluctance of speakers or R.E. seniors approached to commit themselves to a fixed date for participation on the course. Proposal (1), above, may improve the gathering and allocation of outside resources. The result of this administrative mistake meant that the speakers participated towards the end of the course; the community had little opportunity to work in depth with the issues which arose from these sessions. Interaction between speakers and the community was characterised by openness and a sensitivity to conflicting views. A measure of the success of the development of community support was the ease with which speakers were welcomed and invited to open with community members.

5.   COMBINED METHODS: SECOND ILLUSTRATION

Professional training has tended to focus narrowly on particular methods of intervention and also to employ limited sources of learning and to exclude others. It has been found that training courses that integrate a variety of learning methods, focusing systematically on cone subjects round which secondary dimensions can be constructed, are most effective (Truax and Carkhuff, 1967; Carkhuff and Berenson, 1967). It may be that the use of combined methods speeds up the learning process. The next illustration is of a series of short courses which seem to have been influenced by this idea. Management courses for nurses have been provided by Slough College of Technology since 1968. The information about their aims and methods given here can be compared and contrasted with the material of the University of Surrey. It is derived from an explanatory paper for Training Officers (Nevard, 1972).

Objectives and assumptions

Before any course of training programme can be designed,

fundamental assumptions have to be made. Because the assumptions made in different types of course in management training vary widely, we thought we ought clearly to state our own. We have assumed:

(a) that many men and women do not make adequate use of their resources;

(b) that both perception and utilisation of resources can be improved;

(c) that resources are of many kinds, some internal and some external to the individual;

(d) that this improvement initiates a process of development;

(e) that training in the perception and utilisation of resources cannot be conducted satisfactorily by static and formal methods of instruction;

(f) that the training experience must not be destructive in character, must rather be a dynamic, releasing, creative experience, providing great satisfaction.

Having declared our basic assumptions, we can set objectives at three levels; *first,* the *general* objectives of the programmes; *second, course* objectives for course members (so that they have acceptable "targets" at which to aim), and *third, sessional* objectives for use by tutors and others interested in the content of the courses.

As a result of the discussions we had with senior members of the Health Service, we think courses should do three things. They should *firstly* make course members more aware of their own inner resources and the ways in which they can be used; *secondly,* they should convey factual information about management techniques and the structure of the Health Service; and *thirdly,* they should provide opportunity for members to experiment in the use of the insight and techniques acquired or discussed during the course. The course thus becomes a kind of management "laboratory", in which experiment is followed by free discussion. When we worked these ideas out in detail, the "general objectives" for each programme became:

(a) to increase the total awareness of course members, so that perception of their resources is heightened, and they become more aware of potential uses;

(b) to give course members an understanding of the principles of organisation;

(c) to convey factual information about the structure of the Health Service, and changes in approach to major problems in the field of health service provision;

(d) to enable course members to carry out tasks in groups under controlled conditions, so that they can better assess their own behaviour and understand the behaviour of others;

(e) to provide training in social skills (e.g. interviewing, committee work, etc.) through a balanced programme of experiences and seminars;

(f) to facilitate the application of newly acquired skills in the working environment.

These objectives specify the kind of learning situation we are trying to create, and we hope that as the result of learning which has taken place on the course, members will have:

(a) diagnosed his/her own training needs in relation to the course syllabus and the managerial aspects of his job;

(b) acquired such knowledge and skills to meet these needs as the limited duration of the course will allow;

(c) designed an on-going programme of self-development so that the training can be continued back "on the job";

(d) arranged an interview with a senior responsible officer to discuss and facilitate the implementation of the personal development plan, i.e. by projects, tutorials, guidance, study days, etc.

Many of the ideas discussed in the course are known to some members of the course before they come, and we think that the main function of the tutor is to enable course members to identify their own ideas and to make them available for use by the whole group.

Plan of the programme

The Programme consists of four major sections:

1. *An "Induction Day"* (sometimes called an Orientation Day), during which course members introduce themselves to each other, examine the methods of the course, discuss the problems associated with projects, and consider the implications of the basic assumptions of the course.

2. *A three-week course* — referred to here as "the main course" — consisting of a balanced set of seminars, group discussions, experiments and short lectures.

3. *A project*, preferably chosen by the course member in conjunction with a senior member of his organisation.

4. *Two Review Days*, when course members' projects are presented to the course and action plans are examined.

Each of these elements is important, and the value of the whole experience will be lessened if a member is unable to take part in any one of the sections.

The Induction Day is *essential* to course members and to tutorial staff. We try to "tailor" courses to meet the needs of each group of members, and we cannot do this unless we meet members on an Induction Day. Although the techniques used on the course have been thoroughly tested, they are very different from the formal teaching methods most people have experienced in the past. It is essential to explain to course members *what* we are doing, and *why*, and to give them a chance of exploring the value-judgements implicit in the "general objectives". *The main course* has been built up over a period of time on a sound experimental basis. This does *not* mean that we change the course around "to see what happens" — we do not want change merely for its own sake. We try to "tailor" the course and sessions to the needs of members, but we are not always successful. If there is an unfavourable reaction to one particular session do not necessarily scrap the session, but try to identify what went wrong and rectify it. If there is a similar reaction to the same session during later courses, we can modify the session further in the light of the new information we have received, or drop it altogether. We try to remember that the men and women who join our courses have had far more experience of health service management than we shall ever have, and we cannot claim to be "management experts" who will show the erring manager the folly of his ways! We will not *teach* management; we will try to help members to *learn* management, and to increase understanding and performance through the exchange of ideas and information.

While we have been developing the course, we have had to overcome certain problems. The capacity of members for statistics is limited, and attempts to devote one whole day to this subject were a notable failure! The capacity of office reproduction facilities is also limited, and certain work is carried out at a particular time in the course so that material produced by members can be reproduced and used in further practical sessions later (e.g. Staff Selection I and II, and Preparation of Statements for Panel). A complication of a different type is a characteristic of all learning and is sometimes called "the learning plateau". It is summarised in the comment "You learn to skate in the summer, and to swim in the winter". There is usually a period of time between the point at which material is made available for learning and the point when the material is understood or used. If a student needs to acquire certain facts about the History of Tudor England, or the English Legal System, if it is a subject which interests him, the period will probably be relatively short. On the other hand, where the material to be learned may cause the student to examine and perhaps change his/her attitudes and value-judgements, the period may be very much longer, and may have to be measured in weeks or even months. This is especially the case in management training, where the discovery of new attitudes, new kinds of information and different approaches taken by members of other disciplines may be a painful process. This kind of sensitivity to course material increases the difficulties faced by tutors when trying to assess the effect and impact of courses, because during the course the student may openly reject the material presented. However, when the course is over, the process of assimilation and change may take place without the student having been aware of it, and an observer at a later date may find him using the material he had previously "rejected".

The present courses have been designed on the basis of this kind of thinking, and the current plan looks like this:

GROUP A

General theme	*Subject heading*
Starting where the course member is	Methods. Course/Personal Objectives
	Hospital Management Problems
	What is Management?
	Roles in hospital organisation

GROUP B

Processes of Thinking, and their use	Learning for Leadership Management and its functions Problem-solving Work on Projects
Thinking and *other people*	Communication

GROUP C		**GROUP D**	
Theme	*Subject*	*Theme*	*Subject*
Groups and their Problems	Barrier Problems Study of Group Structure Preparation of Studies for Panel	*Organisation* — theory and techniques	Interviewing and Appraisal Measurement and Management Staff Selection (1) and (2) Human Relations Committee Procedures

(GROUPS C AND D RUN CONCURRENTLY)

GROUP E	*Subject heading*
General theme *Application* of material learned in study of groups, and organisational techniques	Effective use of Committees Group Pressures in Committees Practical Selection Interviewing Trend Valley Hospital Group Human Relations (2) Delegation Management by Objectives
Application of all course material to the *individual's working situation*	Discussion with Panel Preparation of Action Plans Presentation of Action Plans Project Work

Action plans

During the course, members are asked to keep a diary of the material they hope to be able to use when they return to the hospital. On the last day they are asked to prepare "action plans" from this material, i.e. "What plans do you propose to make for yourself, for the team you work with, for your department, for your involvement in the life of the hospital in the short, medium and long term?" They are asked to comment on the way in which they have implemented these plans when they return to the Review Day(s).

Sensitivity training

We hope that the process of sensitivity training will go on throughout the course, but there are four major sessions in which this aspect of training is emphasised. They may be regarded as "centres of interaction", strategically placed so that they relate to the more formal activity taking place in the course at about the same time. The tasks suggested for these sessions deliberately minimise structure, but the task requires course members to relate to each other. The relationships so created can be examined when the task is completed, using the valuable insights and approaches derived from training experiences known as "T-groups". During "T-group" training, group members have no prearranged time-table. The discussion sessions are entirely unstructured, and the members examine the way in which relationships form within the group, the emergence of leadership and its rejection, the differing forms of authority which members try to use, and the various "devices" used by group members to gain acceptance of their ideas. This course is not a "T-group" course, nor are "T-groups" arranged as part of the group experience. Past experience, however, shows that "T-groups" often develop as a natural consequence of course work. In our opinion, it is better to allow such discussion to develop from a "task-centred" activity than to run a T-group as a "thing-in-itself". The organisational environment is highly structured, and the speedy removal of this structure in a "pure" T-group situation has seemed undesirable to us. Some have found the emotional pressure of a T-group excessive and not everybody can learn in such a situation. Even when learning takes place, there may be difficulty in transferring learned responses from the almost unstructured environment of the T-group to the highly structured working situation. A statement of the objectives of each of these sessions has been prepared, although the nature of the sessions makes it impossible to frame these too tightly. A detailed description of the exercises, together with an analysis of some of the lessons provided by past experience, has also been prepared and will gladly be made available if it is wanted.

Some notes on "projects"

These notes try to summarise the views of college staff as to the use and value of project work carried out by members of middle management courses, and some of the difficulties found to be associated with its execution. Some suggestions for overcoming some of the difficulties are also briefly discussed.

The project and training. In the field of education and training, projects methods are now widely used. This is because we have realised that if you let people put theory into practice, they understand it more clearly. In the view of college staff, it is a most valuable training "tool".

1. It is a waste of money sending staff on management training courses unless there is some tangible improvement, certainly in the long run and preferably also in the short run. The successful execution of a project which may, even in a small way, increase efficiency of some aspect of the working situation is thus a logical result of such a course.

2. Ideas have to be transferred from the "course" situation to "real life", and the execution of a project helps this process of transfer. It also reinforces learning which has taken place on the course.

3. Provided that the project is one to which the "trainee" is able to commit him/herself, the project reinforces the process of personal development started by the course, and new insights, new powers of thought and a deepening of personality may result.

4. It is hoped that new analytical skills will have been acquired as part of the training process of the course. The application of these to the work situation may present problems to those who have had no previous relevant experience. The project makes it possible for these to be exercised under the guidance of skilled tutorial staff, concerned with the application of social science insights.

5. The successful completion of a project is a clear demonstration, both to the individual concerned *and* to those working with him/her of the value of a positive approach to management and other problems; it is an example of the "ripple effect"! All projects will not be successful, but, rightly handled, the "trainee" can learn from his/her failure.

6. The nature of the projects tackled by past course members shows wide variation — as it should. Many of them have been closely related to the working situation of the course member, and the completion of the project has resulted in improvement of the immediate working environment.

Reactions to project work

We are able only to record the comments of course members about hospital reactions to "projects". Not all these comments are made objectively but making adequate allowance for any bias in reporting, we are left with a very wide variation in the apparent attitude of senior staff to project work. They range from warm acceptance of the idea and positive interest in individual projects, through "get-on-with-it-if-you-must-but-don't-let-me-catch-you-doing-it-in-hospital-time"   to   the highly negative reaction which alleges that the whole process is a waste of time, and that the social scientist is an intruder. These negative attitudes on the part of senior management have created despondency among some members of management courses, and this clearly reflected in their attitudes to project work and implementation of action plans, when these are discussed at Review Days. Yet other comments of course members returning for Review Days relate to the problems associated with *time* to carry out project work, and the availability of essential *resources*. The "time" problem varies greatly from one individual to another, but there is no doubt that for some it creates serious difficulties. An increasing proportion of senior and middle management staff are married women, and the need to reconcile the competing claims of home and job may cause much pressure. In these circumstances, it may not be possible to find the extra time and energy to carry out a project unless there is a genuine interest and concern on the part of the appropriate senior officer. Even then, some staff members may already be over-stretched in attempting to carry out their normal duties, and in consequence this "extra thing" is seen as a nuisance. The resources made available by different organisations also shows wide variation. Some make clerical assistance available, arrange to handle the typing of any documents necessary for the execution of the project, and finally type the final draft. On the other hand, some course members have found it impossible even to get their final draft typed. On one occasion, a course member reported that a typist doing secretarial work for her colleagues said that she would type the project — during working time — provided that she was given an extra £5 for doing so!

The projects we have seen to date fall into these main groups. A nursing officer was concerned about patient waiting time in a busy ante-natal clinic, and her project was to study the cause and to suggest remedies. Another nursing officer had long wanted to write a book. She wrote it as her project, and a publisher is now being sought. An administrator had become a member of a joint liaison committee, and found that it took up so much of his time that he could not start his original project. He chose a new project — a description of his work on the Committee. Below is a short list of some of the projects undertaken recently in connection with management courses:

Security Problems in a Hospital Group.

Introducing a system of Ward Pharmacy in a large general hospital.

The value of the Voluntary Worker in hospitals.

An Orientation Course for Overseas Learners.

The value of the Nursing Auxiliary in a Maternity Department.

Introduction of In-service training for Nursing Auxiliaries.

The work of a Joint Liaison Committee in the creation of the new NHS management structure.

Transport Problems in a widely scattered hospital group.

The rationalisation of patients' moneys in a large psychiatric hospital.

Where do we start management training? Report on an experiment to give third-year nurses management experience in the ward.

Industrial Relations on the Hospital front.

Improving night-duty conditions in a large psychiatric hospital.

Drug checking by night sisters.

A Typical Course Time-table

Week 1

MONDAY	a.m.	Methods of Objectives. Problems.	Course. Syndicate	Personal work	and on	Course Hospital

	p.m.	What is Management? Role Problems in a Complex Organisation.
TUESDAY	a.m.	Case Study and Seminar — Management and its functions.
	p.m.	Learning for Leadership.
WEDNESDAY	a.m.	Some approaches to Problem-solving.
	p.m.	Measurement and Management.
THURSDAY	a.m.	Communication — Theory and Practice.
	p.m.	Structure of Organisations.
FRIDAY	a.m.	Barrier Problems in Human Relations.
	p.m.	Lecture — Barrier Problems Discussion and Evaluation.

Week 2

	p.m. / a.m.	
MONDAY	a.m.	Structure of Groups.
	p.m.	Staff Selection I (Job Descriptions, etc.).
TUESDAY	a.m.	Principles of Interviewing and Appraisal.
	p.m.	Staff Selection (II).
WEDNESDAY	a.m.	Preparation of Group Studies.
	p.m.	Human Relations (I).
THURSDAY	a.m.	Management and Reorganised National Health Service.
	p.m.	Project Work.
FRIDAY	a.m.	Committee procedures.
	p.m.	Formal and Informal Meetings.

Week 3

MONDAY	a.m.	Making effective use of Formal and Informal Meetings.
	p.m.	Industrial Relations and Health Service.
TUESDAY	a.m.	Practical Selection Interviewing.
	p.m.	Delegation — Techniques and Problems.
WEDNESDAY	a.m.	The structure and management problems of the Trend Valley H.M.C. Human Relations (II).
	p.m.	
THURSDAY	a.m.	Management of Objectives.
	p.m.	Panel of Senior Hospital Managers to consider Group Studies Review.
FRIDAY	a.m.	Preparation of Action Plans.
	p.m.	Action Plans — Presentation. Discussion of Projects. Final Evaluation.

The Slough courses are action centred; they start with the members'
own jobs and then move quickly on to develop new areas of interest.
Case studies are used for group discussion and they all refer to a
fictitious hospital management committee and a local authority. This
material has taken years to produce. One important reason for its use is
that it helps to overcome the idea that course members are being

disloyal to their own organisations if they say that they have problems. It also leaves open the question of what could have happened thus avoiding the possibility of a student saying, "this is wrong. I know what happened." Two of these case studies are reproduced here, as being of potential interest to social workers and in particular workers in social service departments.

CASE STUDY 1

Trend Valley H.M.C.

Some of the Group Officers (Catering, Transport, Building, etc.) some times meet in "The Flying Horse", Market Overt. The following is a short summary of one of their recent discussions:

In our view, there is insufficient staff participation in the general management of the hospital. There are many symptoms of this "sickness of the organisation":

(a) At the moment, staff are very reticent in bringing forward problems or ideas to their department heads. In some cases, those who represent the department know little or nothing about the daily working of the department, and do not even consult senior staff. Frequently, when problems are brought to the notice of a departmental head, there is no further communication from him, to indicate how or when the problem is likely to be solved.

(b) Departmental heads appear to have little or no idea about the way in which decisions are reached or procedures evolved at either hospital or group level.

(c) There is often complete lack of interdisciplinary communication within the unit. This applies especially when the unit in question is part of a section in a smallish hospital. This lack of communication had led to a considerable waste of money, and equipment has been bought and remained idle for nearly a year because the electric power supplies are not adequate to supply the equipment, and there is not enough money available to install a new cable.

(d) There is little or no consultation between group officers and departmental heads on the practical consequences of ideas and recommendations made at group and regional level.

CASE STUDY 2

Case Study — Mrs. Eileen Watson

The background

Mrs. Eileen Watson, widow, living at Twine Cottage, Hemp Lane, Quirk (a small town in Wisselshire). Husband killed some years ago in car accident. Since then, has made a home for her brother, William Pearce, and his daughter, Janet. (Mrs. Pearce died at childbirth. Second child still-born.)

The house

Small town cottage, which has been in Mr. Watson's family's ownership for generations. Well maintained, with small but colourful gardens. Three rooms downstairs, including Mrs. Watson's "workroom" (containing her sewing-machine, ironing board, "bits and pieces" for embroidery, etc.); new kitchen, lavatory and bathroom built on by Mr. Watson; three small bedrooms upstairs.

Mrs. Watson

Not well educated, but widely read and well known in the neighbourhood for her unobtrusive acts of kindness. Member of Quirk United Free Church, but readily offered to accommodate the new Roman Catholic priest until suitable permanent lodgings could be found for him. Age: 55 years.

Mr. Pearce and Janet

Mr. Pearce — foreman in Repair and Service Department of Quirk

Motors Ltd., a small garage owned by local man. Has worked there for nearly twenty years. Garage's high local reputation owes much to Mr. Pearce's skill and conscientiousness. Quietly spoken; well regarded by owner and men. Regular member of Parish Church. Age: 59 years.

Janet — a charming and intelligent girl of 18-19 years of age. Has nine "O" levels and one "A" level. Seems unable to decide on a career, and is at present working in local factory. Father "can't make head or tail of her". Has always had excellent relationship with her aunt.

Shortly after 55th birthday Mrs. Watson noticed lump in right breast. Her general practitioner, Dr. John Sutton, sent her to Overt Royal Hospital in the the County of Upshire, about 15 miles away. Consultant diagnosed advanced mammary carcinoma, but thought a radical mastectomy was practicable. Operation was successful; patient recovered; discharged after period of convalescence.

About 8 months later, complained she felt very unwell. Dr. Sutton called, suspected development of secondary carcinoma. Again admitted to Overt Royal Hospital; preliminary diagnosis was confirmed, prognosis poor, surgical intervention impracticable. Admitted to Carlisle Ward (general medical ward) as a terminal case. Morphine prescribed.

Three weeks later, Senior Registrar discussed with Ward Sister the intense pressure on beds and shortage of staff. Decided to recommend that two patients go home for week-end, one of the two being Mrs. Watson. He hurriedly wrote note to Dr. Sutton to say that Mrs. Watson would arrive home "tomorrow", that she had hitherto been on morphine, that she should return to hospital on Monday evening, and that this pattern of procedure would probably be repeated in the future.

The following day, Saturday, Mrs. Watson left the ward with Janet. Ward sister (Sister Green) told Janet: "Everything will be all right over the week-end; her doctor will take care of her. We would like her back about 6 p.m. on Monday, please."

Dr. Sutton did not call on Saturday. Mrs. Watson was in great distress by Sunday morning, and about 8 a.m. the Vicar looked in on his way to the early Communion service. Very shocked by Mrs. Watson's obvious distress. Called at doctor's house on way to church.

Doctor away for week-end, locum in next village *(Dr. Mills)* four miles away. Vicar called locum from church vestry. Had been called out to serious accident on motorway, M549, by police. Time of return uncertain. Would come when he could.

9 a.m. Vicar returned from service. No doctor yet. Went home, rang police. They would try to contact a doctor.

10 a.m. *Dr. Sanders* arrived at Twine Cottage. Asked to come by police, who were not able to contact Dr. Mills. Knew nothing at all about the case. Administered morphine, assured Mr. Pearce that Dr. Mills would be in later in the day.

1 p.m. Dr. Mills rang Vicar to find out nature of the problem at Twine Cottage. Had just returned home to find messages from Dr. Sanders and police. He would have a meal, come over to Quirk as soon as possible. Did not know anything about the case, but would do what he could.

2.15 p.m. Dr. Mills arrived at Twine Cottage. Administered morphine.

8.30 p.m. Dr. Mills called at Twine Cottage. Administered morphine. Left note at Sutton Lodge for Dr. Sutton.

10.45 p.m. Dr. Sutton called at Twine Cottage. Had just returned home from week-end visit to friends to find letter from hospital and note from Dr. Mills. Mrs. Watson asleep. Left instructions that he should be called if patient awoke and appeared to be distressed.

Monday, 8.45 a.m. Dr. Sutton visited. Patient in coma. Advised against return to hospital. Rang hospital from the cottage, reported worsening of condition.

6 p.m. Dr. Sutton visited. Patient weakening rapidly. Morphine administered.

Death took place at 5.30 a.m. Tuesday morning.

What were the *management* problems which affected this family?

What are functions of Management?

Which of those functions were not carried out by the management (a) of the hospital, (b) of the community nursing service?

What steps would you take to see that this sort of breakdown did not occur again?

(The District Nurse, Mrs. Salmon, attached to the practices of Dr.

Sutton and Dr. Mills was involved in a car accident about 8 weeks ago, and is in Overt Royal Hospital with a fractured femur.)

6. FIELD EXPERIENCE

Many social work training courses include either a supervised group work placement or opportunities for group work while students are on a fieldwork placement. One student spent part of a placement working with a group of prisoners' wives, their children and some voluntary helpers. The student wrote the following account of this work (Central Training Council in Child Care, 1970).

My contact with the group and what I learned from this experience could be divided into work with children, wives and volunteers. Talking to the children was always a good means of contacting the mothers although on one occasion the child of a new member bit another child's hand! For some of the children this group was their first experience of playing with other children. Some refused to leave their mothers for even a few minutes while others were very boisterous and needed to be kept occupied. If one of the volunteers was playing with the children then most of my time was spent talking to the wives. Initially all the wives were visited by the Probation Officer or myself and they would approach us about any particular problem that they might have, while they would talk to the volunteers about more general matters. The sudden increase in numbers affected the group dynamics. The members who were unsure of their position in the group did not immediately accept the newcomers but the more secure members with encouragement would welcome the others and help them feel at home. A great deal of time was spent talking to the more reserved members and helping them to form relationships. It was often the withdrawn, introverted person who attended most regularly and appeared to gain the most support from the group.

I was given the task of organising a mini bus to take the wives and children to visit their husbands in prison. Co-ordination was necessary to arrange visits and travel warrants to the particular prison on the same day. The arrangements for these visits involved both old and new members and as a result of this a number of friendships were formed. From this contact with volunteers I realised how important it was that there should be agreement as to what the group was seeking to achieve. Many of the volunteers wanted to organise rather than work with the group and they distinguished between wives and volunteers. I found that it was important to have only a few volunteers who felt a sense of commitment and attended regularly. The more informal method of communication adopted often meant that the volunteers were not aware of what was being arranged, e.g. the mini bus. I learnt the importance of involving volunteers with as much as possible and have regular meetings with them to discuss what was happening. The volunteers needed to gain some sense of satisfaction from attending the group. Some times they found this by mixing with the wives and on other occassions they wanted to sit and talk with the other volunteers. As this was quite a large, informal group it was often difficult to see all the group interactions. A number of sub-groups were formed and the changing membership affected the structure of the group. I was able to observe the different roles that members assumed or were pushed into.

7. CONCLUSION

It is not easy to make a balanced assessment of the uses of unstructured groups in training, although the idea that many people are able to learn through analysis of their current psychological experience and social encounters seems to be a reasonable basic assumption. Through observing people's feelings and reactions towards each other in groups it is possible to develop understanding of how communication can be inhibited. Essentially such inhibitions are learned. In a training group the forces against communicating attitudes and feelings about other people can be overcome. In combined training programmes (i.e. programmes using lectures, role play, and project work in addition to unstructured sessions) similar assumptions are made. Two illustrations have been given. These courses showed some similarities but points of contrast were also identified. In both courses group members' communication with each other was facilitated by the leaders who found ways to encourage frank discussion. Members gradually "open up", show more about themselves and find that bonds between them are strengthened. Groups are able to exchange views and decide on action in relation to their jobs (in hospitals in the examples given). Feedback from participants in these and similar courses seems to indicate that some people find their group experience painful and continue to feel hurt for some time while others find it rewarding. A great deal depends on the trainers who vary from taking passive roles (thus frustrating the group into taking action) to being more active in facilitating communication. Two case studies used in discussion groups in one combined methods course are reproduced because of their possible interest to social workers.

CHAPTER 8

Communication Skills in Teaching and Social Work

1. COMMUNICATION AND SOCIAL CONTEXT

In this last chapter it will be helpful to retrace our steps and review the questions we have studied earlier. In particular I want to develop the discussion of feedback and two-way communication in learning. It will be quite clear that there are many useful indications from researchers on topics such as making communication more efficient, or speeding up the process of learning and making it "less" mechanical and "more" human. But at present we lack the tools to build a convincing synthesis. There are few clear principles which can be applied to making learning and interviewing "efficient". At present we use a great deal of art and little science. I have not attempted to argue the desirability or otherwise of this state of affairs. What I do want to try to do now is refer to the earlier discussion of communication and social context. The importance of social and cultural variables in the interview has been emphasised by Cross (1974). He also stated that an interview is an instrument for communication and invokes the use of verbal language and non-verbal symbols. It is an essentially human situation in which social interaction must occur. Characteristics of social interaction in the wider society are focused in this specific situation, so that factors extraneous to the interview are reflected in it. In taking all this for granted I will attempt to look at other aspects of relationships. Then I refer to earlier discussion of the nature and organisation of learning, then proceed to some questions about two-way communication in training and then return to skills in learning and communication again.

Robinson (1972) suggests that to ask questions about the functions of communication can be a useful framework for inquiry. It seems appropriate to ask simple questions about man-made systems and to try to understand the functions of human communication. All human groups have norms or rules of behaviour such as conventions about clothes, social customs, formalities of behaviour, rules of the road and rules of membership and function in institutions and families. They provide guides to people's tasks and the roles they play. Thus they are functional relationships which decide patterns of communication to a great extent. Codes of behaviour, such as legal systems, develop organically as linguistic conventions do. They provide guidance about what can be expected of particular people and what they ought to do. A social system has a structure of relationships between individuals. It can be described in terms of rules and its functioning depends on communication. I now discuss some questions about the acquisition of language, language functions and social context.

Language is the most highly developed, subtle and most complicated form of symbolism. There is no necessary connection between the symbol and that which is symbolised, between words and things or situations. You can say "I'm hungry" but without actually being hungry. Also, just as social status is symbolised in many different ways according to where you live, the fact of being hungry can be expressed by many different noises, i.e. in different languages. This may seem obvious when it is stated but it seems that people often feel and behave as if there necessarily are connections between symbols and things symbolised. A boy said "pigs are called pigs because they are such dirty animals". Some people regard snakes as nasty slimy creatures and see the word snake as a nasty slimy word. With regard to some topics many societies give systematic encouragement to the habitual confusion of symbols with things symbolised. In the days of emperor worship in Japan you had to rescue the emperor's picture if there was a fire at the risk of your life. Nowadays we are encouraged to possess credit cards, to get into debt, in order to show off our symbols of prosperity. It almost becomes more important to possess the symbols than the things they stand for. We tend to take language very much for granted. We assume that a child learns the language of the group in which he is reared and gains increasing fluency as his central nervous system matures. We tend to assume that which language a child learns is relatively unimportant since each provides a way of expressing his needs and ideas (Lidz, 1963). What is the effect of particular languages on the way people think and deal with their environment? It is an illusion to imagine that a person adjusts to reality essentially without using language and that language is just an incidental means of dealing with problems. The "real world' is to a large extent unconsciously built up on the language habits of the group. The language which we learn influences profoundly the ways we perceive and experience (Sapir, 1949).

In a sense people live in two worlds. First there is the world that consists of things seen, felt and heard, the flow of events constantly passing before our senses. This world of happening which we know at first hand (the extensional world) is small. Most of our knowledge from parents, teachers, books and television is received verbally, we know of Brazil, even if we have not been there, and about the Battle of Trafalgar, because we have been told about them. This is our verbal world. The verbal world ought to stand in relation to the extensional world as a map does to the territory it is supposed to represent (Korzybski, 1933). If a child grows up with a false map, that is, with a map which does not correspond to the extensional world but which contains error and superstition, he will be constantly running into difficulty. A map is useless to a traveller if it does not give accurate information about the relationship of places to each other, the structure of the territory. Using imaginary or false reports, or by making false inferences from good reports language can be used to make maps which have no relation to the world of happenings experienced at first hand (the extensional world). People acquire a great deal of erroneous information; maps formerly thought to be accurate require correction. There are two ways in which false maps are acquired: first by having them given to us; second, by creating them ourselves (e.g. by misreading the true maps with which we are provided). The distinction between the extensional meaning of words (pointing to things) and their intensional meaning (ideas or notions) is between their denotations and their connotations. Connotations are informative and effective. The informative connotations of a word are its "impersonal", socially agreed, meanings. They may include the definition of a term and its denotation (i.e. which one of a group you are talking about). Denotations raise problems of interpretation because the same word may mean different things to people in different social groups, or different geographical areas. In a B.B.C. Brains Trust Bertrand Russell gave the following conjugations: "I am firm. You are obstinate. He is a pig-headed fool." A *New Statesman* competition invited similar conjugations of "irregular verbs": "I am sparkling. You are unusually talkative. He is drunk." "I am fastidious. You are fussy. He is an old woman." "I am righteously indignant. You are annoyed. He is making a fuss about nothing." The affective connotations of a word are the aura of personal feelings it arouses. There is no necessary agreement about these feelings (for example, about pigs or snakes), but under some circumstances words can be used for their affective connotations alone. When we are very moved emotionally we express our feelings using words without giving attention to their connotations. When words are used as equivalents of expressive actions or gestures such as crying in pain, or snarling in anger, language is being used in presymbolic ways. If someone is in danger the actual words shouted in warning matter little; what conveys the warning is the loudness and tone of the cry. Very small children understand the warmth or invitation in a mother's voice long before they can understand her words. This sensitivity to presymbolic communication survives in later life to a greater or lesser degree. Social conversation, for example, at parties may have little informative content as far as the topic is concerned. The prevention of silence itself seems an important function of spoken language: it is impossible to talk only when we have something which is highly informative to say. The purpose of this kind of talk is to promote friendly relations or "social smoothness", and the topics are carefully chosen; they are ones about which agreement is likely to be possible, for example, the state of the weather. Language thus has two tasks. One is instrumental in conveying information. The other is its use for the direct expression of the feelings of the speaker. From the hearer's point of view report language informs him while the expressive or presymbolic functions of language affect his feelings. Affective language affects the hearer in a forceful way: a spoken insult provokes an insult in return; a loud command compels attention if not obedience.

The child's progressive mastery of language forms and their

meanings occurs, at least partly, through imitation. Imitation itself changes in the course of a child's development and it is only one element in a complex process (Lewis, 1951). Simple mimicry happens early in development but for the most part words are acquired as they heard and uttered in familiar situations. The child does not mainly imitate words as labels for objects; he soon hears and responds to words as means of communication. The need to communicate keeps the child imitating; he improves his imitations because of this. At the same time as he is imitating the child is exploring. He adapts verbal actions to his situation. Past experiences enable him to adapt himself to a new situation. It is a process of transposition of the pattern (rather than the entire detail) of the child's past experience to a new situation. The main social reinforcement comes from the child's realisation of his success in communication. He sees that he is being understood or is understanding others. He acquires language not mainly by imitation, not mainly by learning the names of objects, but in trying to use language to communicate (Skinner, 1957). The process of exploration in the acquisition of language can be illustrated by the way a child builds words. A mother asked her son what had happened to an apple. "I taked it and eated it" he replied. These forms of the past tense are probably the result of reasoning by analogy. He has heard "walked" as the past of "walk"; "talked" as the past of "talk". He will usually be correct and receive reinforcement if he uses the present tense with the *d* or *t* endings to obtain the past tense. When he makes mistakes he will usually be corrected. These experiments show how the child produces new forms and meanings, that he has not met before. The child is not necessarily aware of the relationship between the present and past forms of verbs and he does not produce new forms by a process of reasoning. It seems more likely that repeated experience will be sufficient to establish a tendency for him to indicate the past in this way. It is a characteristic way in which past experience generally influences present behaviour. Successive experiences establish schemata, or patterns of behaviour potential which become active in subsequent situations alike or different from those previously met. A person may often be unaware of this persistence of the past. It seems that this may be what happens when a child learns language. The unconscious effects of past experience produce a habitual pattern of speech which he uses when he has to indicate a past event (Lewis, 1963).

If a person's communication is to embrace a wider range of experience and is to enable him to make finer distinctions and comparisons he has to pay more attention to the language he uses and responds to: this is often seen in children's questioning of language. At first they are interested in naming objects: "what is this?" Later they are interested in finding the meanings of words: "what does that mean?" Meaning rather than structure becomes the more important factor in the child's language development and differences among children become most marked in semantic rather than structural development. When an individual first learns language this is a way of being a member of a group. It is part of communication with the family. With increase in age the child becomes a member of other social groups and learns to use language in fitting in to them and influencing others. As knowledge of language develops it is used for personal purposes. From the age of 4 to 7 the child uses egocentric speech, talking audibly to himself about what he is doing but not intending to communicate with others. Egocentric speech, it is suggested, does not disappear but becomes part of a person's thinking. A person comments to himself on what he is doing, to explain past events, to make plans for the future and to make sense of his actions or fit them into a framework of meaning. This use of language by the child becomes an essential part of thinking and feeling: what is learned as part of communication with other people is later specialised to more private purposes (Vygotsty, 1962; Piaget, 1959). The forms of a child's language and their meanings come nearer and nearer to the language of his social environment through both imitation and exploration. Mutual adjustment in communication with others proceeds constantly; the child adjusts to others and they adjust to him and through this process the child's language develops. This process of mutual adjustment is one of communication between the child (or the adult) and his social environment. One function of language is the definition of role relationships, "role" referring to the set of behaviours prescribed for or expected of a person occupying a particular place in a group. Although role expectations vary in different sub-cultures and roles allow different degrees of individual discretion as to how they may be played, there are written or unwritten rules that govern people's behaviour. In this discussion we are dealing with the problem of the relationship between symbolic and social systems.

The area of interest of sociolinguistics (sociology of language) is best illustrated by the question "who speak or writes what language (or what variety of language) to whom, when, and for what purpose?" It attempts to develop understanding of the norms of language use, i.e. the generally accepted social patterns of language use and of behaviour toward language in a particular community. How and why do differences occur in the same community in the social organisation of language and behaviour toward language? Chomsky (1965) called linguistic competence a person's implicit knowledge of his language and contrasted it with performance, the actual use of the language in particular situations. Competence referred to the speaker's ability to produce an infinite number of grammatical sentences out of a finite set of rules. It is helpful to distinguish competence and performance in the use of language, that is between code and message and between language and speech. We are able to speak to each other effectively because the rules of language systems are flexible and develop from speech. We need to bear in mind that there are social rules and rules of grammar: both affect speech. As far as speech is concerned there is a plurality of codes in the same linguistic community. The idea of language repertoire refers to all the linguistic forms regularly employed in the course of socially significant interaction (i.e. to all the accepted ways of formulating messages).

The type of social relations does not directly influence linguistic codes but constrains speech. The type of speech used reinforces the selective perception of the speaker. In the process of socialisation the child learns overt or implicit attitudes towards language and the requirements of a certain social structure. This is Bernstein's (1959) hypothesis. He said that the important linguistic differences between the lower working class and the middle class result from entirely different modes of speech which are dominant in, and typical of these social strata. One form of speech which is available to both groups but typical of the first group he referred to as the restricted language code (or public language). The typical speech mode of the middle class he called an elaborated code (or a formal language). In lower working-class families the child learns the restricted speech system which is appropriate to his own environment but not suitable in relationships with middle-class institutions such as schools, hospitals and other social agencies. The restricted code is characterised by a reduced number of adjectives and adverbs, especially those which qualify feelings. The organisation of speech is relatively simple and the use of the code is generated by social relationships which are characteristically emotionally close involving strong identifications, common assumptions and shared interests; these all reduce the necessity for a person to be verbally explicit and to elaborate his intentions. It should be noted that this code is not exclusive to the working class. This speech system in which feelings are taken for granted (and not verbalised) operates whenever social relationships are close, for example in peer groups and between friends, and in closed communities such as prisons. The restricted code is available to and used by all members of society but some people are limited to it and have no other speech mode. The restricted system cannot be used to communicate unique experiences which emphasise individuality: the pronoun I is used less than others: uniqueness is expressed non verbally. The code does not permit a person to discriminate between different feelings and motives in himself and others. This lack of perceptual discrimination can be illustrated in the different ways in which middle-class and working-class parents discipline their children. Middle-class parents use rational discussion related to their feelings about the child's behaviour and the consequences of his actions. Working-class parents, on the other hand, employ impersonal, status-orientated appeals in a very direct way quickly followed by punishment. In general, the middle-class child is distinguished not only by the size of vocabulary but by sensitivity to a way of organising and responding to experience. From the earliest years of conversation the tendency is for him to be oriented to future goals. His life is planned and he lives in a stable framework of rewards and punishments. His behaviour is commented on so that he learns to see himself as a self-regulating, responsible individual. The working-class child tends to live much more in the present: rewards and punishments tend to be arbitrary and may be inconsistent and he has no clear future plans and sense of personal status.

In the restricted ode thoughts are strung together rather loosely and ungrammatically. Much of a person's meaning is conveyed by gesture, vocal intonation and by uninformative (redundant) but emotionally reinforcing phrases. (For example: "He's like that you know", "It's life", "That's the way it goes".) Its main function is the expression of feeling and the enhancement of social solidarity and it is inefficient for tracing cause and effects relationships. Tensions are less subject to verbal control and tend to be dissipated quickly through actions. The person will tend to "act out" rather than to "talk out" his problems. He will tend to deny having them rather than try to make excuses for himself. The working-class child is relatively uninhibited in the direct expression of anger and other feelings. He reacts overtly to frustration and hits out not just because he has not learned to repress instinctive tendencies; he imitates the way adults react to him when he annoys them. His parents are more likely to use physical punishment or coercion. The middle-class child's verbalisation in contrast is bound up with the process of internalising moral values and prohibitions. He is controlled in his conduct more by his own guilt feelings. He turns aggression in on himself more and reacts to conflict situations by repression. The working-class child is more likely to put blame on the environment rather than himself. The contrasts between public and formal language are brought out in this table (Bernstein, 1961).

Public language
1. Short, grammatically simple, often unfinished sentences with a poor syntactical form stressing the active voice.
2. Simple and repetitive use of conjunctions (so, then, because).
3. Little use of subordinate clauses to break down the initial categories of the dominant subject.
4. Inability to hold a formal subject through a speech sequence; thus, a dislocated informational content is facilitated.
5. Rigid and limited use of adjectives and adverbs.
6. Infrequent use of impersonal pronouns as subjects of conditional clauses.
7. Frequent use of statements where the reason and conclusion are confounded to produce a categoric statement.
8. A large number of statements/phrases which signal a requirement for the previous speech sequence to be reinforced: "Wouldn't it? You see? You know?", etc. This process is termed "sympathetic circularity".
9. Individual selection from a group of idiomatic phrases or sequences will frequently occur.
10. The individual qualification is implicit in the sentence organization: it is a language of implicit meaning.

Formal language

1. Accurate grammatical order and syntax regulate what is said.
2. Logical modifications and stress are mediated through a grammatically complex sentence construction, especially through the use of a range of conjunctions and subordinate clauses.
3. Frequent use of prepositions which indicate logical relationships as well as prepositions which indicate temporal and spatial contiguity.
4. Frequent use of the personal pronoun 'I'.
5. A discriminative selection from a range of adjectives and adverbs.
6. Individual qualification is verbally mediated through the structure and relationships within and between sentences.
7. Expressive symbolism discriminates between meanings within speech sequences rather than reinforcing dominant words or phrases, or accompanying the sequence in a diffuse, generalized manner.
8. It is a language use which points to the possibilities inherent in a complex conceptual hierarchy for the organizing of experience.

Lawton (1968) gives some written illustrations which show similar differences to those found in speech. Boys from different social backgrounds were asked to write essays, two of which are given now.

Working-class 15-year-old boy's essay on

My life in ten years' time

I hope to be a carpenter just about married and like to live in a modern house and do a ton on the Sidcup by-pass with a motorbike and also drinking in the local pub.

My hobby will be breeding dogs and spare time running a pet shop. And I will be wearing the latest styles of clothes.

I hope my life in ten years time will be a happy life without a worry and I have a good blance behide me. I am going to have a gay and happy life. I am going to work hard to get somewhere in the world.

One thing I will not do in my life is to bring disgrace and unhappiness to my family (in Lawton, 1968, p.112).

Middle-class 15-year-old boy's essay on

My life in ten years' time

As I look around me and see the wonders of modern science and all the fantastic new developments I feel a slight feeling of despondency. This is because I am beginning to wonder who will be in control of the world in ten years time, the machine or man. Already men are being shot around earth in rockets and already machines are being built that will travel faster and faster than the one before. I wonder if the world will be a gigentic nuthouse by the time I'm ten years older. We are told we will be driving supersonic cars at fantastic speeds, with televisions, neds, and even automatic driving controls. Do we want this, do we want to be ruled by machinery. Gone will be the time when the family go out for a picnic on a Sunday Afternoon, we will be whisked along wide flat autoroads we will press a button in a way and out will come a plate of sandwiches ready prepared. You may think that this is a bit far fetched but if things keep on improving men will not have to think for themselves and we will become a race of bos-eyed mawrons. There is, if this is going to happen, no way to stop it. Men say we will have just one or two more luxuries and it never stops. I enjoy the luxuries of today, but in my opinion there is a limit. But who decides what the limit will be. No one knows its just a lot of men all relaying on someone to stop this happening, but non-one is going to. We're doomed. No prayers can save us now, we'll become slaves to great walking monstrosities. Powerless in the hands of something we helped to create. I'm worried about "my life in ten years time".

One problem with Bernstein's theory is the danger of taking it too literally. A theory formulated in terms of contrasted types may lead people to exaggerate, or to form the impression of an unbridgeable gulf between two social groups rather than seeing people on a continuum. If we took Bernstein's theory literally this would just about rule out the possibility of social mobility. This would hardly fit the evidence that the largest number of grammar-school pupils are down from the working classes. We need to bear in mind the great variety in patterns of socialisation and family life and in the character training of children. Accepting that there is a relationship between the shaping of experience, social structure and symbolic systems it is still not clear how this shaping occurs (Bernstein 1970a; see also 1970b). Different speech forms or codes symbolize the form of the social relationship, regulate the nature of the speech encounters and create different orders of relevance and relation for the users. The experience of the speakers is then transformed by what is made significant by the speech form. Bernstein consistently emphasised the form of social relationship, i.e. the structuring of relevant meanings. He regarded role as a complex coding activity controlling the organisation of specific meanings and the conditions of their transmission and reception. Sociolinguists attempt to explore how symbolic systems are both realizations and regulators of the structure of social relationships. The particular symbolic system is that of speech not language. The idea of sociolinguistic codes points both to the social structuring of meanings and to their related contextual realisation (or existence). He thought later that he should have written of sociolinguistic rather than linguistic codes, the latter giving the impression that he was specifying grammar at the expense of meaning or suggesting that there was a one to one relationship between meaning and a given grammar.

The following incident also illustrates how communication defines peoples' roles. In this case only two people are involved.

Mrs. Smith is a patient in hospital, she is unable to sleep. The nurse on the ward telephones the duty doctor at 1 a.m. The doctor does not know Mrs. Smith. The conversation proceeds like this:

Nurse: Hello Dr. Brown, this is Nurse Jones, Ward 2. I have a patient Mrs. Smith who learned that her father died today. She is unable to go to sleep.

Doctor: Has she had any medicine to help her sleep before?

Nurse: Pentobarbitol (100 mg) was quite effective the night before last.

Doctor: Pentobarbitol 100 mg before bedtime as required for sleep — got it?

Nurse: Yes I have. Thank you very much doctor.

From the point of view of communication you can discuss two levels in the nurse's first message. Overtly it describes a woman who cannot sleep and who that morning had heard of her father's death. Less overtly the message contains a diagnosis and a recommendation. "Mrs. Smith is unable to sleep because she is grieving and she should be given a sedative." The doctor accepts the diagnosis. He does not know Mrs. Smith and he asks the nurse for a recommendation about what sleeping medicine should be prescribed. He recognised that the nurse knows Mrs. Smith but his question does not *appear* to be asking the nurse for a recommendation. The nurse replies with a disguised recommendation. The doctor responds with a note of authority in his voice and then the nurse says she is grateful. What can one observe about the social context and the participants in this short story? I suggest that it illustrates some of the points made earlier about our systems of expectations of people in social groups. As described in my anecdote (which may well be antique or unrealistic or non-typical — this does not matter for our present purpose) the nurse is required to have initiative, to act decisively and responsibly, and at the same time to appear passive or, at least, not to seem to challenge the doctor's authority. Part of her role consists in making it look as if it is the doctor who initiates any recommendations. One of the rules governing the relationship is to avoid open disagreement between the professions. For this to happen the doctor can be expected to ask for recommendations without appearing to do so: the nurse has to learn how to give recommendations without seeming to. The hospital (in common with other social systems) appears to have significant effects on relationships between patients, doctors and nurses. It is not easy to abandon or change familiar role definitions in order to ease communication or to make it more open or direct (Stein, 1967). Codes illustrate how communication is incomplete. They represent shared shortcuts in meaning provided the users of codes are clear about their meaning. When they got off the communication track through using codes they must be able to get back on the track by being able to determine when the game, or the use of the code, is over. When people share a code they share a specialised and potentially private or secret way of communicating. When they have shared experiences they tend to condense many of them into codes. Examples are "family jokes", e.g. when a family is aware of the special meaning for them of a particular phrase or word. Here is another incident. A visitor to a home for elderly people noticed a group of men in the living room. One of the men said "27" and everyone laughed. Then another one said "18". Everyone laughed again. Someone else said "29". There was silence. The visitor asked the warden what was going on. "What's going on here? You hear all these numbers and then everyone laughs." "Oh", said the warden, "you see these men have been here for some time and they know each other's jokes so well that instead of telling them over and over again they must give the number." "Well", said the visitor, "What happened to number 29? No one laughed." "Oh, that fellow", said the warden, "he never could tell a joke." Every communication thus has a content and a relationship aspect. The two modes of communication both exist side by side and complement each other in every message. The content aspect is conveyed digitally. Digital message material is of a much higher degree of complexity, versatility and abstraction than analogic material. Analogue communication is not comparable to the logical syntax of digital language. In analogic language there are no equivalents for "if . . . then . . ." "either . . . or" and it lacks an expression for "not". Digital communication is important for the sharing of information about objects and for the transmission of knowledge. The area of analogic communication is that of relationships rather than making denotive statements about objects. Analogic communication has no qualifiers to indicate which of two discrepant meanings is implied nor any indicators that would permit a distinction between past, present or future. There are tears of sorrow and tears of joy: the clenched fist may signal aggression or constraint. It is virtually all non-verbal communication. Objects, in the widest sense, can either be represented by a likeness such as a drawing or they can be referred to by a name. Whenever a word is used to name something the relation between the word and the object is arbitrarily established. Human beings communicate both digitally and anologically. Digital language has a highly complex and powerful logical syntax but lacks adequate semantics in the field of relationship. Analogic language possesses the semantics but has no adequate syntax for the unambiguous definition for the nature of relationships. The laws of logic do not hold for processes in the id: contradictory impulses exist side by side. The id is virtually equivalent to analogic communication. A similarity can be seen between the psychoanalytic concepts of primary process and secondary process and analogic and digital communication respectively (Watzlawick, 1968). Sapir (1967) refers to communication as a verbal and non-verbal process of making requests of the receiver. The receiver has to be aware of his own receiving system or interpretation system. A sender communicates through his gestures and facial expression as well as with words. The communication occurs in a context and one wants to know when it took place, and about the relationships between the people involved. Thus the receiver assesses both the verbal and non-verbal content of a message so that he can draw some conclusions about what the sender meant. Content of messages may be about anything that is communicable regardless of the validity or truth of the information. The other aspect of communication refers to what sort of message it is and to the kind of relationship that exists between the people who are communicating. Whenever a person communicates then, he is (a) making a statement, (b) asking something of the receiver and (c) trying to influence the receiver to give him what he wants. A range of responses may be hoped for, however, from just asking the receiver to show that the message was heard to a specific kind of response such as performing a particular act. If all behaviour has message value (i.e. is communication) no matter how hard you try you cannot *not* communicate. Activity or inactivity, words or silence, all have message value: they influence others and these others in turn cannot *not* respond to these communications and are thus themselves communicating. You cannot say that communication only takes place when it is intentional, conscious or "successful", i.e. when mutual understanding occurs (Watzlawick, 1968). We are all aware that messages can be constructed, especially in written communication, in ways which are highly ambiguous. An example is a notice in a restaurant which can be understood in two entirely different ways: "Customers who think our waiters are rude should see the manager." This kind of ambiguity is not the only possible complication which arises out of the level structure of all communication. Another notice read "Disregard this sign". These notices convey information — even if it is that the people writing them were confused, or were setting out to deceive or mislead . . . you could continue trying to puzzle this out. The notices also tell you to do something. I would like to extend the discussion to these two aspects. A metacommunication is a communication about a communication: it qualifies it, modifies it, or denies it. It may be non-verbal, e.g. being expressed by shouting or a gruff tone, smiling, or posture. Or clues may be obtained from the context of the communication. Verbal examples are; "This is an order" or "I am only joking." An example is when a mother says angrily or gruffly to her crying child who is seeking comfort "Oh come here then". The tone of voice conveys that the invitation is given grudgingly or that she does not want the child to come to be comforted. Communications and metacommunications provide a dual flow of information. They may be congruent or, as in the last example, incongruent. The problem with such incongruent messages is the necessity to decide which aspect of the message to respond to. All messages could be characterised as requests for validation. They are frequently interpreted in such terms as "Go along with what I am saying"; "Be on my side"; "Show me you value my ideas"; or, simply, "Agree with me". People rarely verbalise these requests that others agree with them or that others want what they want. The wish to be valued and for co-operation leads them to try to persuade others or to try to elicit the response that is wished for, by indirect means. A person can label the kind of message he sends, telling the receiver how he wishes him to receive it (e.g. to take it seriously or frivolously) and how he should respond. He can say "It was a joke" (laugh at it), "It was just a passing remark" (ignore it), "It was a question" (answer it). "It was a request" (consider it). "It was an order" (obey it). He can say why he sent the message by referring to the other person's past actions: "I was showing consideration or courtesy towards you in response to your kindness towards me." He can say why he sent the message by referring to his expectations about the other person's future behaviour (i.e. what actions he wanted the other person to take or *not* to take): "I was asking you to leave the room." "I did not want you to tell her about my illness." If a message and a metacommunication are incongruent (do not fit) the receiver has to reconcile the discrepancy by translating the two communications into a single message. In order to do this satisfactorily he has to be able to comment on the presence of the discrepancy. For example, a husband is trying to repair an electrical fitting and says, irritably, "Damn it, the fixture has broken". In this situation the wife may go through the following process (described here in slow motion), in reacting to what he said. (1) "He is telling me about the condition of the fixture he is working on." (2) "But he is doing more than that. He is also telling me he is irritated. 'Damn it' and his tone of voice indicate this." (3) Is he criticizing me? Is he suggesting that I am responsible for the condition of the fixture?" (4) "If he is criticizing me what does he want me to do? Take over the job for him? Apologize?" (5) Or is he criticizing himself, irritated that he is having a frustrating time with the job, and that he only has himself to blame for the fact that the fixture broke?" (6) "If he is primarily criticizing himself, what is he asking me to do? Sympathize with him? Listen to him? Or what?" (7) "I know that he regards electrical jobs as his best skill. So he is criticizing himself and he must be primarily asking me to sympathize with him." (8) "But how do I sympathize? Does he want me to help him with the job, bring him coffee, or what? What behaviour on my part that he could see and hear would mean to him that I am sympathizing with him?" (Satir, 1967). If instead of saying "Damn it the fixture has broken" the husband had said "I'm fed up. I'm having a hard time with this job. Bring me a cup of coffee" the wife would have little trouble assessing his message. He would be telling her overtly what he wanted from her (sympathy and coffee) and why. (Or should it have been tea and sympathy?) This example illustrates that what a person means by his communication can be said to have at least two levels: (a) the denotative: the literal content and (b) the metacommunication level: a comment on the literal content as well as on the nature of the relationship between the persons involved. The request, which is part of every message, may, or may not, be expressed denotatively. There are degrees of directness to which requests can be spelled out denotively. Because of the complexity and incompleteness of human communication receivers have to try to complete the sender's message by trial and error or intuition. This is not always possible. Even the most clairvoyant of receivers guesses incorrectly at some time. When this happens the sender's next message usually informs him of his mistake. When the wife heard her husband express his irritation about the electrical job she might have sought further information in various ways. She could have moved towards him and looked attentive or questioning. He might have continued his communication by grunting, groaning, swearing or bashing at the fitting. The wife might have asked "Is there anything I can do?" In this way she would be seeking clarification directly. She would be asking her husband to be specific about his request. The husband's reply would help her to reduce her uncertainty. For example, he might say "No, I just have to work out how to do it" and this could indicate that he was dissatisfied although the wife could still not be sure what he expected of her. She might then ask "Would you like a cup of coffee?" If he answered affirmatively and she provided the coffee this particular communication sequence would be closed. Receivers vary in their ability to perceive the needs and wishes of other people. We have seen that the wife could mistake her husband's irritation with himself for a criticism of her and she could end up trying to take over the job for him, instead of sympathising with him. If this wife in all situations and in all her relationships at all times decides that senders are criticising her or praising her, she would be regarded by other people as egocentric, deluded or paranoid.

2. LEARNING: ITS NATURE AND ORGANISATION

It is thus possible to recognise some of the ways in which speech and writing may contribute to certain kinds of learning. Teachers can influence and prevent the use of language for learning. They can influence the context for talk and writing, and the nature of participation in dialogue or discussion. If people are to talk and write about what they are learning in a way which encourages assimilation and accommodation the social context has to be planned to make this possible. Earlier it was observed how communication involves the organisation or structuring of experience or ideas. In the first two chapters of this book the organisation of learning and the processes involved were discussed. I now return to those chapters and extrapolate the following salient points. If learning is regarded as changed behaviour the change occurs as a consequence of three basic factors. These factors are (i) what to do and how to do it (knowledge or information), (ii) the desire or willingness to practice what has been learned (attitude) and (iii) the ability to apply the knowledge acquired in training to particular tasks (skill). The three factors are interrelated but learning any one does not necessarily imply the automatic development of the others. It is an over-simplification, but a useful guideline to keep in mind, that knowledge can usually be effectively acquired through reading and lectures. Attitudes are influenced by many methods and cultivated through discussion in particular. Skills are usually best developed by means of demonstration, rehearsal and performance. Simulation exercises may have an important part to play here.

If it is assumed that the aim of teaching is to produce changes in students' behaviour (i.e. changes in thinking, feeling and acting) some implications for the organisation of learning can be seen. The desired changes have to be specified and then particular learning experiences can be selected. They will relate to specific areas of content and types of educational method likely to result in changed behaviour. When they are specified the learning experiences are systematically organised (in a syllabus). The formulation of training objectives is a complex task, some influences on it being the identification of the future roles of students when they have completed the course, and the need to encourage or develop an ability to be "flexible" or "adaptable". The task of specifying the kinds of knowledge, attitudes and skills required in present and possible future professional roles involves controversy among social workers and educators. Planning learning experiences to help students attain objectives involves reformulating the objectives into specific areas of content and then selecting methods of instruction, including practical work; this has to be related to the needs of the students and the resources that are available. The experiences are planned to form a pattern which facilitates learning. This system is made up of experiences which are mutually reinforcing and have a cumulative effective. They are related to each other so that later learning can be built on earlier learning, and links connecting experiences are built into the syllabus. These links can be theories or concepts (e.g. hierarchies in learning and hierarchical communications systems), common skills (oral and written communications) and common attitudes and values (e.g. human dignity). The principles on which learning is organised is considered. It may proceed from part to whole, from the concrete to the abstract, or from the simple to the complex, for example. Having specified and organised training objectives and learning experiences and exposed students to them the results are evaluated and the students' performance is assessed. This evaluation process is to see to what extent the desired changes in behaviour have been achieved. It goes on continuously from the time a student is selected for training; it involves evaluation of the student's current knowledge, skills and attitudes, previous experience, level of education and capacity for learning.

Human communication may be studied in terms of its elements. For example, the following variables may be identified: (1) someone (2) perceives an event (3) and reacts (4) in a situation (5) through some means (6) to make available materials (7) in some form (8) and context (9) conveying content (10) of some consequence. The components are regarded as the basic elements in each phase of human communication. In the analysis of each phase the relationships among the components have to be studied to see if they are complementary or if their influence is distinctive. The behavioural approach to the study of attitude change treated the component of communication, source, message, channel and receiver as separate variables. This approach demonstrated the relationship between attributes of a component and a receiver's attitude change. The elements' distinctiveness is important. But it is as a whole, rather than as separate elements, that they make sense of communication. Probably the best-known communication model is Shannon and Weaver's (1949) who applied electrical engineering to human communication. Such models differentiate source and receiver but it is generally recognised that communication is a two-way activity. At one time one person is in the position of receiver: at another time he is the source. In interpersonal communication it is the rule rather than the exception that relationships are reciprocal; in learning feedback or knowledge of results is crucial. This aspect of training is controversial and problematic. It has not been discussed in detail earlier: we must take it up now.

3. TWO-WAY COMMUNICATION IN LEARNING: FEEDBACK AND ASSESSMENT

Experiments which have been used to study factors influencing the efficiency of small groups in problem-solving and of the satisfaction of group members involve controlling the number of channels of communication which can be used. In an experiment the number of channels used can easily be restricted by isolating each person by erecting vertical partitions round a table. They are allowed to communicate with each other by passing written notes through slots. In adapting this experiment this may not be practicable so people participating should be told that the point of the experiment will be lost if they communicate in other ways than those laid down. Five people sit round a table and each has a numbered card in front of him. The experiment is explained as an attempt to see how efficient various methods of problem-solving are. The participants are then given the rules of the exercise. (1) They may only communicate by passing notes on the cards provided, each must contain only one message, and each must be marked with the number of its origin and destination. (2) People must not pass on cards they have already received themselves and they must not read notes passed between other people. (3) They are told by the experimenter to whom they may pass messages. (4) They will be given a list of five symbols and they have to find out which symbols are common to the whole group. The problem will be solved when each person knows the correct answer. Four kinds of communication sets can be used: (1) the circle in which there are five communication channels; each person may only communicate with the person on his left and with no one else. (2) The full circle in which each person may communicate with people sitting on each side of him. (3) The wheel: one person can communicate with all the others but they can only communicate with each other by going through him. This provides eight channels. (4) The situation in which all the channels are open. The same participants can be used in each situation. Each is given a card which contains five symbols and they are told which kind of network is to be used. The time that is taken to produce correct answers can be recorded and as the cards are filled in the number of messages sent can be counted. After each experiment the participants can be asked to complete rating scales. These can indicate how efficient they think the network is 1 indicating "very inefficient", 7 indicating "very efficient", 4 being a midway rating. They can also be asked about how satisfactory they found their membership of the different kinds of groups 1 indicating "great dissatisfaction", 7 "great satisfaction" and 4 again indicating neutrality. Discussion afterwards will be about the time taken to solve problems and the number of messages sent in each type of situation, and people's ratings of the efficiency and their feelings of satisfaction with the different situations. A number of findings have been reported quite consistently from these experiments. The greater the possibilities of communication open to members the greater will their satisfaction be. The individual member who is most involved in communication will derive the most satisfaction. The group in which all channels of communication are open appears to be the most satisfying to members. It also seems to be the most efficient in problem-solving. Some cards with the problems to be solved are illustrated here. The original experiments were by Leavitt (1951).

The idea of knowledge of results or feedback has a long history. The idea is important because it suggests some basic characteristics of behaviour. Simple and complex behaviour can be seen as being governed by results; the notion of feedback, (and the ways in which the results of behaviour are seen to be significant) seems to account for some of the complexities of behaviour and flexibility of behaviour. The suggestion that rewards and punishments were basically responsible for changes in behaviour has been expressed in different ways and often it has aroused controversy. One question has been about the possibility of distinguishing incentives and reinforcers. Rewards are regarded as reinforcers when more or less permanent changes in behaviour are studied. But when changes in behaviour are more transitory you usually find people talking of incentives. Rewards and punishments may have incentive effects, in increasing motivation and leading someone to make greater effort. Feedback may have three functions then; these are the informative function (information about the results of an action),

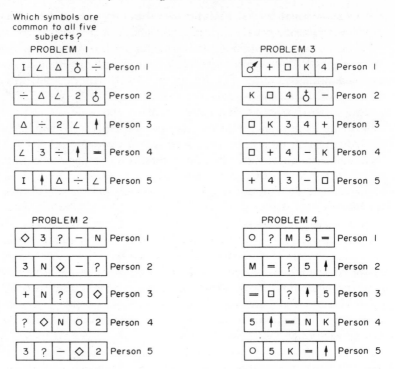

Fig. 13. Common symbols.

the reinforcement function and the incentive function of reward and punishment. It is also important to distinguish different kinds of feedback. Intrinsic feedback is normally present as an organism maintains equilibrium; for example, muscle movements always involve two or more sets of muscles: one set contracts when the other expands. This kind of reciprocal system is required for smooth bodily movements. This basic level of feedback is intrinsic to the movement and it is not easily susceptible to external manipulation. In many situations, of course, external manipulation (e.g. by an experimental psychologist, a parent or a teacher or anyone else for that matter) is possible. In experiments on steering tasks (steering a mock-up model for example) visual feedback is intrinsic but is subject to manipulation by the experimenter: distorting mirrors or television pictures might be used for example. In training or teaching situations comments like "Not so good", "You are doing well", "That is much better" may not be usual results of doing a task: they are also examples of extrinsic feedback. As a technique used in training feedback is present only during the period of training; after that the trainee has to rely on evaluating results himself. How extrinsic feedback can be used to facilitate transfer to ordinary conditions where intrinsic feedback only is available is a question teachers have to bear in mind, but at present there are few suggestions from research to help them. (See Miller, Galanter and Pribram, 1960, for a systematic discussion of these problems.)

Two main purposes of systems of assessment are (a) to provide feedback to students on their learning (for them and for their teachers) and (b) to provide a "measure" of achievement (for the purposes of awarding a qualification very often). The short-comings of traditional methods have been studied. It was found that physics papers in G.C.E. examinations emphasised note learning of descriptions of experiments and simple problems at the expense of questions requiring understanding of principles (Spurgin, 1967). A study employing taxonomies of educational objectives in relation to medical students' tests obtained rather similar results. The largest category of the test items depended on reproduction from memory. Only a small number of test items required recognition of learning of a fact or a concept or ability to generalise (McGuire, 1963). In another study of physics examinations it was found that 40% of questions could be answered entirely from memory (Black, 1968). Another problem is that agreement among examiners or essay markers is often poor (Bull, 1956; Cox, 1967) and this is also found in oral and practical tests in some subjects. Measures which have some success in overcoming this problem are (a) to require shorter answers (agreement on marking is better) and (b) reduce the number of grades (Mowbray and Davies, 1967). It is sometimes possible to provide students with information about their performance quickly. Teaching techniques such as games and simulation exercises and programmed learning facilitate this but the problem is that they are not applicable to all kinds of learning objectives as far as can be seen at present. Forms of continuous assessment (including student peer group assessment) are ways of shaping learning. Fairly constant criticism and, as mentioned above, reinforcement of correct or desirable responses, with other methods of continuous assessment, could supersede traditional methods of examinations or tests. Continuous assessment which involves frequent (i.e. weekly or fortnightly) tests appear to be counter-productive. It seems to have an adverse effect on teaching and it puts a continuous strain on both students and teachers (Burke, 1968). However, a modified form of assessment of all aspects of a student's work are taken into account leads to ways of planning courses so that there is adequate feedback. It appears to have the advantage of enabling students to be active both in their own learning and in assessing it. In this procedure course work is assessed at regular intervals, students and tutors decide on the five (or however many it is) best pieces of work to be used in assessment. Opportunities for *viva voce* discussion can be built into this method. One of its disadvantages is that students may not work to their full capacity all the time. But it seems preferable to continuous assessment which leaves students unable to pursue special interests, or feeling that they are on a kind of treadmill. To illustrate these points the structure for the assessment procedure of one course is now reproduced. The operation is still at an early stage but as one of the assessors involved I find it an intriguing and challenging scheme. At this very early stage my personal reaction has been to identify as problematic (i) the responsibilities of students, tutors and assessors and (ii) to clarify the assessors' role and to differentiate it from that of the professional adviser. This illustration is reproduced by courtesy of C. R. Akhurst of Bristol Polytechnic.

REGULATIONS FOR ASSESSMENT

A. *Assessment procedure*

1. The assessors will review the performance of all students during the final year of the course.
2. The material to be submitted for review will be as follows. (See note 1.) One essay in each major subject area in each academic year.

(Social work, Psychology, Sociology and Social Policy. See note 2.)
A case study from each field-work placement.
A study on other field-experience during the course.

3. The assessors will also consider the following matters:
The reports of field-work supervisors.
The tutor's assessment based upon the joint evaluation records of tutor and students compiled throughout the year.

4. The assessors may ask for additional evidence in relation to any student.

5. Students may submit additional material if they so wish.

6. All written assignments submitted to the assessors will be accompanied by a detailed critique prepared by the appropriate tutor.

B. *Recommendation for the award of the Certificate of Qualification in Social Work*

1. The recommendation for the award of the CQSW will be made unless objection is made.

2. It is the responsibility of tutors to satisfy themselves that a student has reached an appropriate standard in both field and academic work. If they are not so satisfied it is the duty of the tutor to make out a case to the Assessment Panel that the student should not be recommended for the award of the CQSW.

3. Where an objection is made the Assessment Panel shall consider all the relevant material, including additional material submitted by the student at his own request or the request of the assessors. The assessors may also interview tutors, supervisors or students where appropriate.

4. Having considered the material presented to them and such additional material at the final assessment as the student wishes to present, the assessors shall be recommended to the evaluation panel:
either   (i)   the student's performance has been satisfactory;
or   (ii) that the student's performance is not of a sufficient standard and there is no reasonable expectation that they will achieve that standard through further study and/or field experience;

or   (iii)   that the student should undertake a further period of study, not exceeding one academic term;

or   (iv)   alternatively or additionally that the student should undertake a further period of supervised practical training not exceeding a period of sixty (60) days;

or   (v)   require the student to undertake a *viva voce* examination to be conducted by a member of the panel on the basis of which the panel shall make a decision in accordance with sections (i) to (iv) above.

5.   In any case where the decision to defer recommendation for the award of the CQSW the assessors shall review the additional material or supervisors' reports before a final decision is made.

6.   A student shall not normally be deferred more than once.

7.   Re-submissions shall normally be completed by the end of the Autumn Term immediately following the conclusion of the course.

C. *Interim review of student's work*

At the conclusion of the first year of the course the assessors will review the work of a sample of all students during the year. They shall also review the work of any student whose work appears to be below the level expected at that stage in the course. As a result of this review the assessors may either review the educational needs of any borderline (or below) student or require the student's work to be brought before them for the final assessment.

D. *The Assessment Panel*

The panel will consist of the assessors, a teacher whose primary concern is with an academic subject, the Principal Lecturer in Social Work and the Head of Department of Social Science as Chairman. The Faculty Administrative Officer shall act as Secretary.

Members of staff who have taught in the social work course shall be in attendance.

The panel shall hear the case of any student in relation to whom an objection has been made.

The assessors will also present to the meeting a report on the work of the students and in compiling their report may have access to any evaluation material produced by students.

Note 1:   The material to be submitted for review will be selected by the student in consultation with his/her tutor.

Note 2:   These essays are selected from programmes of work set by the relevant subject tutors during the course of the two years.

Memorandum on Evaluation Scheme

In designing an evaluation scheme we have been guided by a number of principles that we see as fundamental to the educational processes that we are trying to implement.

First   the assessment procedure should arise from the methods and objectives of the educational processes rather than dictate them. Examination and continuous assessment tend not to fulfil this requirement in so far as they over-focus the attention and efforts of the student on the evaluation and give rise to unproductive levels of anxiety.

Second   the student should be involved in all aspects of his own evaluation. One of the objectives of his education is to develop the capacity to identify and manage the standards of his own performance. Examinations and to some degree continuous evaluation, tend to exclude the student and do not lend themselves to becoming educational experiences.

Third   while equity demands that the assessment should be the same for all students we do not see that it is necessary to create a series of hurdles for all students in order to identify the one or two who are not of a satisfactory standard. Neither do we believe that assessment is necessary as an incentive to study. The pass rate in social work courses is generally better than ninety-five per cent (95%). This implies a high degree of effectiveness in selection and educational procedures and that assessment processes are concerned with the identification of a very small number of students. There is general agreement that social work students are highly motivated to learn and the relevance of teaching to social work practice helps to sustain this.

Finally since evaluation processes are often implicitly related to the assessment of the course this relationship should be made clear. Most procedures place responsibility upon the student to pass and (except where there are specific objections) assume the educational methods and opportunities sufficient. External assessors should therefore be enabled to take account of the educational processes in evaluating student performance. There is obviously a necessity for some clarification of the respective roles of assessors and professional advisers.

Students are encouraged to take increasing responsibility for the content and organisation of their own learning. Within this context they are encouraged to evaluate teachers' performance as well as their own.

Written Evidence for Evaluation

Each student is required to complete a minimum number of assignments during the course. These are evaluated by the appropriate members(s) of staff and detailed comments are recorded. Marks are not given unless specifically requested although the standard of performance should be clear from the comments. Essays are retained by students and copies of the marking sheet are held on the student's file.

Where a member of staff wishes to express a qualification about the level of performance reached at the conclusion of a course he must arrange for the allocation of marks to the presented material.

Students will not be eligible for assessment who fail to fulfil assignments or to produce required evaluated material. Material presented in other than written form (video tapes, etc.) may be assessed if this is requested by the student in advance of the presentation. A written evaluation report compiled by tutors and signed by the students as an agreed evaluation will then be retained in the evaluation record.

A student subject to an objection is entitled to submit additional material from his work during the course as evidence on his own behalf and may ask for this to be evaluated.

The Function of the Field-work Supervisor's Report

The field-work supervisor's report occupies its traditional place in social work assessment. While the question of pass/fail is still present it is less explicit perhaps because the educational task is more evidently shared. In practice too, the likelihood of success seems to be more assumed than in normal academic evaluation procedures.

Two aspects of the practice of evaluation are designed to build a bridge between field and academic assessment. First is the practice of conducting a three-way discussion between the student, tutor and supervisor at the time the final report is compiled. The second is the tutor's assessment of the detailed case study prepared by the student. This provides the opportunity for an alternative assessment of some aspects of field-performance by the tutor, a bridge between field and academic assessment.

The Role of the External Assessors

The traditional function of assessors has been to moderate the judgement of staff in situations where staff are responsible for the implementation of assessment procedures. This is the role which we are seeking to maintain but it leaves to be answered the question of how this role may be fitted into the proposed evaluation structure.

It is proposed that assessors should review samples of students' work in the first year. These samples shall be structured in such a way as to ensure that some work of every student is reviewed each year. They should also be invited to consider especially the work of any student about whom a staff member feels anxious.

In relation to a student regarding whom an objection has been made the assessors shall consider the relevant evidence and make recommendations to the assessment committee.

The Role of the Personal Tutor in Evaluation

The first function is to help the student to develop his own evaluation capacities. This he does by drawing the student's attention of criteria of organisation and content in the presentation of material. He also acts by encouraging the student to use evaluation to improve his productive skills both in relation to understanding himself and others.

In carrying out this first function the tutor will also be measuring the student's progress towards professional competence. It may be that the first function will entail helping the student to recognise that his skills and capacities are not appropriate or sufficient for the role of professional social worker. We view it as important that, whenever possible, the decision to withdraw from social work should be seen as a positive one rather than carry implications of failure.

The tutor is responsible for consultation with other staff on the student's performance each term and for conveying this information to the student. This feed-back is essential both educationally and in order to ensure that the student is aware of any doubts that may lead to a suggestion that he should withdraw or not be recommended for the award of a professional qualification.

Where a member of the staff forms the view that student's performance is of an insufficient level then he has the obligation to gather and present the evidence of this to the assessment panel.

The Tutor's Report

This report, which has featured in C.S.W. assessment procedures, will contain the following material:

1. A summary of the tutorial assessments discussed and agreed with the student throughout the course. This will include an assessment of the student's personal development.
2. An account of the student's academic performance; his approach to learning and actual achievements as evidenced by his presented material. (Copies of marking sheets are maintained on the file.)
3. A summary of the student's field-work performance.
4. An assessment of the student's overall performance and a

statement of the grounds upon which any objection to the award of a qualification is based.

The tutor's report will be compiled for every student during the final term of the course.

This form of assessment also provides valuable feedback for teachers. Although, like examiners, students observe different things, and their ratings of teachers' performances are unreliable, their comments on failures in teaching and ways of improving teaching are very important aspects of an assessment procedure.

In conclusion perhaps one point about evaluation should be underlined. It needs to be related to learning objectives. Although, as I have tried to show, learning objectives may be stated rather vaguely or in rather general terms assessment should still be related to them. A person who has learned a new subject or skill and then discovers that little importance is given to this and that it is not assessed, feels frustrated. Further enthusiasm for developing knowledge or skill may be dampened. The purpose of evaluation is to discover the extent to which the objectives of a course of training have been achieved. It involves assessing changes in knowledge, skills and attitudes on the part of students at various times during the course, and if possible, discovering how permanent the learning has been by assessing performance some time after the end of a course. If one expectation of mature students on a professional course is that they should develop a capacity for evaluation of their own work, they should be helped to do this during their training. Problems arise in developing appropriate methods of assessment because it is often difficult to specify the knowledge, skill and attitude changes that are expected. It is necessary to consider the results of evaluation in terms of their implications for course objectives, content and teaching methods. It is also worth examining how accurate an evaluation has been.

4. SKILL IN INTERVIEWING AND COMMUNICATION

In her discussion of the skills to be learnt in interviewing training

Heywood (1964) describes the two primary *tools* of casework as relationship and interviewing. In the agency the student should be helped to use the worker-client relationship in a professional way as a primary tool, seeing it as a corrective or enabling experience for the client. In any two-way relationship the communication which occurs helps the people involved learn about each other's roles. This process is enhanced as they become able to share the meanings of the terms and other symbols they use. They may agree or disagree with each other but there must be a degree of understanding of what the other person means. For the client, problem-solving has elements of learning in it which are not very different from the learning process in childhood. In adulthood people tend to learn best from people they like and identification is a better basis for development than submission. Initially we assume that the client will explain the difficulties in his current situation, not necessarily as clearly as he perceives them, but as fully as he believes the social worker needs to know about them. The social worker needs to demonstrate that he is "available", receptive and non-blaming before the person in trouble may feel free to talk more freely. However, both the client and the social worker communicate more than this. Heywood refers to "the sensitivity in both people, the quality the creative artist has par excellence to feel into the person beneath the battered or sophisticated exterior and to respond to this". Social workers have different temperaments and they vary in having this quality of imaginative sympathy and in the capacity to develop it further. Other nuances affect the relationship: such things as the social worker's demeanour, attitude or thoughtfulness. Thus, as the client defines his position the social worker communicates about the reciprocal role of interviewer and indicates the potential for help that is available. The way of working with the client helps to forge the relationship, and this is the tool which may strengthen the client to work on his problem himself. Everything is interrelated in social work. From the point of view of communication, however, it is apparent that in interviewing clarification and re-clarification of the conditions under which the two people are in a professional relationship proceeds continuously. The social worker demonstrates his role by explicit statements and by his actions. The client clarifies his position and expectations.

The skills that can facilitate communication in an interview are common to all interviews, although in different professional or social contexts the emphasis may well vary. Nevertheless, it is argued, there are basic regularities in all interviews and they provide the basis for common denominations of skill. The core elements which form the technique of interviewing can be learnt. However, just learning the technique does not in itself turn someone into a perfect interviewer. Interviewing is an art which cannot be learnt from a book and has to be perfected by practice. Cross (1974) analyses the skills involved in terms of the processes in interviews: (1) the pressure of social and cultural factors; (2) role expectations; (3) encoding and decoding of both verbal and non-verbal communication; (4) manipulation of the course of the interview to maintain and increase the motivation of the interviewee to participate and (5) the psychodynamics of interviewer-interviewee interaction. Skills related to these components include (1) purposiveness, emphasis on individuality and emphasis on common themes; (2) "teaching" role expectations, maintaining adequate role distance and reflecting social understanding; (3) ability to listen, careful observation, clear question formulation and communication control; (4) encouraging the client to communicate and express his problems, and persuading him to believe that the social worker is fully aware of his difficulties; (5) establishing rapport and showing warmth. It is important to recognise that an interview has a beginning, middle and an end, it is usually seen as a whole and not as separate elements. This suggests the possibility of chronological analysis of the interviewing process, seen in the literature (for examples see Kahn and Cannell, 1957; Perlman, 1957). Communications, including interviews, may be analysed in terms of the phases through which they pass.

The initial phase of human communication is the process by which a specific piece of information and the receiver(s) are linked through a particular medium. It can be analysed in terms of the extent to which information is transmitted successfully to the receiver (i.e. the information system) and in terms of the network through which the encounter takes place (i.e. the delivery system). The study of social interaction is required for an understanding of all kinds of human groups. In the course of interaction norms emerge and are enforced, relationships are defined and status is differentiated in various ways. The term social interaction refers to the reciprocal influence of people's social actions on each other (Blau, 1960). Aron (1970) refers to the element of meaning in social interaction, which, he says, occurs when, given several actors, the meaning of the action of each is related to the attitude of the others. The actions are reciprocally orientated towards one another. The term thus refers to communication of a symbolic kind which forms a basis for much of the patterned nature of social experience. This element of meaning implies significance. The meaning of a situation is an interpretation of its significance, but meaning is only established when the response to a symbol is the same for the person who produces it as for the person who receives it. Meanings are socially transmitted: they derive from social institutions and language. The importance of language seems to be self-evident. It is in and through language that the actions and psychological life that define human beings as human take place. Actions have significance through being named and located in language, but it is also through social interaction that people change and modify social meanings. Through language "self" and "not-self" can be stated and experienced, and through social interaction personal identities are formed and maintained (Berger and Luckmann, 1971).

The participants in communication try to maintain sharing of meaning through a set of symbols. Exchange is defined as the flow of shared meaning and it is because this sharing is possible that encounter can be transformed into exchange. Exchange is not just a matter of "talking" or "listening" but also of "understanding". The major concern is the message or the meaning contained in the symbols. Thus it involves more than the information measured by "bits" and network factors; it involves the meaning of the symbols as it is shared by the participants. There are many situations where people engage in exchange just because they are together in time and space. Exchange serves many different functions. It may promote and integrate groups, effect status differentiation among participants or signal the disintegration of groups. The next communication phase is the discrepancy between a person's attitude or behaviour before participating in encounter or exchange and his attitude or behaviour after encounter or exchange. The assessment of attitude change is difficult; it is affected by the ability of people to recall facts and opinions. Although there is evidence that attitude change leads to behaviour change and vice versa some discrepancies have been observed (e.g. between a person's attitude toward a minority group and his actual behaviour). A variety of theoretical approaches are found in the study of influence under such headings as persuasion, judgement and various cognitive theories. The effectiveness of the mass media has been compared with interpersonal communication in studying behaviour change. The effectiveness over time of encounter, exchange or influence depends to a large extent on control, the process by which the fidelity of information flow and the efficiency of message flow and induced changes are achieved and maintained. Control can be regarded as the organisational phase of human communication. It can be achieved by the feedback mechanism and by the dissemination mechanism. The dissemination mechanism can be regarded as the enforced transmission where the transmission intent of the source is strong, the delineation of the receiver system is relatively complete and the manipulation and maintenance of transmission are deliberately carried out by the source. The two mechanisms are related. Negative feedback provides information about those aspects in the system which have not performed effectively relative to the sources' expectations. The dissemination, with the feedback, improved the probability of system success by correcting the defective aspects of the system (Lin, 1973). Skills may possibly be identified in relation to these different phases.

An interview consists of a process with a beginning, a middle and an end. Just as the steps of data collection, data assessment and intervention in the problem-solving process are not clearly separated, the phases of an interview overlap each other. It is helpful to think of the process consisting of (1) the introduction phase when the participants get to know each other and decide on the purpose of the interview, (2) the development phase, the main part of the interview and (3) the termination phase. These phases have different aspects and tasks for the participants. For example, during the beginning phase the authority of the worker's position is more important than the personal-relationship authority. The interviewee's uncertainty, unfamiliarity and confusion are likely to be greater. The interviewer may have to provide more direction and structure and also more support and empathic understanding in the early part of the interview. In the second phase there is relatively more concern with instrumental problem-solving activities. Open-ended questions and perhaps non-directive comments occur early in the interview; in the later stages there may be more detailed explanation and discussion of specific areas. In the development phase the social worker helps the client to talk about the board range of concerns relevant to the purposes of the interview. He helps the client to discuss some subjects in greater depth and also to move to discussion of another topic if necessary. One simple way to encourage communication is to express interest in and to show attentiveness to, what the other person says or does. Nodding, leaning forward, and smiling when appropriate all act as verbal reinforcements encouraging the client to continue to talk about the particular subject. Comments which suggest that what has been said "is important and I would like you to continue" indicate readiness to discuss a particular subject further. Clarification and interpretation go beyond this. The first translates what the client has said into words in such a way that it can be understood more clearly. Interpretation involves making explicit something that has been said but at a low level of consciousness so that the speaker was not aware he said it. Clarification is more concerned with understanding at the cognitive level; interpretation emphasises understanding more at a feeling level.

Questions are probably the most frequently used ways of encouraging communication. They are often necessary in achieving the purpose of an interview. Although social workers may try to develop skill in using alternatives (such as reflective statements) questions are asked to obtain information, to help a person communicate more fully with himself as well as the social worker, and also to help the client tell his story. Good questioning helps in the organisation of ideas and the inclusion of relevant information. However, interviewers need to learn that leading questions have dangers. They are least appropriate when the client is anxious to please the social worker or who does not want to appear to disagree. Questions may be formulated in ways which allow a simple positive or negative reply rather than encouraging further elaboration. This can lead to deeper discussion of some subjects. Encouraging this involves explicit concern with how a person feels about something. It may also involve sanctioning the discussion of socially unacceptable feelings or attitudes, as well as using euphemisms to ease communication. These soften the apparently threatening impact of questions and thus keep the anxiety level down. Asking about how a child is disciplined or punished may be less provocative than references to hitting or "belting" him. Changing to a new subject occurs if it is clear that a topic causes a person too much anxiety; it is also initiated if it is clear that further discussion is not related to the purpose of the interview.

Although it is not clear how the estimate was made, if an interviewer spends less than two-thirds of an interview listening and more than one-third talking he is talking too much, according to Kadushin (1972). Perhaps the proportions depend on the kind of social work interview one is considering. Kadushin emphasises that "good listening requires following carefully what is overtly said as well as the latent undertones". Effective, perceptive listening is an art. The same principles of learning apply both to reading and listening. From the point of view of training much of the material to be learned comes from books. But oral explanations and interpretations comprise a large part of training and it is important to know how to listen properly. The first step in any learning is being motivated to learn. Effective listening depends on motivation, i.e. wanting to learn, or seeing why a particular topic is of importance. Then deliberate effort is required to capture, examine and analyse the ideas put out by the speaker or tutor. This effort to concentrate is important because in reading a book it is possible to refer to earlier points that have been forgotten. This is not possible with a discussion or a lecture. Of course sometimes this has advantages, but the general point about making a deliberate effort to concentrate pays dividends. If silence is seen by an interviewer as hindering the progress of the interview, or, perhaps as an expression of hostility by the interviewee, this narrow view may lead to premature termination. A silence may communicate hostility or resistance but it may signify many other things, such as requiring a pause to collect one's ideas, to reduce tension, or simply that a topic has been exhausted; there seems to be nothing more to say. If an interviewer is silent the client has the problem of interpreting what this means. It may enable him to continue his discussion of a particular subject, and this might be a positive function. But silence on the part of the interviewer may add to the client's role problems and increase his anxiety. The interviewer's problem is to assess when a silence is "productivity" and when it is not. It is an aspect of the problem of interpreting non-verbal communications (Wolberg, 1954 discusses this).

Many different roles are expected of the practitioner in the helping process. He responds differently to different persons, i.e. he may be one person with A, a different one with B, and still another with C. There is a danger that role playing may become over-rigid, in the sense that an insecure helper will seek rules for guidance with particular people or in particular situations. Carkhuff (1969) argues that an insecure helper is always asking whether his role calls for institutional allegiance or allegiance to his client. Such a helper is not as helpful as the person who is committed to his own growth as well as that of others. The latter rejects the imposition of roles beyond those dictated by the helpee's needs. Effective helpers do not deny the power implicit in their role in the therapeutic relationship, i.e. they are functioning at more effective levels than their helpees and they accept the helpees' recognition of them as agents of change because they can involve the helpees in a therapeutic process leading to constructive change. "Their movement in all of their human relations, however, is from role to person." They avoid the potentially deleterious effects of premature communication of counsellor values. The often very conditional quality of healthy human relationships is one in which neither person allows himself or the other to be less than he can be. The social worker in a group is involved in many of the same activities as in the one to one interview, including the maintenance of an atmosphere that will foster the achievement of goals. They also include influencing interaction, asking questions, providing information, facilitating the communication of ideas and feelings clarifying communications and giving advice. Ideally he demonstrates a model of a constructive communicator who is tolerant and accepting.

5. LEARNING SKILLS IN COMMUNICATION

I now draw together some ideas from the preceding discussion to make some concluding points about some of the problems of learning communication skills (including their identification). It might be thought to be possible to consider and define some of the core communication skills involved in teaching and learning. It may first be helpful to think about instruction from the point of view of communication. It is often necessary to use a simple communication model. The fact that this is done in many books on the subject seldom implies that real-life complexity is ignored; but we often have to take it for granted. One aspect of communication is the process by which an individual transmits stimuli to another to modify the receiver's behaviour. A message (stimulus) must be understood (in terms of the sender) by an audience (a receiver or receivers) who are influenced by the variable cultural and social contexts in which the message is received. The effects of communications are not easily predicted or controlled in some contexts. The teacher creates messages which he sends to his students. With the development of radio and television the educational audience grows more rapidly in size and variety than knowledge of the effects of these communications on it. The use of such media as tape recordings, video tapes, records and films adds to communication problems in training. Teachers have to remember that the messages they send should be both received and understood. They are understood when the receiver(s)' behaviour is changed in the way that is expected or desired. Like other senders teachers do not always discover the effects of their communications even in face to face relationships. It is not always clear whether a lecture has conveyed the ideas that were intended or whether it was misinterpreted. The effects of a teacher's general style of speaking and the accompanying posture and gestures are not necessarily known to teachers of long experience. Often there is little awareness of the effects of messages sent in the course of education in terms of achieving or not achieving learning objectives. The high redundancy of the English language, however, increases the likelihood that messages will be accurately received. Redundancy is a type of repetition which attempts to ensure that certain changes of behaviour occur in a receiver. For a long time we have known that there is a need for repetition as practice to consolidate learning. Repetition, as redundancy in communication, might be investigated in giving instructions to students, in demonstrating skills, and in explaining principles.

In the interchange between the speaker and his audience the comprehension of the communication involves not only understanding the content of what is said, but also what sort of person the speaker is and what his motives and expectations are. Variations in the content and the speaker will produce different effects in different individuals and different groups. Differences in the speaker's gestures or use of aids will not produce uniform effects in the listeners. Differences in education, or social or economic status, in emotional maturity and in motivation will produce different results in the members of an audience. We have repeatedly seen that one of the greatest difficulties in communication is that the sender makes assumptions about the receiver's ability to understand the message. If he knows the meaning of a word, understands a topic, or responds to a particular stimulus, he may implicitly assume that the receiver also will understand, appreciate or be motivated. These implicit assumptions may well be erroneous. It is safer to assume that an audience is variable in ability, knowledge and motivation, except in two-way conversation. The effects of communication always have an element of uncertainty.

One example of a pragmatic approach to the identification of teaching skills is given by Allen and Ryan (1969). They said they had no set rules about the nature of "good teaching"; the skills chosen were ones that they felt would be of most use to beginning teachers. They aimed to extend the range of communications skills that students brought with them to training. Examples of chosen skills were stimulus variation (because boredom is a major problem in schools), skills involved in maintaining interest and attention, e.g. set induction, reinforcement of student participation, silence and non-verbal cues, fluency in asking various kinds of questions, recognising attending behaviour, using examples, and completeness of communication. These are general skills which can be applied at many levels and in teaching many different subjects. Two further points should be added. One refers to the learner as both sender and receiver. The second point refers to communication models discussed earlier, and directs attention to reciprocity in human relationships. From the point of view of psychology the idea of transmitting stimuli to modify receiver's behaviour covers the situation where a sender may be his own receiver. He may modify his own behaviour by talking to himself, or writing for himself, as well as for others.

Carkhuff (1969) provides some further ideas both for teachers and students of human relations as they undertake the preparation of the student to be a helper. These ideas are not mechanistic. The focus is on changes in the person of the trainee and not on the acquisition of techniques. The effective factor in the training is the person of the trainer, not gadgets like videotapes, simulation devices and so on. He suggests that the direct training of clients or patients in the conditions of good interpersonal relations is more effective than therapy; perhaps we should educate everyone in the condition of good human relations and make psychotherapy obsolete. He emphasises that in communication training the trainer acts as a model and the requirements of the model are high. He must be genuine and sensitive; he must translate a deep respect for constructive forces by nourishing them and he must be committed to the destruction of destructive forces, both within and without individuals. Without a person with these aspirations to personal integrity who can provide an integrated learning experience, discussion of communication training is meaningless. Carkhuff writes that "high levels of communication" enable the trainee to experience warm and sensitive as well as forceful communications. The trainee experiences having his communications understood in depth and this allows him to understand himself at deeper levels. The effective helper provides a basis of experience within which the trainee can come to respond or react to the trainer's teachings; both parties are then involved in a search for more effective learning. In the early stages of communication training the trainee focuses on empathy. This is regarded as the most critical of all helping process variables and the one from which all other dimensions flow in the helping process. The initial stage of communication training consists of three phases. The first involves responding to recorded material, the second involves role playing, while the third involves contact with someone needing help (referred to by Carkhuff as a helpee). He suggests that successful completion of the first two stages makes possible a viable communication process with a person in need of help, a person who cannot under any circumstances be used of the experimental purposes of the earlier stages.

Notes

An editor recently remarked on the way in which writers on communication seem to prove that the subject is inexhaustible. This may account for the feelings of exhaustion experienced by students having to cope with more and more material. On the other hand it seems that both readers and writers often come to the end of an article or book regretting that a particular topic, or a specific part of an argument, has been omitted or curtailed. However, the positive side to this is the stimulus it may provide to improve matters by further study. The notes below are brief but they are intended to provide some realistic suggestions for further reading.

The book by Rogers (1973) is valuable in providing a down-to-earth approach to adult learning. It seems to communicate genuine interest and concern as well as a common-sense approach. In particular it contains a large number of first-hand accounts of their experiences by both teachers and students. Another very valuable book on adult education is by Cleugh (1962). Tyler's work on the planning of instruction is well established (1949) and continues to yield helpful insights. Research is moving towards finding ways of helping students of all ages to define strategies and orientate to the task of learning. An example of this is a paper by Gal'perin in Simon (Ed.) (1957). Papers by Thompson, Legge and Connor in Stephens and Roderick (Eds.) (1971) are of interest to the student of organising instruction. Education in general, and social work education in particular, owes a special debt to the work of Charlotte Towle (1954). Her work is important particularly because it deals with the learner as a "whole person", the role of motivation in learning, and the relationship between education and the development of personality. In Chapter 2 Towle deals with learning principles, in Chapter 3 with personality development while Chapter 7 discusses the social component in professional education. The compilation by Younghusband (1968) includes a paper by Eileen Blackey on curriculum building, and Leonard's discussion of the place of scientific method in social work education. Younghusband's paper entitled 'The teacher in education for social work' (In Younghusband, E. (Ed.), 1968) pointed to a lack of interest in the way adult students learn, and the need for learners to *practice* skills. Skill learning is seen as occurring (1) through perception and the application of knowledge and (2) through practice or action. To regard the art of human relations as a series of techniques is not the whole story. Attention should also be drawn to the importance of periods of depression as important parts of the learning process. Readers wishing to read more on student supervision will find Young (1967) helpful. In Chapter Five she refers to learning from social work records and points out how the student may learn from records he has written himself and from records made by other social workers. Young's discussion of Style is relevant to references to social context and language in this book. The paper-bound books by Beard (1972) and Bligh (1972) contain provocative and stimulating ideas about tools of learning. More work on simulation exercises is now becoming available. A paper by Stock on role playing and simulation techniques (in Stephens and Roderick (Eds.),

1971) is useful background reading. There is a variety of literature on group experience. Of more recent work the book by McLeish, Matheson and Park (1973) can be recommended with confidence.

A useful discussion on English language and literature which refers to various literary forms including novels and plays is provided by Davies (Chapter 7 in Dees, N. (Ed.), 1965). The article by Lee (1974) is specially recommended here since it contains useful further suggestions and more references. An authoritive survey of general linguistics which is comprehensive in scope is by Robins (1970). Contemporary theoretical issues in linguistics are discussed by Black (1972) who refers to two of the most important texts, De Saussure (1960) and Bloomfield (1935). Chapter Five of Black's book deals with language functions and can be read in conjunction with Crystal (1971) to study the interaction between language and social events. Black (Chapter Seven) is also recommended for discussion of problems of meaning. Kadushin (1972) discusses communication and relationship in social work; his discussions of the interview process, cross-cultural interviewing and non-verbal communication should also be consulted. The book edited by Cross (1974) is a useful source. The work pioneered by Mullen to which I refer in Chapter 1 may well be of particular significance for social work research of communication skills.

Some of the learning experiences described in the text are relevant to study of organisations and also to political and social action which I have discussed elsewhere (Day, 1972). There is increasing interest in the management of social services among social workers and others. But the way in which services have been reorganised has not always been based on empirical research findings. This topic is discussed in an article by G. Smith (1974) in which suggestions for reading are included. Argyle (1967) discusses aspects of work supervision and Schein (1965) is a useful basic book recommended for further study. The role of communication skills in social action is another topic which has not been fully covered in the text. For reading on this, as on many other topics mentioned here, current journal and newspaper articles are often more helpful than books. A document which deals with advocacy and social and political action has been issued by the British Association of Social Workers (1974). This refers to implications for social work training. Machiavellianism is to do with manipulative approach towards personal relationships. The idea is that one is more likely to achieve one's goals by not revealing one's motives and by concealing one's feelings. It involves exploiting other people when the opportunity presents itself and using any methods to attain one's goals. Treating people as pawns is not to everyone's taste but this reference is included for the sake of repairing this particular omission. Some social workers hold to the view that it is undignified in these ways. The use or abuse of communication skills is not only a matter of taste of course: moral and political judgements and personal integrity are inextricably involved. A questionnaire has been devised to assess Machiavellian traits. People are asked whether they agree with statements like "the best way to handle people is to tell them what they want to hear"; "It is hard to get ahead without cutting corners here and there". Agreement with statements like these would imply a "high Mach." score. In experiments involving competitive games "high Machs" seem to be superior because they remain less emotionally involved than "low Machs". High Machs seem to have more accurate stereotypes, seem more able to maintain eye contact when lying and seem to be less suggestible than low Machs. The evidence appears to suggest that "high Machs" are more effective in their social behaviour. Christie and Geis (1970) have summarized the research.

A small book which is a useful source of references as well as one which raises questions about the varied purposes of the mass media in government was published by Carter in 1971. As I indicated before (Day, 1972) social workers are conscious of the need for sound public relations and Carter's introduction is a useful starting-point also in discussing political questions and how they are handled, public opinion and the mass media and social change.

References and Bibliography

Abercrombie, M. L. J. (1969) *The Anatomy of Judgement*, Penguin.

Allen, D. and Ryan, K. (1969) *Microteaching*, Addison Wesley.

Alvarez, A. (1971) *The Savage God*, Weidenfield and Nicolson.

Argyle, M. (1967) *The Psychology of Interpersonal Behaviour*, Penguin.

Aron, R. (1970) *Main Currents in Sociological Thought*, Vol.2, Penguin.

Asch, M. J. (1951) Non-directive teaching in psychology. *Psychological Monographs*, **65**, 4.

Asch, S. (1946) Forming impressions of personality. *Journal of Abnormal and Social Psychology*, **41**, 258-290.

Asch, S. (1952) *Social Psychology*, Prentice Hall.

Baldwin, A. L., Kalhorn, J. and Breese, F. (1945) Patterns of parent behaviour. *Psychological Monographs*, **58**, 268.

Bandura, A. (1962) Social learning through imitation. In: Jones, M. R. (Ed.) *Nebraska Symposium on Motivation*, University of Nebraska Press.

Bandura, A. and Walters, R. H. (1963) *Social Learning and Personality Development*, Holt, Rinehart and Winston.

Banton, M. (1965) *Roles*, Tavistock Publications.

Barker, R. (1963) On the nature of the environment. *Journal of Social Issues*, **19**, 4.

Barnes, D. (1973) *Language in the Classroom*, The Open University Press.

Bartlett, F. C. (1932) *Remembering*, Cambridge University Press.

Beard, R. (1972) *Teaching and Learning in Higher Education*, Penguin.

Berger, P. L. and Luckmann, T. (1971) *The Social Construction of Reality*, Penguin.

Bernstein, B. (1959) A public language: some sociological determinants of linguistic form. *British Journal of Sociology*, **10**.

Bernstein, B. (1961) Social structure, language and learning. *Educational Research*, **3**, 163-76.

Bernstein, B. (1970a) Social class, language and socialisation. Lecture to the Institute of Contemporary Arts, 3rd February.

Bernstein, B. (1970b) Education cannot compensate for society. *New Society*, **387** (February).

Black, P. J. (1968) University examinations. *Physics Education*, **3**, 2.

Black, M. (1972) *The Labyrinth of Language*, Penguin.

Blau, P. M. (1960) Social integration, social rank and processes of interaction. *Human Organisations*, **18**, 152-157.

Bligh, D. A. (1972) *What's the Use of Lectures?*, Penguin.

Bloomfield, L. (1933) *Language*, Holt Rinehart and Winston.

Bowlby, J. (1971) *Attachment and Loss*, Vol.1, Penguin.

British Association of Social Workers (1974): *Social Action and Social Work* (Publication No. 6) (30th May).

317

Brown, S. *et al.* (1973) *Training for Change,* Vol.2, University of Surrey.

Bruner, J. S. (1961) The act of discovery. *Harvard Educational Review,* **31,** 21-32.

Bull, G. M. (1956) An examination of the final examination in medicine. *Lancet,* **2,** 368-372.

Burke, R. J. (1968) Student reaction to course grades. *Journal of Experimental Education,* **36,** 11-13.

Campbell, J. P. and Dunette, M. D. (1968) Effectiveness of T. Group experiences in managerial training. *Psychological Bulletin,* **70,** 73-104.

Campbell, J. and Yarrow, M. (1961) Perceptual and behavioural correlates of social effectiveness. *Sociometry,* **24,** 1-20.

Carkhuff, R. (1969) *Helping and Human Relations,* (2 vols.), Holt, Rinehart and Winston.

Carkhuff, R. and Berenson, B. (1967) *Beyond Counselling and Therapy,* Holt, Rinehart and Winston.

Carter, M. D. (1971) *An Introduction to Mass Communications,* Macmillan.

Central Training Council in Child Care (1970) *Working with Groups,* Study group on field work training; Discussion paper 5.

Chomsky, N. (1965) *Aspects of the Theory of Syntax,* M. I. T. Press.

Christie, R. and Geis, F. (1970) *Studies in Machiavellianism,* Academic Press.

Cleugh, M. F. (1962) *Educating Older People,* Tavistock Publications.

Cooper, C. L. (1974) Psychological disturbance following T. Groups: relationship between the Eysenck Personality Inventory and family/friends perceptions. *British Journal of Social Work,* **4,** 1, 39-50.

Cooper, C. and Mangham, I. (1971) *T. Groups: A Survey of Research,* Wiley.

Cox, R. (1967) Examinations and higher education. *Universities Quarterly,* pp. 292-340 (June).

Cross, C. P. (Ed.) (1974) *Interviewing and Communication in Social Work,* Routledge.

Crystal, D. (1971) *Linguistics,* Penguin.

Davitz, J. R. (1964) *The Communication of Emotional Meaning,* McGraw Hill.

Day, P. R. (1965) Rivalry at work. *Case Conference* **12,** 1.

Day, P. R. (1966) The influence of the academic setting on social work students' learning. *Social Work,* **23,** 4.

Day, P. R. (1972a) Aspects of learning and probation treatment. *Probation,* **18,** 1.

Day, P. R. (1972b) *Communication in Social Work,* Pergamon Press.

Day, P. R. (1974) Formal aspects of interpersonal communication. Paper for the Symposium on Communication in Medicine, Exeter University, April (unpublished).

Deese, J. (1958) *The Psychology of Learning,* McGraw Hill.

De Saussure, F. (1960) *Course in General Linguistics,* P. Owen (London).

Diack, H. (1966) *Language for Teaching,* Chatto and Windus.

Drever, J. (1952) *A Dictionary of Psychology,* Penguin.

Edom, R. F. (1965) Do people really matter? *Case Conference,* **11,** 8.

Faw, V. (1949) A psychotherapeutic method of teaching psychology. *American Psychologist,* **4,** 104-109.

Fiedler, F. E. (1953) Quantitative studies on the role of therapists' feelings towards their patients. In: Mowrer, O. (Ed.) *Psychotherapy: Theory and Research*, Ronald Press (New York).
Fraiberg. S. (1952) Understanding the child client. *Social Casework*, **33**, 9.
Freud, S. (1966 edition) *The Psychopathology of Everyday Life*, Benn.

Gal'perin, P. 1a. (1957) An experimental study in the formation of mental actions. In: Simon, B. (Ed.) *Psychology in the Soviet Union*, Routledge.
Gibb, L. and Gibb, J. (1952) The effect of the use of "participation action" groups in a course in general psychology. Paper read at A.P.A. meeting.
Goffman, E. (1959) The Presentation of Self in Everyday Life, Allen Lane.

Halkides, G. (1958) An experimental study of four conditions necessary for therapeutic change. Unpublished doctoral thesis: University of Chicago.
Hallowitz, E. (1965) Group approaches in the helping process. Paper given at the American Social Welfare Assembly, 30th April.
Harlow, H. F. (1971) *Learning to Love*, Albion Publishing Co. (San Francisco).
Harlow, H. F. and Harlow, M. K. (1949) Learning to think. *Scientific American* (Offprint No. 415).
Heine, R. W. (1950) A comparison of patients' reports on therapeutic experience with psycho-analytic, non-directive, and Adlerian therapists. Unpublished doctoral thesis: University of Chicago.
Heron, J. *et al* (1972) *Training for Change: an account of a course for staff from mental handicap hospitals*, University of Surrey.
Heywood, J. (1964) *An Introduction to Teaching Casework Skills*, Routledge.
Hilgard, E. and Bower, G. (1966) *Theories of Learning*, Appleton Century.
Holder, C. (1969) Temper tantrum extinction: a limited attempt at behaviour modification. *Social Work*, **26**, 4.
Holgate, E. (Ed.) (1972) *Communicating with Children*, Longmans.
Hollis, F. (1967) Explorations in the development of a typology of casework treatment. *Social Casework*, **48**, 335-341.
Hollis, F. (1968) A profile of early interviews in marital counselling. *Social Casework*. **49**, 35-43.
Hovland, C. I. (Ed.) (1957) *The Order of Presentation in Persuasion*, Yale University Press.
Howard, J. and Gooderham, P. (1975) Closed circuit television in social work training. *Social Work Today*, **6**, 7, 194-197.

Itzin, F. (1960) The use of tape recording in field work. *Social Casework*, **41**, 4.

Jehu, D. (1967) *Learning Theory and Social Work*, Routledge.
Jehu, D., Hardiker, P., Yelloly, M. and Shaw, M. (1972) *Behaviour Modification in Social Work*, Wiley.
Jung, C. (1936) *Modern Man in Search of a Soul*, Routledge.

Kadushin, A. (1972) *The Social Work Interview*, Columbia University Press.
Kahn, R. L. and Cannell, C. F. (1957) *The Dynamics of Interviewing*, Wiley.
Keith-Lucas, A. (1957) *Some Casework Concepts for the Public Welfare Worker*, University of North Carolina Press.

Kelley, H. and Pepitone, A. (1952) An evaluation of a college course in human relations. *Journal of Education Psychology*, 43, 193-209.

Kohler, W. (1925) *The Mentality of Apes*, Harcourt, Brace and World.

Kohler, W. (1957) *The Mentality of Apes*, Harcourt Brace.

Korzybski, A. (1933) *Science and Sanity*, Science Press; Lancaster, Penn.

Lawrence, G. (1972) Some dangers in group training. *Social Work Today*, 3. 4.

Lawton, D. (1968) *Social Class, Language and Education*, Routledge.

Leavitt, H. (1951) Some effects of certain communication patterns on group performance. *Journal of Abnormal and Social Psychology*, 46, 38-50.

Leavitt, H. (1964) *Managerial Psychology*, University of Chicago Press.

Leavitt, H. and Mueller, R. (1951) Some effects of feedback on communication. *Human Relations*, 4.

Lee, W. (1974) The novel, empathy and helping. *Social Work Today*, 5, 13.

Lewis, M. M. (1951) *Infant Speech*, Routledge.

Lewis, M. M. (1963) *Language, Thought and Personality in Infancy and Childhood*, Harrap.

Lidz, T. (1963) *The Family and Human Adaptation*, International Universities Press.

Likert, R. (1961) *New Patterns of Management*, McGraw Hill.

Lin, N. (1973) *The Study of Human Communication*, Bobbs-Merrill Co. Inc. (New York).

Lindsley, O. R. (1956) Operant conditioning methods applied to research in chronic schizophrenia. *Psychiatric Research Reports No. 5*, American Psychiatric Association.

Luchins, A. S. (1957) Primacy-recency in impression formation. In: Hovland, C.I. (Ed.) *The Order of Presentation in Persuasion*, Vol.1, Yale University Press.

McGeoch, J. and Irion, A. (1952) *The Psychology of Human Learning*, Longmans.

McGuire, C. H. (1963) A process approach to the construction and analysis of medical examinations. *Journal of Medical Education*, 38, 556.

McKeachie, W. J. (1954) Student centred versus instructor centred instruction. *Journal of Educational Psychology*, 45, 143-150.

McLeish, J., Matheson, W. and Park, J. (1973) *The Psychology of the Learning Group*, Hutchinson.

Mead, G. (1934) *Mind, Self and Society*, University of Chicago Press.

Miller, G. A., Galanter, E. and Pribram, K. (1960) *Plans and the Structure of Behaviour*, Holt.

Miller, N. E. and Dollard, J. (1941) *Social Learning and Imitation*, Yale University Press.

Ministry of Health (1959) *Report of the Working Party on Social Workers in the Local Authority Health and Welfare Services*, H.M.S.O.

Mowbray, R. and Davies, B. (1967) Short note and essay examinations compared. *British Journal of Medical Education*, 1, 356-358.

Mowrer, O. H. (1960) *Learning Theory and the Symbolic Processes*, Wiley.

Mullen, E. J. (1968) Casework communication. *Social Casework*, 49, 546-551.

Munn, N. (1961) *Psychology*, Harrap.

Nadler, E. B. and Fink, S. L. (1970) Impact of laboratory training on socio-political ideology. *Journal of Applied Behavioural Science*, 6, 79-92.

Nevard, L. (1972) *Management development programmes for the National Health Service*, Slough College of Technology.

References and Bibliography 321

Osgood, C. E. and Suci, G. J. (1955) Factor analysis of meaning. *Journal of Experimental Psychology*, **50**, 325-338.

Paterson, R. W. K. (1970) The concept of discussion. *Studies in Adult Education*, **2**, 1.
Perlman, H. (1957) *Social Casework*, University of Chicago Press.
Perlman, H. (1968) *Persona*, University of Chicago Press.
Perlman, H. (Ed.) (1970) *Helping: Charlotte Towle on Social Work and Social Casework*, University of Chicago Press.
Pettes, D. E. (1967) *Supervision in Social Work*, Allen and Unwin.
Piaget, J. (1959) *The Language and Thought of the Child*, Routledge.
Picardie, M. (1967) Learning theory and casework. *Social Work*, **24**, 1.
Pinkus, H. (1968) Casework techniques related to selected characteristics of clients and workers. Doctoral dissertation: Columbia University, School of Social Work, New York (unpublished).

Quinn, R. (1950) Psychotherapists' expressions as an index to the quality of early therapeutic relationships. Doctoral dissertation: University of Chicago (unpublished).

Reid, W. J. (1967) Characteristics of casework intervention. *Welfare in Review*, **5**, 11-19.
Revans, R. W. (1965) Involvement in school. *New Society*, **152** (26th August).
Robins, R. H. (1970) *General Linguistics: An Introductory Survey*, Longmans.
Robinson, W. (1972) *Language and Social Behaviour*, Penguin.
Rogers, C. (1942) *Counselling and psychotherapy*, Houghton Mifflin.
Rogers, C. (1959) Client centred therapy. In: Arieti, S. (Ed.) *American Handbook of Psychiatry*, Vol.3, Basic Books (New York).
Rogers, J. (1973) *Adults Learning*, Penguin.
Ruddock, R. (1969) *Roles and Relationships*, Routledge.

Sapir, E. (1949) *Selected writings of Edward Sapir in language, culture and personality*, University of California Press.
Sapir, E. (1967) *Conjoint Family Therapy*, Science and Behaviour Books.
Scharzmann, B. (1966) paper given at a conference of the Family Service Association of America.
Schein, E. H. (1965) *Organisational Psychology*, Prentice Hall.
Schein, E. and Bennis, W. (1965) *Personal and Organisational Change through Group Methods: the Laboratory Approach*, Wiley.
Seeman, J. (1954) Counsellor judgements of therapeutic process and outcome. In: Rogers, C. and Dymond R. (Eds.) *Psychotherapy and Personality Change*, University of Chicago Press.
Seidenberg, R. (1971) *Marriage in Life and Literature*, Philosophical Library Inc. (New York).
Shannon, C. E. and Weaver, W. (1949) *The Mathematical Theory of Communication*, University of Illinois Press.
Simon, H. (1957) *Administrative Behaviour*, Free Press and Collier-Macmillan.
Skinner, B. F. (1957) *Verbal Behaviour*, Methuen.
Smith, G. (1974) Changing methods and approaches in organisational study. *Social Work Today*, **5**, 10.

Smith, H. C. and Johnson, D. M. (1952) An experimental study of attitudes and achievement in the democratic classroom. Paper read at A.P.A. meeting.

Smith, P. (1969) *Improving Skills in Working with People: the T. Group*, H.M.S.O.

Solzhenitsyn, A. (1971) *The First Circle*, Fontana.

Spurgin, C. G. (1967) Who earns the marks? *Physics Education*, **2**, 306.

Staines, G. L. (1969) A comparison of approaches to therapeutic communications. *Journal of Counselling Psychology*, **16**, 5, 405-414.

Stein, L. (1967) Doctor-nurse game. *Archives of General Psychiatry*, **16**, 6.

Stengel, E. (1971) Poetry of Death. *New Society*, 477 (18th November).

Stevens, M. D. and Roderick, G. W. (Eds.) (1971) *Teaching Techniques in Adult Education*, David and Charles.

Stevens, S. (1950) A definition of communication. *Journal of the Acoustical Society of America*, p.22.

Stevenson, O. (1963) The understanding caseworker. *New Society* (1st August).

Tagiuri, R., Bruner, J. and Blake, R. (1958) On the relation between feelings and perception of feelings among members of small groups. In: Maccoby, E., Newcomb, T. and Hartley, E. (Eds.) *Readings in Social Psychology*, Holt.

Tagiuri, R., Kogan, N. and Bruner, J. (1955): The transparency of interpersonal choice. *Sociometry*, **18**, 624-635.

Timms, N. (1969) *Casework in the Child Care Service*, Butterworths.

Towle, C. (1954) *The Learner in Education for the Professions as seen in Education for Social Work*, Chicago University Press.

Truax, C. (1966) Reinforcement and non-reinforcement in Rogerian psychotherapy. *Journal of Abnormal Psychology*, **71**, 1-9.

Truax, C. and Carkhuff, R. (1967) *Towards Effective Counselling and Psychotherapy*, Aldine Publishing Co., Chicago.

Tyler, R. W. (1949) *Basic Principles of Curriculum and Instruction*, University of Chicago Press.

Valk, M. (1973) Learning to feel the client's predicament. *Social Work Today*, **4**, 5 (31st May).

Verplanck, W. S. (1955) The control of the content of conversation: reinforcement of statements of opinion. *Journal of Abnormal and Social Psychology*, **51**, 668-676.

Vroom, V. (1960) *Some Personality Determinants of the Effects of Participation*, Prentice Hall.

Vroom, V. and Mann, F. (1960) Leader authoritarianism and employee attitudes. *Personnel Psychology*, **13**, 125-140.

Vygotsky, L. S. (1962) *Thought and Language*, Wiley.

Watzlawick, P. *et al.* (1968) *Pragmatics of Human Communication*, Faber.

Whitehorn, J. and Betz, B. (1954) A study of psychotherapeutic relationships between physicians and schizophrenic patients. *American Journal of Psychiatry*, Vol.III.

Whiting, J. W. M. (1960) Resource mediation and learning by identification. In: Iscoe, I. and Stevenson, M. (Eds.) *Personality Development in Children*, University of Texas Press.

Winch, R. J. (1962) *Identification and its Familial Determinants*, Bobbs Merrill.

Wishner, J. (1960) Re-analysis of "Impressions of Personality". *Psychological Review*, **67**, 96-112.

Wolberg, L. (1954) *Techniques of Psychotherapy*, Grune and Stratton.

Young, P. H. (1967) *The Student and Supervision in Social Work Education*, Routledge.
Younghusband, E. (Ed.) (1968) *Education for Social Work*, Allen and Unwin.
Zillig, M. (1928) Einstellung und Aussage. Z. *Psychol*. **106**, 58-106. Cited by Heider, F. (1944) Social perception and phenomenal causality. *Psychological Review*, **51**, 358-374.

Index